Expressive Therapies Continuum

Expressive Therapies Continuum

A Framework for Using Art in Therapy

Lisa D. Hinz

Routledge
Taylor & Francis Group

New York   London

Routledge
Taylor & Francis Group
270 Madison Avenue
New York, NY 10016

Routledge
Taylor & Francis Group
2 Park Square
Milton Park, Abingdon
Oxon OX14 4RN

© 2009 by Taylor & Francis Group, LLC
Routledge is an imprint of Taylor & Francis Group, an Informa business

Printed in the United States of America on acid-free paper
10 9 8 7 6 5 4 3 2 1

International Standard Book Number-13: 978-0-415-99585-6 (Softcover) 978-0-415-96347-3 (Hardcover)

Library of Congress Cataloging-in-Publication Data

Hinz, Lisa.
    Expressive therapies continuum : a framework for using art in therapy / Lisa Hinz.
        p. ; cm.
    Includes bibliographical references and index.
    ISBN 978-0-415-96347-3 (hardback : alk. paper) -- ISBN 978-0-415-99585-6 (pbk. : alk. paper)
    1. Art therapy--Textbooks. I. Title.
    [DNLM: 1. Art Therapy. WM 450.5.A8 H666e 2009]

    RC489.A7H56 2009
    616.89'1656--dc22   2008030581

**Visit the Taylor & Francis Web site at
http://www.taylorandfrancis.com**

**and the Routledge Web site at
http://www.routledge.com**

Contents

SECTION 2   Characteristics of the Expressive Therapies Continuum and Its Components

SECTION 3   Assessment and Clinical Applications

Dedication

This book is affectionately and gratefully dedicated to Vija Bergs Lusebrink, PhD, ATR-BC, HLM, Professor Emerita. She carefully read each chapter of this book as it was finished and offered advice and encouragement; her thoughtful comments honed my thinking and greatly enriched my work. Vija's support sustained me during the two-year odyssey of research and writing that it took to complete this endeavor. She has inspired me, taught me, encouraged me, challenged me, supported me, questioned me, and always believed in me. I am proud to have written this book that honors Vija's creation, the Expressive Therapies Continuum.

Acknowledgments

My good friend and colleague Kathy Gotshall, ATR-BC, first recognized my passion for the Expressive Therapies Continuum. In 1993, she allowed me to speak as an "expert" on the subject to her eager undergraduate art therapy students at the University of Indianapolis. Over the years my passion has grown into real expertise, and since 2000 I have been teaching graduate courses in the master's degree program in art therapy at Saint Mary-of-the-Woods College, the first distance-learning graduate program in art therapy, where Kathy is the program director. I thank Kathy for her unfailing support of me as an expert on the Expressive Therapies Continuum, and for her belief in the importance of this book.

My students also have encouraged me to write this book and speak on the subject of the Expressive Therapies Continuum. Through teaching I have been challenged to present my thoughts as plainly as possible, and consequently, I have been able to clarify and simplify many ideas presented in this text. I thank my students, past and present, for their lively exchanges and unsparing sharing of ideas. I also thank my clients who have invited me into their hearts and minds and nurtured me with their generous spirits. I have used their artwork and words with their permission to help others.

The editorial assistance of Alona Hinz is gratefully acknowledged. The split infinitive in the previous sentence would have been routed out if she were in charge of editing these remarks. Alona's sharp eye and sharp wit made the editing process engaging and enjoyable.

Writing this book would not have been possible without the selfless aid of Judy Tribble, director of the Saint Mary-of-the-Woods College library. Judy procured for me countless books and articles and sent them across the country to me as quickly as was humanly possible. A librarian like Judy makes distance learning (and teaching) straightforward and easy.

Finally, I thank my family for their patience and understanding, especially in the last few months of this process. Sophia, George, Elena, and Andreas, your rooting for me sustained me; I could not have finished this book without your constant support. Thank you.

Foreword

It has been 30 years since the theoretical concept of the Expressive Therapies Continuum (ETC) was published in *Art Psychotherapy* in 1978. The ETC synthesizes and summarizes the essential steps involved in the visual expression, processing of information, and creative integration, with focus on the different applications of the basic tools specific to art therapy, namely, art media. The ETC incorporates many concepts of art therapy, but it does not emphasize any specific approach to psychotherapy or art therapy. When this concept was first presented at the Ninth Annual Conference of the American Art Therapy Association in 1978, some of the audience were questioning how did this concept fit within the existing framework of art therapy, because it introduced a different way of applying art therapy. The first introduction of ETC may have been too dense and too complex in the information presented, but the basic elements of ETC were soundly based on knowledge of the development of mental imagery available at that time. In 1990, I tried to elaborate the different levels of the ETC in my book *Imagery and Visual Expression in Therapy* (Lusebrink, 1990), but the text was still judged as too condensed. Over the years, though, the basic concept of ETC has continued to be supported by increased knowledge in information processing and brain processes (Lusebrink, 2004).

With her book *Expressive Therapies Continuum: A Framework for Using Art in Therapy*, Dr. Lisa Hinz provides a much needed elaboration of ETC, its different levels of visual expression, and application of art media in individual, group, and family art therapy. Dr. Hinz combines her knowledge and training as both a clinical psychologist and art therapist, with many references to current art therapy and clinical psychology literature, illustrated with case examples from her own clinical experience. Her book elaborates on the different levels of ETC, and explores in depth their different clinical applications. In her approach to art therapy, based on the concept of ETC, Dr. Hinz uses a nondirective approach to art expressions in the assessment phase of art therapy followed by directions to the use of different media on different levels of ETC. Her case examples illustrate that different clients may start out using different media on different levels of ETC, depending on their preferences, whereas the explorations and enhancement of the expressions and information processing on different levels of ETC can be influenced by directed change in art media. The strength of Dr. Hinz's presentation lies in the clarity of her writing and systematically organized approach to the applications of each level of ETC. Her approach renders the concept of ETC easily comprehensible and applicable, elaborated with informative tables at the end of each chapter. For those readers who may wonder about the diverse strands of knowledge and approaches to art therapy incorporated into the concept of ETC, Dr. Hinz provides the historical background information in her Chapter 2.

Last, but not least, the ETC was conceptualized as reflecting the parts innate specifically to art therapy, based on the understanding of the underlying principles of the development of mental imagery, processing of information, and integrative power of creativity. Certain theoretical approaches to art therapy would seem to be more compatible with some of the levels of ETC than others, but the concept is applicable regardless of the practitioner's personal theoretical preference for a specific approach to therapy. Art expressions are multileveled, and they deserve acknowledgment of the different processes involved in their creation. Dr. Hinz has been able to present her own view of the ETC honoring the multileveled nature of visual expressions.

Dr. Hinz's book offers a new and informed look at ETC, including rich resources from art therapy and clinical psychology literature for practitioners and students alike.

Vija B. Lusebrink, PhD, ATR, HLM, Professor Emerita
Palo Alto, California
April 2008

Preface

As a student in a clinical psychology graduate program in the early 1980s, I was trained in behavior modification techniques and cognitive behavioral therapy. Learning these approaches to psychotherapy affected me in two ways. First, the orientation led me to believe that control of emotions was a worthy goal. From this perspective, I deduced that I should be able to provide clients orderly formulas with which they could improve their mood; yet I often felt uncomfortable telling clients what to do. Second, I felt these approaches frequently left clients wanting more. Many craved not just behavioral change, but a deeper self-understanding.

In addition, behavioral approaches did not seem appropriate for those who were grieving significant losses. Nor did they appeal to clients who spoke a metaphorical language—those with visual, symbolic, or poetic orientations to life. As I went through my schooling, I learned that there was no objective evidence for psychoanalytic theories, but I often wondered, "Could everything that Freud said about the unconscious be wrong? Does nothing that Jung said about archetypes and symbolism remain relevant?" I sought out experiences to appease my curiosity and supplement my education. Most of these experiences were independent readings, but I also found a professor who was willing to teach projective personality testing.

This interest led me to another professor, who had been hired by a local community to study the psychological effects on children of a toxic chemical spill caused by a train derailment. The professor chose to assess the children using the human figure drawing and Koppitz's (1968) scoring for emotional indicators. The children were given two sheets of paper in random order: one containing a predrawn train track and "chemical spill" and the other containing cross-hatching in no particular pattern. All children drew two human figures, one on each paper, and served as their own controls. The papers containing the railroad track and chemical spill elicited human figure drawings with significantly more emotional indicators than the standard human figure drawing. The community used the study results to win a class action lawsuit to fund counseling services for children who had been displaced from their homes and whose lives had been severely disrupted by the toxic chemical spill (Siegel, Gottfried, & Lowe, 1988).

Like the judges who presided over the lawsuit, I too was convinced of the power of drawings to help children express pain they could not otherwise articulate. Subsequently, I was ready and willing to supervise an art therapy intern during my first professional position. The counseling center at the University of Louisville had not previously supervised art therapy interns because the director had not studied art therapy. However, based on my past interest in projective drawings, I wanted to find out more about the field.

As I began my supervisory duties, I also was seeing 25 to 35 clients per week individually and in groups. I was trying my best to help them shape their behaviors and moods with cognitive behavioral therapies. I wanted to provide formulas and answers for my clients, but often felt such answers fell short of meeting clients' needs, or were rejected outright. Meanwhile I was witnessing, while observing and supervising the art therapy intern, how images often held truths that clients provided for themselves. Their own image answers were not rejected, but rather regarded with reverence as they revealed the clients' own inner wisdom. Images provided a vehicle for the metaphorical language that appealed to so many. Images helped clients understand, express, contain, and soothe emotions. Images also could be used behaviorally or cognitively, and they could aid in tracking client growth and progress in therapy.

Images provided a way to address clients for whom the behavioral approach fell short. I watched with growing respect as the intern provided various media and experiences that regularly gave her clients the emotional, cognitive, or behavioral information they needed. How did she know what to do and when? Each experience, different from the one before it, seemed to provide and evoke what the client required from therapy at the time. From my observations, I was impressed with the flexibility and power of art therapy, but I knew that there was so much more that I needed to learn. I wanted to know how and when to use certain media, how to decide what experiences would be beneficial, and the best ways to approach clients using art. I joined an art therapy group in which I experienced firsthand the healing power of art. I enrolled in the University of Louisville graduate art therapy program. There I had the privilege of being taught by Vija

Lusebrink and Sandra Kagin Graves, the two creators of the Expressive Therapies Continuum (Kagin & Lusebrink, 1978a, 1978b).

The Expressive Therapies Continuum provided an organizing structure for the art therapy information that previously had seemed so powerful and mysterious to me. It gave form to my thoughts and feelings about this new mode of therapy I was learning. The Expressive Therapies Continuum helped explain how art media could be used in so many ways—from behavioral to symbolic, affective to cognitive. It provided a framework for approaching the what, when, and why of what to do in art therapy. From the perspective of the Expressive Therapies Continuum, I had a method of assessing client preferences and needs, as well as determining directions for therapy. I had a structure, but I did not have to impose it on anyone; clients provided their own answers through their creative experiences and images. This approach to therapy felt informed and respectful. I did not have to be the expert with all of the answers. I knew that the clients held the answers to their questions and challenges and that art gave them a vehicle for uncovering them.

It is my desire that this book about the Expressive Therapies Continuum will honor its creators, as well as integrate, expand, and enrich the body of knowledge already available on the subject. Dr. Lusebrink's book *Imagery and Visual Expression in Therapy* has been out of print for several years. I have long thought that the concepts of the ETC needed to be presented in a new format to emphasize to readers that there is an effective way to structure the sometimes confusing, but always powerful ways in which art media and experiences can heal. Embrace the Expressive Therapies Continuum just as you "embrace the mystery" of art and its symbols (Moon, 1992). Trust the ETC just as you "trust the process" of creating art (McNiff, 1998).

List of Figures

List of Tables

Section 1

Historical Perspectives and Foundations

1

Overview of the Expressive Therapies Continuum

Introduction

Every therapist who uses art in therapy faces decisions when working with clients similar to those of an artist facing a blank canvas or an unformed lump of clay. These are questions such as: How do I begin—how do I break into that inviting yet intimidating untouched surface? What direction shall I take—how can I make the best possible use of time and resources? How do I decide when the process is complete? There are no hard-and-fast rules in art or in therapy, and no easy answers to these and other questions. This book demonstrates that the Expressive Therapies Continuum (ETC) can provide a framework for addressing difficult therapeutic decisions. Just as the muse inspires the artist but does not dictate, the ETC animates and directs, but does not command or require a specific course of treatment. The organizing structure of the ETC is underscored by an understanding that working with the complex nature of the human psyche requires great latitude for individual differences.

The art therapy literature demonstrates that various media and methods can work effectively with all clients, whether they present in similar or different ways. For instance, Cox and Price (1990) in their 12-step approach to working with substance abuse disorder used tempera paint on paper to break down resistances and help clients recognize their powerlessness. The authors chose to work with paint because it is difficult to control, and they wanted the art experience to reflect the concept of unmanageability from the first step of the Alcoholics Anonymous 12-step recovery program. In a less emotional and more cognitive approach to the disorder, Horay (2006) used collage and oil pastels to help clients evaluate the pros and cons of their current situation, determine feeling states, and plan a future course of action. Feen-Calligan (1995) used art therapy in an addiction recovery program to help participants experience the spiritual aspect of their journey. The author described using drawing with the eyes closed, drawing with the nondominant hand, and translating physical gestures in the air into drawings on paper. Feen-Calligan used these experiences to help clients give up notions of how images *should* look and instead allow the healing images to come from within. Each practitioner mentioned above was using art in therapy to help clients with similar presenting problems. However, the different media and approaches used evoked decidedly different therapeutic experiences.

Answering the question of how to decide the appropriate media for clients and under what circumstances their use will be therapeutic has been one crucial aspect involved in defining the field of art therapy (Junge, 1994; Malchiodi, 2003c; Wadeson, 1980). Wadeson stated that students often ask to be taught specific techniques. She explained that what is more desirable than isolated descriptions of techniques is a theoretical framework from which to select appropriate materials and methods. Ulman (1975a) added that not only is a theoretical foundation necessary, but also that it should be so well ingrained that it can inform the "lightning quick decisions" that characterize therapeutic work. The Expressive Therapies Continuum (ETC), developed by Kagin and Lusebrink (1978a, 1978b) and further elaborated by Lusebrink (1990, 1991b, 2004), provides such a framework; it explains the healing dimensions of various expressive experiences and the restorative power of creativity. This is a theoretical and practical guide, which provides a way to answer questions about what media to use, under what circumstances, and with which particular clients. In addition, because the ETC has a comprehensible visual structure, which is presented in Figure 1.1, it can easily be internalized by visually oriented practitioners to provide needed guidance for moment-to-moment therapeutic decisions.

Expressive Therapies Continuum at First Glance

The Expressive Therapies Continuum represents a means to classify interactions with art media or other experiential activities in order to process information and form images (Kagin & Lusebrink, 1978b; Lusebrink, 1990). The ETC organizes media interactions into a developmental sequence of information processing and image formation from simple to complex. Image formation and information processing are categorized in

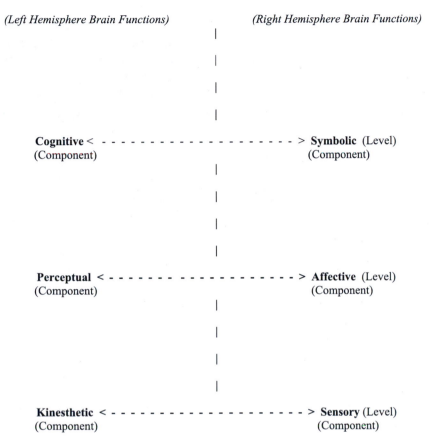

Figure 1.1   The Expressive Therapies Continuum. Reprinted with permission of the American Art Therapy Association from Hinz, L. D., "Walking a Thin Line: Passion and Caution in Art Therapy," *Art Therapy*, 25, 38–40, 2008.

a hierarchical fashion from simple kinesthetic experiences at one end to complex symbolic images at the other. The ETC is arranged in four levels of increasingly complex processing. The first three levels are bipolar or complementary, as shown in Figure 1.1. The two components of these first three bipolar levels represent functions or ways of processing information. The fourth level, the Creative level, can occur at any single level of the ETC, or can represent the integration of functioning from all levels. A single and simple interaction with art media or experiential activity has the power to be a creative experience, or a creative experience may involve the integration of functioning on all levels of the ETC.

Starting at the bottom of Figure 1.1, information processing begins at the preverbal level with kinesthetic and sensory experiences, and thus is called the Kinesthetic/Sensory level. Information gathered through these channels does not require words; it is rhythmic, tactile, and sensual. Developmentally this is the first way in which babies process information. Infants up to the age of 18 months take in information through their senses and receive feedback about their behavior predominantly through their own movement, but also through internal and external sensations. For this reason, experiences on the Kinesthetic/Sensory level of the ETC are indispensable in therapeutic work with children. Children need to physically manipulate and handle materials in order to form internal images of them (Lusebrink, 1991a). The Kinesthetic/Sensory level of the ETC represents the simplest form of information processing.

Moving up the developmental hierarchy, information processing and image formation occur on the Perceptual/Affective level. Information processing may or may not need words at this level. It is beginning to take form or be absorbed in the creation of formed images. Information processing at this level can be emotional and raw, expressed in image without regard to form. Alternatively, it can be characterized by attention to the formal elements of visual expression.

At the third level of the ETC, the functions represented are cognitive and symbolic. Information processed on the Cognitive/Symbolic level of the ETC is complex and sophisticated; it requires planning, cognitive action, and intuitive recognition. Verbal input is often, but not always, required to gather meaning about complex cognitive operations or multidimensional symbols involved on this level.

Although ETC components and levels are conceptualized and presented here as discrete functions, it is at times difficult to provide pure experiences with one component. More complex functioning at a higher level of the ETC often emerges from a creative endeavor, and is referred to as the emergent function (Lusebrink, 1990). The emergent function of each ETC component will be discussed in detail in later chapters.

The component processes represented on the left and right sides of the Expressive Therapies Continuum can be seen as parallel with functioning and information processing differences in the two hemispheres of the brain (Lusebrink, 2004). The *left hemisphere* processes information in an organized, sequential, and linear fashion. Verbal information also is processed in the left hemisphere; it is where logical thought and the labeling and categorizing of information takes place (Carter, 1998). The Kinesthetic, Perceptual, and Cognitive components representing the left side of the ETC can be seen as being involved with information processing predominantly in the left hemisphere. Similarly, the dimensions of the ETC represented on the right side of Figure 1.1—the Sensory, Affective, and Symbolic components—can be viewed as representing processes occurring predominantly in the *right hemisphere* of the brain. The right hemisphere is where the majority of emotional and conceptual information is processed, and where spiritual connections are made (Edwards, 1989; Riley, 2004). Creative experiences have the potential to integrate information from *both hemispheres* of the brain (Riley, 2004; McNamee, 2004). The Creative level of the ETC is believed to have an integrative function (Lusebrink, 1990).

Jill Bolte Taylor (2008) provided a profoundly personal explanation of the distinct functions of the two hemispheres of the brain. Dr. Taylor is a neuroanatomist who suffered a stroke that rendered the left side of her brain nonfunctional. With only the right hemisphere operating, the author said she experienced herself as at one with the world—awash in sensations—emotional, expansive, and mute. The left hemisphere is the part of the brain that holds language, organizes activity, and gives instructions. Dr. Taylor is a stained glass artist, and she used the artistic process as one integrative aspect in her rehabilitation following the stroke. Through creative action, left and right hemisphere functions found congruent and harmonious expression.

As was stated above, the creative level of the Expressive Therapies Continuum can exist at any or all of the levels. For example, finger paint can be used in a soothing, sensory manner to help an individual create an inner sense of calm. This simple experience is a creative one; an individual can bring forth something new (a relaxed state) as the result of the sensual use of finger paints. A sense of calm can be *created* without the formation of an external image; the media experience itself can induce serenity.

Additionally, a creative experience could combine elements from all levels of the Expressive Therapies Continuum. The same interaction with finger paint might begin as a simple sensory experience as described above, and evolve into something integrative and richly creative. As the fingers move paint around the paper, white lines are produced that allow forms to emerge from the background color. From an activity using the Sensory component, an experience on the Perceptual dimension evolves when forms are perceived. Further, the Symbolic component is engaged when a perceived form takes on special meaning and a personal symbol is produced. In this instance, all levels of the ETC are represented in one creative experience. This coexistence will be explained in more detail when the Creative level of the ETC is discussed in Chapter 9.

The two components forming each level of the Expressive Therapies Continuum have been described as having a curvilinear relationship in the form of an inverted U (Lusebrink, 1991b). Lusebrink explained this curvilinear relationship by stating that opposite components of each level at first enhance the functioning of each other. When both components of an ETC level are contributing optimally to an experience, expressive functioning is most favorable. Lusebrink has termed this "creative transition functioning" (V. B. Lusebrink, personal communication, February 24, 2008). In the creative transition area, functioning is optimized by the combined and interactive influences of both types of input. For example, when both kinesthetic and sensory input guide an experience, the creative transition is characterized by dynamic kinesthetic expression with concurrent sensory feedback.

As information processing increases with one component of an ETC level, it necessarily decreases and eventually blocks functioning with the opposite component. In the creative transition area of the Perceptual/ Affective level, a moderate amount of emotional investment will imbue a perceived form or a created image with vitality—emotions bring forms to life. However, persons who are overly emotional have been described as being "caught up in emotion" and "unable to see clearly." These common expressions describe the bipolar nature of the Perceptual/Affective level of the ETC. As emotional involvement increases past an optimal level, involvement with form (ability to see clearly) decreases.

On the other hand, the process of using the formal qualities such as shape, size, direction, and implied movement requires visual representation, but very little emotion. At first, emotional involvement might provide the needed motivation to begin to use this visual language. However, as affective involvement increases, perceptual processing abilities decrease and eventually become blocked. The same relationship is true for each bipolar level of the ETC. As involvement with one function increases, processing with the opposing function is at first enhanced, then decreased, and ultimately is blocked. Later chapters of this book explore using the bipolar nature of each ETC level to therapeutic advantage.

Each component of the Expressive Therapies Continuum has a unique and definitive healing function (Kagin & Lusebrink, 1978b; Lusebrink, 1990, 1991b). The healing function is explained as the activity that is distinctly therapeutic about each component process. According to Lusebrink

(1991b), the healing dimension "denotes optimum intrapersonal function-ing on the particular level" (p. 395).

A particular emergent function (Kagin & Lusebrink, 1978b; Lusebrink, 1990) also is characteristic of each component of the Expressive Therapies Continuum. The emergent function is the process that arises from using a component function. It is said to potentiate more complex processing of information or images, and often suggests or provokes movement to a higher level of the ETC. As was mentioned earlier, the fact that one type of functioning can evoke a higher-level process can complicate the prescrip-tion of "pure" expressive experiences. However, projecting the progress of emergent functions, along with knowledge of healing functions, helps guide art therapists in providing the most effective therapeutic experi-ence for each individual. Emergence of a higher level of functioning also helps clients experience a more integrated sense of self, which also can be healing (Lusebrink, 1991a). The healing and emergent functions of each component of the ETC will be discussed fully in subsequent chapters.

A Developmental Hierarchy

Kinesthetic/Sensory Level

Infants and toddlers process information through sensation and move-ment. Indeed, this has been called the sensorimotor stage of cognitive development (Piaget, 1969). Feedback loops support learning through the senses and through repetitive movement. If art activities are engaged in at this stage, the medium is used for its sensual aspects, or as a passive facilitator of kinesthetic action. For example, a two-year-old happily bangs a piece of paper with a marker and after pounding for a few minutes prob-ably notices that the marker left an image, but the focus of the activity was on the *kinesthetic action* rather than on the product or image.

A toddler using finger paints usually is much more interested in the *sensory experience* of daubing, spreading, and smearing the smooth paint than in making an image with it. Similar kinesthetic and sensory experiences are accessed through the developmentally lowest level of the Expressive Therapies Continuum, the Kinesthetic/Sensory level. It is important for people of all ages to have access to kinesthetic and sensory information, as these types of input form the basis of many experiences, and thus greatly influence the understanding of emotion and the development of memory (Damasio, 1994; Lusebrink, 2004; Siegel & Hartzell, 2003).

Between the ages of three and four years, the scribbling characteristic of the art of toddlers gives way to form. Preschool-aged children begin to draw concentric scribbles. These repetitive round forms become differentiated from one another and eventually become identified and named (Kellogg, 1970; Lowenfeld & Brittain, 1987). Mastering form is essential because children use art to inform those around them about their world and their feelings. Drawings are the natural language of children; they are one of the universal ways children express feelings (Lowenfeld, 1952). During the schematic stage of graphic development, from ages seven to nine years, form is vital to children's drawings. Children develop schemas that function like blueprints or plans for drawings, and consequently for communication. Deviations from usual schemas by omissions or elaborations demonstrate the positive or negative emotional significance of a subject (Kellogg, 1970; Lowenfeld & Brittain, 1987; Thomas & Silk, 1990).

Perceptual/Affective Level

The Perceptual/Affective level is the second level of the Expressive Therapies Continuum, corresponding to the schematic stage of graphic development in which children are learning about the world and the forms around them. Children's drawings are infused with emotions that give them characteristic qualities and personal meanings. Certain children find drawing is a significant way to explain and contain their impulses and emotions. Individual perceptions of reality are neurologically based, culturally influenced, and different from other individuals' perceptions. Figure ground drawings such as the Rubin's vase shown in Figure 1.2 illustrate what Siegel and Hartzell (2003) have called "representational diversity," or the ability to perceive reality in diverse manners. In the case of this drawing, reality can be either two profiles or a single vase.

In order to have fulfilling relationships it is helpful if people understand the concept of representational diversity and are open to new perceptual experiences. Art therapy experiences on the Perceptual/Affective level of the Expressive Therapies Continuum can be designed to broaden clients' perspectives and increase their ability to see another person's point of view through a new visual language. Perceptually based experiences can be one method of promoting effective interpersonal communication and satisfying relationships. The vital role of perceptual activities in couples and family therapy will be explained in Chapter 12. In addition, everyone should understand and have access to information about their emotional

Figure 1.2 Rubin's vase demonstrating "representational diversity."

states. Emotions are used in decision making, memory functioning, and motivating behavior (Damasio, 1994; Ekman, 2003; Plutchik, 2003). Experiences on the Perceptual/Affective level can help clients identify emotions, facilitate discrimination among emotional states, and assist in the appropriate expression of emotions.

The Cognitive/Symbolic Level

The Cognitive/Symbolic level of the Expressive Therapies Continuum is the most developmentally sophisticated. It corresponds to adolescence and the development of formal operational thought (Piaget, 1969). This means adolescents can process information outside of their own personal experience. Events no longer have to occur in the adolescents' personal lives to have meaning. Young people increasingly are capable of delaying impulses long enough to plan a course of action, think it through, and then execute the action. This skill continues to develop throughout adolescence and into the early 20s (Siegel & Hartzell, 2003). With increased ability to delay impulses and delay gratification, behaviors that are more complex are available. Art can become more complex as well. Images in the teen years often are infused with subtle humor, irony, or sarcasm (Lowenfeld & Brittain, 1987). Because adolescents are able to think outside their own experience, and their thoughts have achieved a new level of complexity, they are able to use symbols to represent feelings, thoughts, and events.

Potentially, everyone can benefit from the ability to understand and use symbolic thought. Symbols provide access to intuitive functions, and serve as reminders that experiences are not entirely conscious and fully understood. Art therapy experiences with the Symbolic component of the Expressive Therapies Continuum can aid clients in accessing the wisdom of their bodies or the wisdom of the world, neither of which speak in words. Symbol use can allow clients to maintain a healthy sense of mystery in their lives. The opposite pole of this level is represented by cognitive information processing. Cognitive thought is essential for analytical and sequential operations. It allows people to plan and carry out complex functions as well as to make decisions and solve problems. Input from the Cognitive component of the ETC provides reality feedback in all areas of information processing.

The Creative Level

As was mentioned above, the Creative level of the Expressive Therapies Continuum may exist at any or in all levels, and often serves an integrative function. Many authors have discussed the importance of the creative experience. Jung (1964) stated that all persons show a tendency to grow toward wholeness, bringing to light their uniqueness and individuality. For Jung, this tendency was best displayed by the creation of a mandala. The mandala is a circular drawing representing the self, wholeness of the personality, balance, and a desire for harmony (Jung, 1972). According to Johnson (1990), creative experiences can destroy a "false self" developed in response to shame, and can reinforce an authentic sense of self.

In all types of creative experiences, the artist feels intense joy, which Rollo May (1975) defined as "the emotion that goes with heightened consciousness, the mood that accompanies the experience of actualizing one's own potentialities" (p. 45). Access to creative input allows one to feel the joy that infuses original imaginative experiences. Creative involvement itself can be healing without cognitive overlay or symbolic interpretation (Lusebrink, 2004).

A Reverse Developmental Hierarchy

Interestingly, a reverse developmental process can be seen in the art products created by the devolving or degenerating brain (Ahmed & Miller, 2003). As the disease progresses, patients with Alzheimer's disease or schizophrenia show a reverse developmental hierarchy through the levels of the Expressive Therapies Continuum (Grady, 2006; Killick, 1997; Lusebrink, 1990; Stewart, 2006; Wald, 1984; Zaidel, 2005). Patients with significant brain involvement start out with abilities expressed on the Cognitive/Symbolic level of functioning. They are capable of thinking through sophisticated projects and using learned skills in order to render symbolically rich and complex art products. As the disease progresses, patient abilities regress to the Perceptual/Affective level with what seems to be alternating struggles to emphasize form with the expression of attendant affect. Finally, the last stages of the diseases seem to be characterized by Kinesthetic/Sensory activity with notable fragmentation of images, and no true achievement of formal representation. Ahmed and Miller (2003) reported that patients with Alzheimer's disease experience an unremitting loss of "visuoconstructive" ability. They seem aware that their spatial abilities are deteriorating but do not know how to change them (Grady, 2006; Zaidel, 2005).

An example of this devolution of ability characterizes the late work of Willem de Kooning, who suffered from Alzheimer's disease in the last years of his life (Bogousslavsky, 2005; Stewart, 2006). The artist's work at first was characterized by complexity of design, colors, and materials demonstrating work on the Cognitive/Symbolic level of the Expressive Therapies Continuum. With the first impact of the disease, de Kooning's work seemed to become overly involved with the Perceptual component. It has been called emotionally flat and cartoon-like, with an emphasis on outlining of the figures and a limited color palette (Bogousslavsky, 2005). In the last stages, de Kooning's work has been described as simplistic and impoverished, "a regression to the scribbling stage with random marks on paper" (Stewart, 2006, p. 58).

Using the Expressive Therapies Continuum in Therapy

A well-functioning individual is able to process information on all levels and with all components or functions of the Expressive Therapies

Continuum. Each function provides unique input with which the individual can make informed decisions and life choices (Lusebrink, 1990). There is anecdotal evidence that processing information with one component of the ETC enhances processing in other realms. Work in one artistic area enhances another to infuse the whole creative spirit (Friedman, 2007; Goldberg, 1997; Haynes, 2003). Natalie Rogers (1999) coined the term *creative connection* to emphasize her observations that "one art form stimulates and fosters creativity in another art form and links all of the arts to our essential nature" (p. 115).

Donald Friedman (2007) compiled an impressive volume of profiles of 200 well-known authors who also created visual art, and their explanations as to how engaging in painting or drawing complemented their written art. Writer Natalie Goldberg (1997) discovered what a profound enhancing effect painting had on her writing when she stopped painting, in order to devote her full attention to writing. She described her time without painting as being among her least productive writing years. Painting had a synergistic effect on her writing that enlivened the written word and energized the writing process. Goldberg explained, "When I cut out painting, I cut off that underground stream of mayhem, joy, nonsense, absurdity. Without painting, sludge gathered at the mouth of the river and eventually clogged any flow" (p. 60). Some creative arts therapists would go so far as to say that enlightened individuals seek out diverse experiences representing all components of the ETC in order to enjoy the flow, the self-actualizing properties of the creative process (Capacchione, 2001; Lusebrink, 1990; Malchiodi, 2002; McNiff, 1998).

However, most individuals seeking therapy would not consider themselves functioning optimally, but rather as experiencing problems with living. The Expressive Therapies Continuum helps therapists conceptualize these problems in at least two ways. Problems with living that can prompt individuals to seek psychotherapy occur when people are blocked from receiving or processing information from one or more components of the ETC. Difficulties also can arise when individuals demonstrate strong preferences to process information exclusively with one component. When information processing strategies are limited by being blocked or overused in a restricted manner, decision-making skills are impaired and life choices often are too narrowly defined.

The Expressive Therapies Continuum can be used to assess clients' preferred and blocked levels of information processing and to prescribe desired therapeutic experiences. The structure of the ETC can help creative arts therapists assess both their clients' favored components and significant obstacles to optimal functioning. This assessment information is gathered through evaluating media preferences and styles of interaction with the media, as well as graphic indicators and expressive elements from final art products. Further, therapists can use information from the ETC to guide clients through experiences designed to eliminate impediments to effectively using any component, or to reducing overdependence causing rigid functioning. Clients' social and occupational functioning can be improved by removing obstacles, and increasing flexibility in the ways information is processed and decisions are made.

The ETC Components at Work: The Example of the Scribble Chase

The *scribble chase* is an expressive exercise involving only one type of media, but including activity on all levels of the Expressive Therapies Continuum. This experience can be performed individually or in groups (Lusebrink, 1990; Malchiodi, 2003c). When performed individually, watercolor markers and a large sheet of paper are used. Client and therapist choose different colored markers, and as the therapist begins drawing a line, the client is encouraged to "chase" the line with his or her marker. Malchiodi (2003c) explained that a reluctant client could be drawn into this experience by following a line provided by the therapist. This part of the scribble chase is a purely kinesthetic experience. During this kinesthetic activity there is no thought as to what the lines might look like or what they might represent. After the paper is covered with lines, the client is asked to find images in the scribble and make a picture out of them using markers. By finding images in the lines, the client enters the Perceptual component of the ETC. Finally, the client is asked to tell a story about the picture or talk about what the picture means. Putting a story together requires engaging the Cognitive dimension, and finding personal meaning or a personal symbol demonstrates functioning with the Symbolic component of the ETC. The integration of functioning on all levels is an example of one kind of creative experience.

The scribble chase may be performed in a group of four persons, with two dyads taking turns leading the chase with markers on separate sheets of paper. This unstructured movement is the Kinesthetic component of the experience. In the next step, each participant selects and outlines five forms or objects from his or her scribble pictures. When forms are found, the Perceptual component is engaged. The members of the dyads then share their perceived images with each other, and the Perceptual dimension moves to the Cognitive component of the Expressive Therapies Continuum as verbal explanations are provided. Each dyad then selects five objects from the original 10 objects. Two dyads form a group of four and select five forms among them from all of the forms presented. The negotiation required in this step again engages the Cognitive component. Finally, the group of four uses markers to create a mural on a 3-by-5-foot sheet of white paper using their chosen five forms or elaborations of them. The final product is a creative expression, often on the Symbolic level.

The example of the scribble chase experience demonstrates how the power of the Expressive Therapies Continuum can aid therapists in comprehending and prescribing a wide range of appropriate therapeutic experiences. Essential for a complete understanding of the ETC is an appreciation of the Perceptual/Affective level as a bridge between the Cognitive/Symbolic level above it and the Kinesthetic/Sensory level below it (V. B. Lusebrink, personal communication, March 3, 2008). If unchecked, activity on the Kinesthetic/Sensory level has the potential to remain caught up in repetitive movement and formless sensation, while Cognitive/Symbolic processing could become characterized by intellectualization and artifice. Activity on the Perceptual/Affective level can provide the needed constraints to bridge functioning between the ETC levels. Perceptual/Affective experiences formulate action into image, and thus set the stage for contemplation and personalization of meaning.

The transitional aspect of the Perceptual/Affective level is exemplified in the process of symbol formation. According to Piaget (as cited in Lusebrink, 1990), symbols have both figurative and operational elements. Formulating the figurative aspect of symbols requires functioning with the Perceptual component, and the operational aspect involves the Kinesthetic component. The term *symbol* is used in this context to mean a mental representation, and thus applies also to the Cognitive component, with reference to the thought and memory necessary to bring about the mental picture. Similarly, the Affective component forms a transition between the Sensory component and the Symbolic component. Sensations give rise to affect, which fuels the personal meaning and import of symbolic images.

Working with visual expression in therapy often involves the elucidation and working through of symbolic images, which will be discussed in Chapter 9. Briefly, however, working on the Perceptual/Affective level often provides clarity when differentiating symbolic images and cognitive concepts into their constituent parts. Personal symbols have figurative and affective components that can be rediscovered in the therapeutic process, thus leading to the *meaning* of the symbolic images and expressions, and to the *affective charges* contained in the symbols. The figurative aspects of symbolic images can be explored kinesthetically using a Gestalt approach.

The Expressive Therapies Continuum as a Foundational Theory

The field of art therapy is supported by foundational theories and a growing body of literature that demonstrate its power as a unique health service profession (Junge, 1994; Rubin, 1984). The Expressive Therapies Continuum can be considered one such foundational theory. As was demonstrated in this brief introductory chapter, the ETC is a theoretical and practical guide that describes and represents the ways in which people interact with various art media or experiential activities to process information and form images. The ETC attempts to explain the healing dimensions of various expressive experiences and the restorative power of creativity. Knowledge of the ETC and implementation of its principles can distinguish trained art therapists from other health service professionals who use art media in counseling sessions. The ETC helps clarify art therapy as not merely a modality of verbal psychotherapy, but a unique discipline in its own right with a theoretical framework that can guide the use of art media and experiences.

According to Lusebrink in the foreword to this book, when the Expressive Therapies Continuum was first presented to the art therapy community at the Ninth Annual Conference of the American Art Therapy Association (Kagin & Lusebrink, 1978a), the response was one of uncertainty. Many audience members questioned how the concept of the ETC related to established conceptualizations of art therapy, because it involved a revolutionary way of applying art therapy principles. However, in the 30 years since its initial presentation, the ETC has been discussed in the art therapy literature (Malchiodi, 2003b), and adopted by graduate training programs as a foundational and unifying theory in the field of art therapy. The Expressive Therapies Continuum represents a common language for art therapists having diverse theoretical backgrounds. The ETC provides guiding principles that aid in the recognition and discussion of the healing properties of expressive activities and creative experiences. The ETC has the potential to unite art therapists and provide a solid platform upon which the profession of art therapy can continue to grow. Art therapists of varied theoretical orientations can acknowledge the healing and emergent functions of different expressive experiences.

Unifying the Field of Art Therapy

Historically in the field of art therapy, there has been a division between art therapists who define themselves as artists and those who define themselves as clinicians. For more than 30 years this has been known as the "artist as therapist" versus "art psychotherapist" debate (Junge, 1994, p. 272). The artist as therapist camp has been criticized by their detractors as not being grounded in science. The art psychotherapists have been viewed as too clinical and as disregarding their roots in all elements of art: art education, art history, and art making. Currently among art therapists, there is still resistance to making art therapy too clinical (e.g., Allen, 1992). The Expressive Therapies Continuum is not an attempt to make art therapy more clinical or to follow a clinical or medical model in approaching clients and their treatment. On the contrary, the ETC provides a common theoretical foundation based on qualities of art media, expressive styles, and creative activities. It has been my experience, both as a therapist and as an educator, that knowledge and application of the principles of the ETC facilitate therapist understanding of client needs, effectively guide the selection of therapeutic experiences, and can promote understanding and communication among expressive therapists.

The Expressive Therapies Continuum provides unifying principles that demonstrate the uniqueness of art therapists among other types of mental health professionals. A well-meaning therapist who uses art in psychotherapy, but who was not trained in the ETC, might use the same media or the same directive with all clients. As will be explained throughout this book, one media or one therapeutic experience cannot and will not be adequate to meet the needs of all clients. For example, McNamee (2004) reported some success but more client resistance as she tried to employ scribble drawings with the majority of her clients. In fact, research has shown that sometimes art making can exacerbate painful medical conditions such as migraine headache (Vick & Sexton-Radek, 2005). The ETC can serve as a guide for choosing optimal therapeutic strategies.

The Rest of the Book

The next chapter reveals the historical roots of the Expressive Therapies Continuum as it applies to the field of art therapy. The ETC is a systems-oriented approach to the expressive arts therapies, and Lusebrink (1991b) has described how the ETC can be applied to music, dance, and drama therapy as well as to art therapy. The focus of this book, however, will be on the application of the ETC within art therapy. In Chapter 2, the contributions of seven pioneering art therapists to the field are described and their influences on the field of art therapy examined.

Chapters 3 to 9 explore more deeply each component of the Expressive Therapies Continuum. Examples of activities to stimulate information processing with each component of the ETC are provided. Media and methods for use in specific component processes are examined, and the relative reflective distance evoked by working with the components is described. The healing and emergent functions of each level are explained and their therapeutic uses explored. Finally, Chapters 3 to 9 provide a case example that demonstrates treatment guided by the particular component of the ETC under discussion.

Chapter 10 demonstrates how the ETC centers art therapy assessment on its roots in art, and focuses on *how* clients draw rather than on *what* they draw. The chapter outlines the basic types of information gathered in a series of art sessions, including preferred medium, method of interaction with media, stylistic elements from final art products, and verbal communication. Chapter 10 also includes information about ways to employ information derived from the ETC assessment in the formulation of treatment goals. A case example integrates and summarizes the information on assessment at the end of Chapter 10.

The use of the Expressive Therapies Continuum as a framework for organizing therapeutic sessions with individual clients is discussed in Chapter 11. This chapter aids the reader in understanding how assessment information can be used to gauge where to begin in therapy and how and when to change therapeutic focus. The chapter contains an exploration of the ETC as a framework for building a successful client-therapist partnership in the formulation of treatment goals and the conduct of effective therapy. Chapter 11 explains client resistances to the use of art in therapy, helping clients work through therapeutic obstacles, and describes how the ETC can be used to structure the termination of art therapy. Finally, this chapter details transference and countertransference issues unique to the ETC. The final chapter of the book delineates particular advantages when using the Expressive Therapies Continuum as a framework for the use of art therapy with groups of clients, with couples, and with families.

2

History and Evolution of the Expressive Therapies Continuum

Introduction

Art therapy is a unique profession in that it was founded by persons of varied backgrounds, experiences, and occupations. Professionals from the fields of social work, psychiatry, art education, and fine arts came together to form the American Art Therapy Association. Practitioners from diverse backgrounds shared the common goal of promoting art therapy as a unified profession (Junge, 1994). Social movements, political struggles, and the changing nature of art expression at the time created an atmosphere in which art therapy could develop and flourish.

Artistic expression in the early 20th century was evolving such that artists' emotions, political opinions, and dreams were among the themes represented on their canvases (Feldman, 1972). Cary (1958) quotes from a 1956 letter to *The Times* of London discussing the change in aesthetic ideals:

> The representation of natural appearance is no longer an indispensable or even a characteristic function of the art of painting. The criterion of truth to nature, unless interpreted in some esoteric sense, has ceased to be of critical importance. The artist is now at liberty to distort appearances as inspiration or folly may suggest. (p. 36)

This artistic expansion beyond strict representations of reality supported the nascent field of art therapy where clients routinely were asked to use color, line, and form to represent their ideas and feelings.

Following the Second World War there were large numbers of returning U.S. veterans requiring mental health services. From the late 1940s, many artists and art educators, working under the supervision of psychiatrists, offered patients various types of therapeutic art services in large hospital settings. Hill (1945) described how he single-handedly designed, implemented, and advertised a new art therapy program at a sanitarium-turned-rehabilitation hospital during the Second World War. Components of the program included art appreciation, art instruction, and free art expression. The author successfully used art to relieve boredom and despair, and to bring meaning back into the lives of gravely ill and injured patients.

Many artists and art educators are considered the early art therapy pioneers (Wix, 2000). Each art therapy pioneer brought to the field a distinct understanding of the effects of art media properties and task instructions on the creative therapeutic process. Among those developing the profession of American art therapy were Margaret Naumburg, Edith Kramer, Janie Rhyne, Elinor Ulman, Viktor Lowenfeld, and Florence Cane (Junge, 1994). Vija Lusebrink and Sandra Kagin (now Sandra Graves-Alcorn), working in art therapy with acutely psychotic and developmentally challenged individuals, respectively, created a synthesis of their own observations and the existing ideas about art therapy (V. B. Lusebrink, personal communication, April 12, 2006). The individual contributions of each art therapy pioneer to the shaping of the Expressive Therapies Continuum will be discussed below.

The Grandmother of the Expressive Therapies Continuum: Florence Cane

Florence Cane did not call herself an art therapist; she was a self-described artist and art teacher first and foremost (Cane, 1951; Detre et al., 1983). However, others have described her as an art therapy pioneer, and Cane's book, *The Artist in Each of Us* (1951), could be considered the first art therapy textbook. In her book, Cane explained how she came to teach a particular type of art lesson at her sister, Margaret Naumburg's, experimental school, the Walden School. She also described her singular approach to teaching art. Both Florence Cane and Margaret Naumburg were influenced by personal knowledge of Jungian analysis and interaction with many vanguard artists of their times (Detre et al., 1983).

Florence Cane's approach to teaching art was based on her belief that human beings perceive the world and process information from it through three main functions: movement, emotion, and thought (Cane, 1951). She wrote that art might be a way of integrating all three functions, and that if all three were used, "the child would be permitted to glimpse the fourth dimension, his spiritual awakening" (Cane, 1951, p. 35). Cane's movement, emotion, and thought functions are comparable to the Kinesthetic, Affective, and Cognitive dimensions of the Expressive Therapies Continuum. Kagin and Lusebrink (1978b) broadened these concepts when used in the ETC, by their addition of the bipolar nature of each level. For Cane, movement led to feeling that would imbue the artwork with more meaning (thought). This sequence is similar to the developmental hierarchy of the ETC. Lusebrink (1990) described the well-functioning individual as one who could develop and process images on all levels of the ETC. A similar idea is mentioned by Cane (1951), who explained that life's goal is to integrate all functions and become whole and balanced.

An original art therapy aspect of Cane's book is seen in Part IV, entitled "The Healing Power of Art" (Cane, 1951). This final section of the book was written to depict Cane's art approach with students experiencing academic, artistic, and behavioral problems. According to Cane, these problems likely resulted from blocked basic functions. A blocked basic function, either movement, emotion, or thought, was one that was not fully integrated for use, and through which limited or no information was available. Cane wrote about how her work with art was demonstrated to "unblock" students and to integrate buried functions. She described her teaching in the following words:

> I study each individual, his personality and his type. From observing his work
> I usually can judge which are his superior and inferior functions. Then I pro-
> ceed to find ways of developing his inferior side, and thereby balance his work
> and his character. (p. 316)

Thus, one can see that although Florence Cane called herself an artist and an art teacher, she seemed to work as an art therapist. By using movement, feeling, and thought, Florence Cane sought in her considered approach to her students not only to improve their art, but also to balance their characters. In this way, she meant to improve emotional, academic, or behavioral functioning (Cane, 1951). Cane discussed the fact that improvements in functioning were consistently demonstrated through parallel improvements in students' artwork. Cane mentioned that the artwork became more personally meaningful to the maker and more imbued with life and feeling. Although symbolism was not one of the primary ways in which she envisioned people gathering and processing information, Cane recognized the importance of symbolic content in children's artwork and used this content in her work with them.

The Mother of Art Therapy: Margaret Naumburg

Margaret Naumburg was Florence Cane's sister and is considered the mother of the field of art therapy (Detre et al., 1983; Junge, 1994). She worked in mental hospitals before and after establishing the Walden School, and underwent two personal psychoanalyses (Detre et al., 1983). The Freudian and Jungian ideas underlying her own psychoanalyses informed Naumburg's ideas about the function of art in therapy. Working within the context of these theories, she concluded that art psychotherapy was equal or superior to verbal therapy in its ability to release repressed material. For Naumburg, the process of art therapy was based on the belief that an individual's most essential thoughts and feelings are derived from the unconscious. She hypothesized that unconscious content achieved its most complete expression in images rather than in words (Naumburg, 1966). In addition, when the symbolic aspects of imagery as well as the verbal and cognitive aspects of experience were part of an art therapy session, an integrative and healing opportunity occurred. Mastering the art materials was seen as part of the therapeutic process, but Naumburg—and other art psychotherapists—minimized any special contributions to the process deriving from the art materials or the images themselves (Ulman, 1975a). The most important aspect of art psychotherapy was viewed as mastering the meaning of symbolic content that arose from producing an image (Naumburg, 1966).

Symbolic content was seen as central to the psychodynamic approach to art therapy that Naumburg espoused. In practicing psychodynamically oriented art therapy, Naumburg often used art not as the primary modality in therapy, but rather as a springboard into a verbal examination of the unconscious (Naumburg, 1966). In fact, in discussing the three case studies that comprise the bulk of her 1966 book, *Dynamically Oriented Art Therapy*, Naumburg stated that the majority of artwork was done outside of the therapeutic sessions, and the clients chose the images that were discussed in therapy. Thus, witnessing the process of creation—including verbal communication, frustration tolerance, and coping skills as the materials were encountered and used—was not considered an important aspect of the therapy. Naumburg's emphasis on mastering the meaning of symbolic content that emerged from created images influenced the concept of the Symbolic dimension of the Expressive Therapies Continuum.

Art as Therapy: Edith Kramer

Edith Kramer (1971) emphasized the importance of art as therapy in helping children achieve sublimation through the creative process as well as in the finished art product. Kramer also emphasized the importance of symbolism and wrote that when persons were given free reign to create with art materials, the resulting product "inevitably takes on the image of its maker" (p. 29). For psychodynamically oriented art therapists, every art product was a symbol or metaphor of the creator. Kramer also wrote that different ways of using art media had an impact on the person and the art product. Kramer discussed the use of "precursory materials," to mean scribbling and smearing, as ways to explore the physical properties of the art media. She added information about "chaotic discharge," which she defined as spilling, splashing, or destroying, which represented a loss of control in the therapeutic session.

Kramer (1971) described "art in the service of defense" as a child's use of stereotypical symbols, tracing, or copying other persons' artwork as a way to avoid affect or revealing personal information. Kramer (1971) was referring to simple symbols when she discussed "pictographs." She described pictographs as a means of representing thoughts without words. Finally, "formed expression" was seen as art in the full sense of the word, including the process of sublimation. Sublimation was seen as imbuing both the art process and the product with deeper function and meaning, as it helped contain and control aggressive or sexual impulses in socially acceptable ways.

Kramer's work contributed to the theoretical underpinnings of the Expressive Therapies Continuum. Her use of "precursory materials" and "chaotic discharge" helped formulate ideas about types of kinesthetic activities on the Kinesthetic/Sensory level of the ETC. Kramer's elaborations on the use of form to contain emotion is similar to Kagin and Lusebrink's (1978b) definition of the bipolar nature of the Perceptual/Affective level of the ETC in that as involvement with the perceptual aspect of image formation increases, affective involvement decreases. As will be demonstrated in Chapter 5, perceptual activities can be employed therapeutically to help clients contain emotion. Kramer's approach to the use of symbolic expression in more sophisticated artwork is comparable to descriptions by Kagin and Lusebrink (1978b) of image formation with the Symbolic dimension of the ETC. Symbols contain many levels of meaning and can be used with or without words to convey those meanings. Kramer's overall emphasis on aesthetical qualities of the work and assisting clients to produce "formed images" dovetails with descriptions of the creative level of the ETC.

Creating Order out of Chaos: Elinor Ulman

For Ulman (1975a), the creative process itself was often the prevailing curative factor of the nascent discipline that she attempted to define. Ulman wrote that a symbolic interpretation spoken in words was often not necessary in order for clients to gain insight from their artistic endeavors. For Ulman (1975b), sublimation through the creative process was the key to art therapy, and she said that this process "can be *talked about*, but it cannot be *translated* into words" (p. 32). Ulman (1987) revealed that she approached the field of art therapy from her own personal experiences as an artist. She fully understood the power of the creative experience to help the artist understand himself and his world, to bring order out of chaos, and to align one's inner state and outer representation of it. The creative level of the Expressive Therapies Continuum incorporates Ulman's (1987) description of the creative experience as aligning one's inner experience with an external depiction of it. Kagin and Lusebrink (1978b) discuss the creative level of the ETC as not necessarily requiring translation into words, but based on the creative expression itself.

The Value of Creative Learning: Viktor Lowenfeld

Viktor Lowenfeld was an influential art educator who helped define the stages of graphic development as well as clarify the relationships among intelligence, social abilities, and creative growth (Lowenfeld, 1952). Lowenfeld wrote that optimal learning takes place when it is integrated. He went on to explain that he did not mean the integration of two types of subject matter, but rather the integration of information achieved through different modes. He highlighted information received through kinesthetic, sensory, perceptual, emotional, and intellectual channels and said that the integration of these types of information would provide optimal creative and learning experiences. Lowenfeld contended that integrated education is highly individualized, and that it occurs when a child personally identifies with the experience about which he or she is learning. To increase personalization, Lowenfeld wrote about emphasizing the sensory, perceptual, and emotional information given to children about the subject matter being studied. According to Lowenfeld, the more complete the information taken in from all channels, the more comprehensive and creative the internal educational experience.

In formulating the Expressive Therapies Continuum, Kagin and Lusebrink (1978b) expanded Viktor Lowenfeld's framework. The various modes of information processing were formulated into a hierarchical progression of increasingly complex levels. In addition, the overarching Creative level of the ETC incorporated Lowenfeld's idea that the creative experience integrates information from many channels. The increasing complexity of visual expression on the different levels of the ETC echoes the stages of graphic development in children as proposed by Lowenfeld.

The Phenomenology of Expression: Mala Betensky

Mala Betensky (1973, 1995) pioneered the phenomenological theory of art expression. Phenomenological art therapy is based on the immediate experience of creating and perceiving art images. In her early work, Betensky (1973) discussed the nature of art media and clients' varied responses to it. She reported that persons are drawn to certain media and repelled by others based on the media's inherent structural qualities. In addition, Betensky discussed how the use of color helped facilitate the expression of emotion.

Betensky (1995) began phenomenological art therapy sessions with a period of free play in which clients were encouraged to explore, experiment, and get the "feel" of many different media. Secondly in the phenomenological approach, clients were asked to formulate an image that, when finished, was hung up on a wall to be perceived. In a process that Betensky (1995) called "phenomenological intuiting" (p. 17), clients were asked to intentionally look at their picture and see everything that there was to see in it. The work was discussed in terms of its formal artistic properties, such as line, color, and form. Finally, in the third phase clients were asked to concentrate on the question "What do you see?" (p. 17). In this way they were asked to derive meaning from the art product.

Betensky's phenomenological approach to art therapy and the nature of art media influenced several aspects of the Expressive Therapies

Continuum. Parallels to the ETC can be seen in the author's writings about the movement of fluid media, and how from the undifferentiated background, a figure emerges that can be used in art therapy. Similarities to the ETC can be seen in the way in which Betensky described the therapeutic process in the phenomenological approach to expressive therapy. The free play portion of the therapeutic session is similar to the Kinesthetic/Sensory level of the ETC, where the movement and sensory aspects of the art media are emphasized. The next phase, namely, the clients' contemplation of their own artwork, parallels the Perceptual level of the ETC in which the formal elements of visual expression are paramount. Finally, in the third phase, clients are asked to derive meaning from the art product. Connections between art and life are discussed. This type of information processing is similar to that which has been described as occurring on the Cognitive/Symbolic level of the ETC (Kagin & Lusebrink, 1978b; Lusebrink, 1990).

The Role of Gestalt Art Therapy: Janie Rhyne

The Perceptual dimension of the Expressive Therapies Continuum was influenced by Janie Rhyne's Gestalt art therapy approach (Rhyne, 1973, 1987). Gestalt psychology was a school of thought from the first half of the 20th century that placed emphasis on perception and immediate experience (Rhyne, 1987). In her structured Gestalt approach to art therapy, Rhyne emphasized perception and visual thinking. Therapist and client examined client-created artwork in terms of the perceived structures and the dynamics of these structures. The "visual language" used to describe the artwork focused on the formal elements of visual expression of the structures created. Thus, the qualities of lines and forms and the relationships among them were discussed, and parallels to the client's life might be drawn. For example, an image replete with activity might correspond to the frenetic pace of the client's life (Rhyne, 1987).

This focus on the elements of visual expression and their applications to life is a different approach than discussing and analyzing the underlying meaning and emotion of the symbolism in client artwork. A symbolic interpretation is likely more past oriented or future directed. The focus in Gestalt art therapy is on the *immediate* perception of forms and structures, with the client using a visual language to discuss them.

Rhyne (1973) additionally stated that persons gain awareness of their immediate experience from concentrating on sensorimotor experience.

Rhyne suggested different types of sensory activities to enhance a person's full appreciation of the present moment. Rhyne's Gestalt art therapy approach with its emphasis on perception and visual thinking provided a new and different way to view created artwork. This method with its emphasis on the formal expressive elements was incorporated into the Perceptual dimension of the Expressive Therapies Continuum.

The Developmental Aspects of Image and Thought: Mardi Horowitz

Mardi Horowitz (1970, 1983) wrote about the relationship of images and cognition. He studied diverse types of images, conditions conducive to producing images, and the usefulness of images in psychotherapy. For Horowitz, various types of images formed the basis of thoughts, and cognitive growth could be traced from childhood through adolescence based on the concreteness or abstractness of images.

Enactive representation was for Horowitz (1970, 1983) the first type of thought involving muscle activity and reflexive action. According to Horowitz (1983), this type of thought does not disappear with the development of more complex modes of thinking and can be identified in adults through hand gestures that accompany expressions, perhaps as aids to memory. The second mode of thought to develop was image representation. Horowitz wrote that images developed out of input from all sensory channels, and these images were what allowed cognitive processing of a perceptual event to continue after an actual object had been removed. Thus, he stated that cooks might have olfactory or gustatory images, dancers kinesthetic images, and architects and surgeons visual images to aid in their work. This type of cognition was more complex in that it allowed thoughts about images to continue in the absence of a concrete stimulus, and new connections to be developed and elaborated. The last type of cognitive representation that Horowitz described was the lexical mode. This type of cognitive processing involved words and provided for new levels of abstraction, reasoning, and the conceptualization of information.

Horowitz (1970, 1983) wrote that early forms of representation do not disappear as new capacities are gained. Further, achieving the highest level of cognitive/imaginal processing, which he called lexical representation, increases the ability to process information on any level. In addition, the author stressed that information processing in one mode can facilitate processing in others.

Horowitz's theory provided for the Expressive Therapies Continuum the missing link that showed the parallels among imagery formation, cognitive processes, and art expressions on the different levels. His sequence of enactive representation involving muscle activity and reflexive action, image representation as a perceptual event, and lexical mode of cognitive representation was elaborated in the ETC as image formation on the Kinesthetic/Sensory level, Perceptual/Affective level, and Cognitive/Symbolic level in hierarchical succession. Each new level represented an increasingly complex mode of information processing and image formation. Horowitz's (1970, 1983) statement about the influence of one mode of information processing on others also was incorporated into the structure of the ETC and will be further discussed in chapters on the individual ETC dimensions.

The Effects of Media Properties and Task Instructions

Many early art therapists wrote about media properties and their influences on the art process and product (Kramer, 1971, 1975b; Lowenfeld, 1952; Naumburg, 1966; Rhyne, 1973; Rubin, 1984; Wadeson, 1980). In contrast to the typical ways in which media were referenced in the study of art—graphic arts, painting, and sculpture—art therapists began to define media by their influence on the art process (Lusebrink, 1990). Media were identified as fluid and likely to evoke emotion, or solid and likely to evoke internal structure during the creative act. Rhyne (1973) stated that media choice was influenced by personal style, with persons presenting content imbued with particular meaning. Information about the effects of media properties on the creative process in art therapy was more formally presented by Kagin and Lusebrink (1978b) in work that was called media dimension variables, based on Kagin's master's degree thesis (cited in Kagin & Lusebrink, 1978b). Kagin and Lusebrink categorized two-dimensional and three-dimensional media on continua from fluid to resistive and discussed the influence of media choice on image formation and information processing.

Figure 2.1 shows that materials with more inherent solidity or structure (e.g., wood in three-dimensional, pencil in two-dimensional) are called *resistive* because they require the application of pressure, and provide resistance to pressure to be used effectively. Media with less inherent structure are called *fluid* (e.g., wet clay in three-dimensional, watercolor paint in two-dimensional) because they flow easily and quickly during the

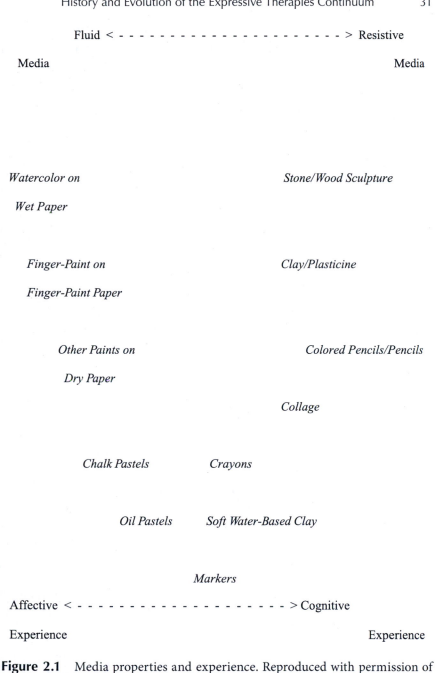

Figure 2.1 Media properties and experience. Reproduced with permission of Jessica Kingsley Publishers from Hinz, L. D., *Drawing From Within: Using Art to Treat Eating Disorders*, London: Jessica Kingsley Publishers, 2006.

creative process. According to Kagin and Lusebrink (1978b), fluid media are likely to elicit emotional responses and resistive media are likely to evoke cognitive responses.

Media Properties

Kagin and Lusebrink (1978b) developed information about media variables and incorporated it into the Expressive Therapies Continuum framework. For example, according to Kagin and Lusebrink (1978b), materials on the Kinesthetic/Sensory level of the ETC can serve as mere facilitators of action or sensation. Materials on the perceptual pole of the Perceptual/Affective level emphasize form dimensions of the media experience. Experiences in which form arises from a background, such as contrasting colored papers or drawing media, help contribute to a perceptual experience. Fluid media, as was mentioned above, can evoke affect. The use of watercolor paint on wet paper is a rapidly flowing activity that often induces an affective experience. Symbolic experiences come from ambiguous forms, such as those produced by sponge painting or blot painting. Ambiguous forms encourage organization into recognizable symbols that can be imbued with personal meaning (Lusebrink, 1990). Materials that involve precision, planning, and complicated thought processes evoke cognitive experiences. Pencils for drawing involve precision, and planning is involved in the cutting and pasting required in creating a collage.

It is not necessary to change media in order to modify the information processing and image formation qualities of an expressive experience. As was demonstrated using the example of finger paint in the first chapter, the same medium may evoke various types of experiences on the Expressive Therapies Continuum, depending on how it is used. Henley (1991) explained this media flexibility with clay:

> At the pre-art stage, clay can be used for play or sensory exploration. Once an appreciation of product is established, the rudiments of pottery making can be taught, following which figurative sculpture can be introduced to explore the expressive mode. (p. 70)

Henley demonstrated how clay may be used in a Kinesthetic/Sensory fashion, a perceptual manner, and finally a Cognitive/Symbolic way depending on the individual needs of the client.

Boundaries, Mediators, and Reflective Distance

In addition to the expressive potentials inherent in the physical properties of art media, Kagin and Lusebrink (1978b) also emphasized that the physical properties of media impose certain limits on an expressive art experience. The authors explained that these limits could be either boundary determined or quantity determined. When media are *boundary determined* the physical boundaries of the materials themselves limit the expressive potential. For example, an individual given a piece of wood to work with is limited by the size of the material. The use of boundary-determined media does not eliminate the expression of emotion in artwork, but rather is one way to contain it safely.

Alternatively, limits imposed by media can be *quantity determined*, such that the amount of a given substance determines the limits of expression. For example, a large jar of tempera paint would impose greatly different boundaries than a tablespoon of the same paint presented in a muffin tin. All other things being equal, the former experience would allow for a much more emotionally engaging experience than the latter.

The use of *mediators* or tools also influences interactions with various media and their expressive potential. Paint applied with a paintbrush (mediator) has a different expressive potential than finger paint applied with the hands. Using the hands would initiate a sensory experience from which an affective occurrence might evolve. The use of mediators also influences the level of reflective distance experienced when working with a particular media. The use of a paintbrush renders the experience less immediately engaging.

Reflective distance refers to an individual's ability to think about or reflect upon the expressive experience (Kagin & Lusebrink, 1978b). In general, the use of tools or mediators (paintbrushes, ceramic tools) increases the reflective distance in an artistic encounter, and thus allows the individual time to ponder the meaning of an expressive event as it is happening. Without mediators, the experience is likely to be too immediate and absorbing to provide for contemplation.

Task Complexity and Task Structure

Kagin and Lusebrink (1978b) indicated that the type of instructions given by the therapist could alter the quality of image formation and information

TABLE 2.1 Complexity and Structure of Task Instructions as Related to Art Project Outcome

Task Instructions	Low Level	High Level
Structure		
(Specific response required or not)	No specific response is required	Specific response is required
	Any or various outcomes expected	Group members would achieve similar outcomes
	Leads to affective functioning or symbol formation	Leads to increased cognitive functioning
	Example: Draw your addiction	*Example*: Draw a floor plan of your childhood home
Complexity		
(number of instructions or steps to completion)	One instruction is given; only one step is required for successful completion of the project	Many instructions are given
	Leads to affective experience, symbolic processing, or both	Many steps are required for successful completion of the project
	Example: Paint the emotion fear	Leads to increased cognitive functioning, as many steps must be remembered and worked through
		Example: Mask making

processing experiences. The two types of task instructions discussed were structure and complexity. Table 2.1 contains information about how both task complexity and task structure are related to Expressive Therapies Continuum component functioning and to the outcome of the final art product. In addition, specific expressive experiences are provided as examples of each type of activity. *High-complexity* tasks are those that involve many steps. *Highly structured* tasks involve specific types of responses leading to specific outcomes at task completion. Experiences with more complex instructions or requiring many steps tend to evoke cognitive functioning. Clients must think through the order of operations and execute many steps in order to reach a desired goal. Therefore, these high-complexity and highly structured experiences evoke information processing with the Cognitive component of the Expressive Therapies Continuum. Art experiences requiring few instructions (*low-complexity* tasks) and those not associated with a specific response (*low structure*) are more likely to evoke functioning with the Affective or Symbolic dimensions of the ETC. Fewer instructions and specified dimensions allow the art experience to flow more freely and liberate emotional potential as well as the opportunity for discovering personal meaning. The influences of task complexity and structure will be discussed in more depth in the chapters on the individual levels of the ETC.

Summary

Early art therapy theorists came from diverse backgrounds that influenced the ways in which they viewed the healing properties of art media and the creative experience. In the early days of the profession, there were disagreements about what characteristics of the creative experience and art product were therapeutic (Junge, 1994; Ulman, 1975a). The Expressive Therapies Continuum represents one way to recognize that numerous features of the media properties, art experience, and finished product are healing. The ETC takes into account many essential aspects of information processing and image formation and relates them to one another in a theory that is developmental and hierarchical. It also reflects a synthesis of Kagin and Lusebrink's own observations, and draws diverse aspects from several different schools of thought.

As shown in this chapter, precursors of the Expressive Therapies Continuum existed in many early writings. Early art therapists felt emotion arising from kinesthetic and sensory activity, saw form emerging from chaos, and wrote about the importance of helping people understand personal and universal symbols. Evolution in the fine arts allowed for emotional expression beyond strict lifelike representations of artistic subjects. In formulating the Expressive Therapies Continuum, Kagin and Lusebrink (1978b) expanded upon previously isolated descriptions of image formation, information processing, and creative activity. Based on their respective work and observations with developmentally challenged and acutely psychotic individuals, they devised a manner of describing the processes taking place within an expressive therapy session among an individual, the art materials, and the image produced. The ETC provides a theoretical structure that describes interactions among person, product, and process in art therapy. The framework of the ETC can guide the assessment process in therapy as well as describe what happens in a therapeutic session. It also provides information to direct the selection of materials and activities from session to session for optimal therapeutic gain. Finally, a client's progression in the therapeutic process can be tracked within the framework of the ETC.

With the Expressive Therapies Continuum, Kagin and Lusebrink (1978b) presented a unifying theoretical construct that cuts across therapeutic orientations to describe how qualities of the media, or the experiences chosen, interact with each person's preferred style of image formation and information processing to convey content or meaning. Although hierarchical from simple Kinesthetic/Sensory to complex Cognitive/Symbolic information processing, there is no implication that one level of the ETC is inherently superior to another. A well-functioning individual is able to receive and process information on all levels and with all components of the ETC. Art therapy can help balance functioning of an individual who tends to over- or underuse one type of information in processing and decision making.

Section 2

Characteristics of the
Expressive Therapies
Continuum and
Its Components

3

Kinesthetic Component of the Expressive Therapies Continuum

Introduction to the Kinesthetic Component

The kinesthetic sense encompasses the sensations that inform people of and accompany bodily movement, rhythms, and actions. Gardner (1999) defines bodily-kinesthetic intelligence as "the potential of using one's whole body or parts of the body (like the hand or the mouth) to solve problems or fashion products" (p. 42). He describes actors, dancers, and other athletes as being particularly in tune with their kinesthetic-bodily sense. According to Cane (1951), the kinesthetic sense is much neglected and many people are largely unaware of the feedback that they get from their bodies or how to use kinesthetic information and expression effectively.

Information gathered and processed on the Kinesthetic/Sensory level of the Expressive Therapies Continuum (capital letters are used throughout the chapter to distinguish the Kinesthetic and Sensory components of the ETC from other uses of the words) is often preverbal. Part of the connection between motor associations and somatosensory associations takes place in the limbic system or old brain, whereas the other part of the connection is through direct transcortical transmission between the two cortices (Lusebrink, 2004). Incidents in our very early childhood occur before we have words to describe and label them. Experiences that occur before the age of three years are likely stored in the right hemisphere of the brain because the corpus collusum does not develop sufficiently to assist in the transfer of information from the right hemisphere to the left, where words and verbal labels dominate, until after the third year of life (Riley, 2004; Schore, 2002). Thus, art therapy performed on the Kinesthetic/Sensory level of the ETC may be particularly helpful in accessing preverbal material (Lusebrink,

1990, 2004; Sholt & Gavron, 2006). Kinesthetic activity is the most basic level of expression, and graphically it is the first mode of expression.

Most art experiences involve movement and motor experiences, but incidental motor activity is not what is intended by the term *kinesthetic functioning* on the Expressive Therapies Continuum. Experiences using the Kinesthetic component of the ETC are those in which motor action itself is used therapeutically to express energy or as a reconstitutive agent (Lusebrink, 2004). Kinesthetic information provides feedback about how the body moves in space and a sense of bodily rhythms. Karen Signell (1990) explained the importance of bodily rhythms:

> From the very beginning of life, how good it feels to move at our own individual pace and in accordance with the wider rhythms around us, and how alienating to our personhood to be restricted in our movement or speeded up, discordant with our surroundings. Finding our own natural rhythm is a crucial experience of the early Self: being attuned to Nature, its rhythms, and attuned to one's own inner nature. These are all early manifestations of being in accord with one's deepest center, one's environment, and even the Great Round of life and death. (p. 55)

In addition to fostering connections with universal rhythms, kinesthetic information is important for nonverbal communication, movement of the body effectively through space, and increasing or decreasing bodily tension.

As mentioned in Chapter 1, components of each level of the Expressive Therapies Continuum are related in a curvilinear fashion, resembling an inverted U (Lusebrink, 1991b). Processing with one component of the level will at first increase or enliven the opposite function, and later inhibit or block it. On the Kinesthetic/Sensory level of the ETC, a small amount of kinesthetic activity will facilitate sensory information processing, perhaps by minimally increasing bodily tension, and thus rendering sensory input more salient. This increase in functioning occurs up to a certain optimal level, and then it begins to decrease and even block opposite component functioning. Thus, *absorption* in kinesthetic activity will obstruct information gathering and processing from the opposite component (Sensory). For example, engaging in vigorous kinesthetic activity such as pounding clay would not allow the absorption of sensory information about the temperature or texture of the clay.

Developmental Hierarchy

Because they are action oriented and tension releasing, there is a tendency for kinesthetic activities to lead to regression (Kramer, 1971). The rhythmic aspects of kinesthetic action comprise the first learning feedback loops, allowing infants to profit from recurring movements. Repeated kinesthetic action can be a method of self-soothing in infants and older children experiencing developmental delays. As was mentioned in the first chapter, when very young children use art materials, they are not concerned with the outcome of their actions. They are occupied solely with the actions themselves. The movements involved in creating art provide stimulation and release tension. The same kind of kinesthetic stimulation can be used therapeutically to reconstitute memory functioning in the elderly (Lusebrink, 2004) and to help clients cut off from bodily sensations regain an appreciation for kinesthetic input. Large muscle movements were used by several early art teachers and therapists to relax their students and allow imagery to flow more freely (Cane, 1951; Lowenfeld, 1952; Ulman & Levy, 1975).

Jackson Pollock seemed to intuitively understand the healing role of movement when, early in his career and suffering from mental illness, he entered analysis with a Jungian psychiatrist and introduced drawings into the therapeutic process (Wysuph, 1970). According to Wysuph (1970), Pollack was withdrawn and found it difficult to verbalize his concerns in therapy; however, the addition of drawings gradually opened up communication about his psychic state. As his art evolved into "action painting," Pollock did away with representations of the psychic state in favor of *enacting* it in physical movement. Through action and movement the artist was able to convey what word and conventional forms could not.

Healing Dimension of the Kinesthetic Component

The healing dimension of the Kinesthetic component of the Expressive Therapies Continuum involves increasing or decreasing clients' amount of arousal and tension. It can involve the *stimulation* of arousal or energy through involvement with kinesthetic action, or the *discharge* of energy that reduces the individual's level of tension (Kagin & Lusebrink, 1978b). Research has shown that pent-up muscular tension can lead to tension headache, lower back pain, and other somatic symptoms (Cooper & Dewe, 2004; Eriksen & Ursin, 2004). Meerlood (1985) claimed that disrhythmias are the basis of psychosomatic disease. He explained that psychosomatic conditions could begin as defenses against the imposition of outside schedules on a person's internal biological patterns. Healing can be promoted by the release of tension using art media and expressive experiences (Cohen,

1983; Slater, 2004). Slater explained the kinesthetic involvement central to stone carving: "The act of using big muscles to remove blocks of stone is a powerful experience. It was cathartic, exhilarating, and relaxing all at the same time" (2004, p. 227).

Lack of awareness of or blocking of kinesthetic information can be a precursor to alexithymia. Alexithymia literally means having no words for emotions or, practically speaking, being out of touch with the experience of one's emotions. Clients suffering from alexithymia can benefit from experiences that introduce them to nonthreatening kinesthetic action and rhythms (Lusebrink, 1990). Gently rolling clay is an experience that taps internal rhythms. In addition, clients can be asked to knead soft dough or tap nails into soft wood or Styrofoam. Therapist direction can help clients maintain a focus on finding and matching internal rhythms.

Examples of Kinesthetic Experiences

Art activities with the Kinesthetic component are those that emphasize rhythm, action, movement, and the release of energy. Used in a kinesthetic manner, art media often act merely as the passive facilitators of action. Pounding, pushing, scratching, stabbing, smashing or rolling clay, pounding nails into wood, cutting, scribbling, splashing paint, and tearing paper are some examples of kinesthetic activities emphasizing movement and release of energy (Lusebrink, 1990; Sholt & Gavron, 2006). Sometimes an identifiable art product is not produced using these methods, but a creative moment can still take place via the principle of *isomorphism*, as an internal state is expressed and matched in a corresponding external experience (Cohen, 1983; Feldman, 1972). In the case of kinesthetic expression, an internal state such as anger can be matched to the external experience of pounding clay.

It should not be assumed that all kinesthetic experiences have to be aggressive or angry. In fact, kinesthetic experiences can be soothing. Poetry therapists emphasize that the rhythm and cadence of words often are more healing than the meaning of the words themselves (Meerlood, 1985). The maternal heartbeat is the original rhythm that infants perceive, and throughout infancy it has a calming effect (Kurihara et al., 1996). Entrainment is a concept that can help explain the soothing aspects of rhythmic kinesthetic activity; it is the tendency for two bodies moving in rhythm to lock into phase so that they move in harmony (Large & Jones, 1999; Rider, 1987). Entrainment also is defined as a synchronization of two or more rhythmic cycles (Etzel, Johnsen, Dickerson, Tranel, & Adolphs, 2006). The principle of entrainment is universal and affects many processes; it is possible to have rhythmic entrainment, melodic entrainment, and dynamic entrainment (Bradt, 2002; Large & Jones, 1999).

Entrainment rhythm or music has the potential to resonate with the listener's feelings and promote a sense of alert relaxation. The principle of entrainment has been used in the treatment of autism to reduce self-harm (Orr, Myles, & Carlson, 1998), in pediatric pain reduction (Bradt, 2002), and in drug abuse treatment (Blackett & Payne, 2005; Winkelman, 2003). Art making processes can be used in a similar fashion using the Kinesthetic component of the ETC to help persons find and express a soothing internal rhythm, to resonate with a relaxing rhythm, or to discharge energy in a slow and rhythmic fashion.

A rhythmic kinesthetic experience can be used in a reconstitutive fashion with schizophrenic or Alzheimer's patients, or persons recovering from stroke (Cottrell & Gallant, 2003; Lusebrink, 2004). The object of such kinesthetic activity would be to help integrate fragmented cognitive experiences, to increase memory functioning, and to promote life satisfaction. Wadeson (2000) recommended painting to the rhythm of music as one type of reconstitutive activity. Forming a clay sculpture to music can have the same effect as long as the clay is soft, warm, and pliable.

Media Experiences That Enhance Kinesthetic Functioning

Media that emphasize movement and enhance the release of energy are often *resistive*; they require effort to manipulate, and provide resistance to that effort. Resistance increases the physical energy needed to perform a function and increases the release of energy. Materials such as stone, wood, mosaic tile, and clay have an inherent structure, and this provides the resistance that makes them good vehicles to enhance energy release. In addition, these materials are also *boundary determined*—their inherent structure (physical boundaries that are limited) restricts the potential for the expression of energy. The release of energy can only take place as far as the boundaries of the media (Kagin & Lusebrink, 1978b).

On the other hand, *quantity-determined media* (boundaries determined by the amount or quantity available to the client) such as paint can amplify the expression of energy. A client can load up a paintbrush with more and more paint in an effort to increase the release of pent-up energy. Kagin and Lusebrink (1978b) point out that therapists must be acutely aware of the amplification potential of quantity-determined media. Quantity-determined or *fluid* media can sometimes detract from the therapeutic value of kinesthetic activities. Because the energy that arises from these experiences is undifferentiated, media without inherent form can lead to increased confusion rather than direction (Lusebrink, 1990). The use of finger paint with children, for example, could lead to smearing and both artistic and behavioral regression (Kramer, 1971).

In order to increase the healing properties of energy release, clients can be led to a conclusion about the experience through discussion. Alternatively, they may arrive at closure through emergence of a form, feeling, or insight about the experience. An open-ended kinesthetic experience can be interpreted as a wonderful release of tension by the art therapist familiar with clay work. But a frightened client, unfamiliar with art therapy or the use of clay, might interpret the kinesthetic experience as one of overwhelming power; clay can evoke too much energy release. It is advisable to conclude kinesthetic sessions with a discussion of the experience, and with a conversation or perhaps an art activity, that helps the client gain closure about the experience and its meaning.

Reflective Distance With the Kinesthetic Component

Because kinesthetic activities are so physically engrossing, the amount of reflective distance is usually minimal. For this reason, a discussion or art activity often is needed to help structure the experience and process its meaning. The undifferentiated energy expressed during kinesthetic action is absorbing, and thus the client's ability to think about the experience while it is happening is quite low. As was mentioned above, sometimes the use of fluid media in a kinesthetic fashion can lead to a regressive use of the media. The introduction of a mediator—a tool interposed between client and media—can help increase reflective distance and reduce the likelihood of regressive involvement if it is unwanted.

Questions and Discussion That Promote Kinesthetic Functioning

In order to promote information gathering and processing on the Kinesthetic dimension, certain lines of questioning can be followed that focus on the action or rhythm involved in the experience. The therapist can ask: "What are you *doing*?" or "What *action* is that?" (Lusebrink, 1990). Therapists can encourage energy release by commenting that an action is physically powerful or really requires muscle. When clients focus on how their muscles are working, the energy release can be even more effective. Questions could focus on rhythm by asking: "Can you concentrate on that beat?" or "Can you repeat that pattern of rhythm?" Discussions can include those that focus on vibrations, patterns of rhythm, regularity, symmetry, and pulse.

Emergent Function of the Kinesthetic Component

As was introduced in Chapter 1, the emergent function of a component on the Expressive Therapies Continuum refers to an experience that is generated from the current mode of information processing. A higher level of functioning generally results from the current experience. The emergent function of the Kinesthetic component is the appearance of form or emotion, leading the client to the Perceptual/Affective level of the ETC. Thus, from a focus on rhythm and action on the Kinesthetic dimension, form can emerge and lead the client toward interaction with the Perceptual component. In addition, the tempo of a kinesthetic activity has an influence on the type of form produced (Rosal & Lehder, 1982). A scribble drawing primarily is a kinesthetic activity, but when a person perceives an image in the intertwining lines of the drawing, the Perceptual component of the ETC is engaged. Focusing on structure can help clients formulate their thoughts and feelings about an event or feeling.

Kinesthetic action can also lead to the emergence of emotion and engagement of the Affective dimension of the Expressive Therapies Continuum (Lusebrink, 1990). Vigorous movement is likely to be associated with increased arousal, excitement, or anger. Slow movement likely will evoke soothing emotions. One strategy for helping persons with limited access to their emotions is to provide a kinesthetic activity directed at first by questions about the *action* and later by inquiries about the *feeling*. Changing lines of questioning is one way to facilitate changing levels of the ETC. Reluctant clients may not be able to respond to questions with the name of an emotion, but they can be encouraged to draw as one way of gaining closure about the experience. Later in treatment, vigorous kinesthetic activity such as throwing clay at a wall could be used to energize the experience of emotion.

When Work on the Kinesthetic Component Is Indicated

In general, art therapists begin their therapeutic work with clients at the level and component of the Expressive Therapies Continuum where the client demonstrates the ability to work comfortably (Lusebrink, 1990). As was discussed previously, client comfort with media and information processing strategies, as well as a typical expressive style, can be determined during the assessment phase of therapy. Assessment issues will be examined in detail in Chapter 10.

Clients who are attracted to the Kinesthetic component generally will begin art therapy with action-oriented activities. They express themselves naturally through their bodies and learn best by involving the kinesthetic sense. Such persons might include those that are naturally athletically talented or perhaps gifted crafts persons (Gardner, 1999). In addition, certain psychiatric diagnoses may lead one to prefer the Kinesthetic component of the Expressive Therapies Continuum. For example, children with attention-deficit/hyperactivity disorder might first approach the art materials in an action-oriented manner. As will be discussed in the following case example, a purely action-oriented approach will be tempered and altered in the course of therapy.

Overcoming Blocks to the Use of Kinesthetic Functioning

Obstacles to functioning on the Kinesthetic component come from many sources, including those generally related to society and those specific to the individual. In general, our society teaches and values linguistic and cognitive processes (Gardner, 1999). From an early age, children are required to sit attentively at school and process information through linguistic channels. Although there is evidence that kinesthetic activity can enhance academic functioning (Jensen, 2001; Miller, 2006), recess is generally viewed not as a time to prepare students for learning, but rather as a time to rid the body of excess energy built up by sitting too long.

When kinesthetic information processing is not valued, it does not develop at the same rate and intensity as other types of information processing strategies. Art therapists must bear in mind that because the body-kinesthetic sense is not as well developed as cognitive forms of information processing, many clients will be uncomfortable with kinesthetic activities, and some clients will show an aversion to them. However, a well-functioning individual is able to value and process information with all components of the Expressive Therapies Continuum. Recovering function in the kinesthetic area can be determined as a goal for art therapy.

Other blocks to kinesthetic functioning may be specifically related to individuals. A person can be so cognitively oriented that she or he is out of touch with the rhythms and wisdom gathered through the body. Clues to the disconnection between cognitive functioning and bodily functioning are rigid body posture and movement. Eating disordered persons frequently ignore kinesthetic cues from their bodies when they overexercise and cause themselves exercise-induced injuries (Yates, 1999).

Increasing Kinesthetic functioning and reorienting a client to the kinesthetic-bodily sense can be one important goal for art therapy. Clients can be encouraged to sculpt themselves in clay miniature or draw a self-portrait and then pose themselves as the product. Processing of the experience involves helping clients find words for how their bodies feel and how the body might move (walk, dance, sit) in the posed position. Family sculpting is a similar activity that can be conducted in a group setting with clients alone, or with clients and their families (Root, 1989). Clients first construct their families out of clay and later take turns posing group members as their families. Clients begin talking about the *physical feelings* associated with the postures (Kinesthetic dimension) and later discuss *emotions* evoked by the experience (Affective component).

Balancing Overuse of Kinesthetic Information Processing

Motor activity can be used defensively as a way not to think deeply or feel emotion (Lusebrink, 1990). Through continuous movement such as repeated toe tapping, overinvolvement with the Kinesthetic component could inhibit involvement on the Perceptual/Affective level of the Expressive Therapies Continuum. Lusebrink (1990) points out that traumatic memories from early childhood are likely stored in memory as images on a preverbal level. Thus, clients unable or unwilling to process the images and emotions associated with trauma can use motor activity such as repeated foot movements as an outlet for mounting anxiety. The physical action can be used to ward off the formation of traumatic images and to avoid experiencing painful emotions. A nonthreatening kinesthetic art activity such as cutting and fitting mosaic tiles into a pattern can provide an outlet for arousal as well as suggest a form for the threatening images.

As was mentioned above, persons suffering from attention-deficit/
hyperactivity disorder, predominantly hyperactive-impulsive type, often are
most comfortable processing information with the Kinesthetic component
of the Expressive Therapies Continuum. According to the DSM-IV-TR
(American Psychiatric Association [APA], 2000), a child with attention-
deficit/hyperactivity disorder (AD/HD) demonstrates restlessness or
fidgety behavior. In class, this child inappropriately leaves his or her seat,
runs or climbs in the class, and has trouble quietly playing or engaging
in leisure activities. The AD/HD child also appears driven or "on the go."
In fact, it would be difficult for him or her to curtail physical activity long
enough to effectively process information in other ways. Often a therapeutic goal for a child with AD/HD is to learn to slow down and use cognitive information processing strategies to control behavior. In addition,
children can be taught to examine cause-and-effect relationships and to
think before they act (Froehlich, Doepfner, & Lehmkuhl, 2002).

According to Safran (2003), art therapy has several advantages with
AD/HD children. Art is an engaging and familiar activity for children
that can help normalize their therapy experience. Art provides a structure
for the therapeutic sessions and provides an immediate visual record of
the thoughts and words expressed in therapy. The image created can be
referred to repeatedly in therapy and with parents to reinforce learning.
Safran used a group approach to the treatment of AD/HD that emphasized
learning social skills and sharing the universal problems and concerns
related to living with the disorder. Each week in art therapy children drew
an image related to a central symptom (e.g., impulsivity, distractibility),
discussed its impact upon family and peers, and proposed potential solutions.
Images helped children in the group stay focused on the problem at hand.

The Expressive Therapies Continuum offers another framework for
the treatment of attention-deficit/hyperactivity disorder. The disorder is
conceptualized as information processing concentrated at the Kinesthetic
component of the ETC, and the goal of therapy is seen as familiariz-
ing the child with other information processing strategies. Beginning
with the Kinesthetic component, other activities of increasing complexity are taught until the child is able to gather and process information
on the Cognitive/Symbolic level of the ETC. Information processing
with the Cognitive component requires thought before action, planning
abilities, and the carrying out of tasks with multiple instructions. As
will be illustrated in the following case example, the child is first met in
therapy at the Kinesthetic dimension and gradually moved to the next
level of functioning—the Perceptual/Affective level—and finally to the

Cognitive/Symbolic level, with the goal of establishing more cognitive control over motor activity and impulsive behaviors.

With the Expressive Therapies Continuum in mind, along with the effects of media properties and task instructions, the therapist could do several things in order to ensure successful treatment of the child with attention-deficit/hyperactivity disorder. The art therapist could limit media choices in order to contain activity. Safran (2003) reported that she limited media choices to markers and colored pencils in order to provide the structure, predictability, and consistency needed to ensure successful therapy. In addition, therapists likely will use low-complexity, low-structured tasks at first so that multiple or complicated instructions do not interfere with successful task completion. With time, and as the child is more able to successfully employ cognitive processing strategies, the complexity and structure of the tasks can be increased to developmentally appropriate levels. The art therapist working with AD/HD children will reduce emphasis on the art product because lack of fine motor control can make the product less pleasing than the child would like. Parents also would be counseled not to focus on the "beauty" of the finished product, but to focus on what the child has learned as a result of engaging in the art process. Finally, the art therapist will introduce slow and careful contemplation of the structure of forms, cause-and-effect thinking, and control over actions as the child begins to gain more cognitive regulation of his or her behavior.

Case Example

Introduction

Adam was an eight-year-old boy in the second grade when he was referred for art therapy. His pediatrician, in consultation with Adam's parents, a psychologist, and his teacher, had diagnosed Adam with attention-deficit/hyperactivity disorder, predominantly hyperactive-impulsive type. Psychological testing demonstrated overall intellectual functioning in the high average range, with deficits on tasks requiring sustained attention and concentration. Adam's parents were reluctant to begin medication and decided to have him work with a psychologist and an art therapist to try to help Adam gain control over his behavior without medication.

The teacher reported that Adam had difficulty sitting in his seat and frequently got up to talk with other children when the class should have been working quietly. She added that he got up to sharpen his pencil several times per day, and raced other children to the front when lining up for any activity. The teacher stated that Adam had difficulty remembering to raise his hand before speaking, and that he frequently shouted out answers and had difficulty waiting to tell a story or relate an event when the class was seated in circle time. Adam's teacher added that he frequently corrected other children when he saw them "breaking the rules" or just doing something out of the ordinary. She thought that his impulsivity caused him to have few friends.

Adam's parents stated that at home Adam often was argumentative and frequently wanted to have the last word. They noticed that he talked excessively and always was moving until he fell into bed exhausted at night. Adam's parents said that they were worried that he had few friends and said that his impulsivity caused him to poke, tickle, or nudge children on his baseball and soccer teams until they were annoyed and moved away, hit Adam, or told the coach. Adam himself stated that he was sad he did not have more friends. He played with a cousin, two years older, who lived nearby and with his younger sister, who was in kindergarten.

Kinesthetic Activities

The art therapists initially proposed seeing Adam for two half-hour sessions per week, feeling that longer sessions would inordinately strain his ability to attend and concentrate. The frequency and duration of sessions would be monitored, and changed when the therapist thought it appropriate. When Adam first came to the art therapy room, he had difficulty settling down and beginning the task at hand. During the first 15 minutes of the session, Adam walked around the room exploring the furniture and materials, looking out the window, and commenting on everything. When he finally sat at the art table, the art therapist described a *scribble drawing* and encouraged Adam to try it.

The rationale behind the choice of the scribble drawing was that it is an activity that begins on the Kinesthetic dimension of the Expressive Therapies Continuum, but that could encourage functioning with the Perceptual component as forms are identified in the overlapping lines. Adam refused to participate in the planned art activity, stating that he disliked drawing because he was not good at it. However, he did engage in conversation about himself and his disorder. While talking about himself and having AD/HD, Adam began dropping a thick watercolor marker on a sheet of paper. He was excited by the tiny splash of paint that the marker created as it hit the paper. Adam repeatedly dropped a black marker on a white piece of paper, and the therapist joined in the activity on a separate paper while continuing the conversation about the problems caused by AD/HD.

Kinesthetic to Perceptual Functioning

In the second session Adam settled down more quickly to the art materials and once more began dropping a marker on the paper. The therapist again joined in with her own marker and paper. After a time the therapist took a different colored marker and said that she was going to "connect the dots." Starting on the left side of the paper and moving to the right, a continuous line connected the dots and formed an image. The therapist contemplated the image and named it. Adam connected the dots on his own paper, found an image, and named it. According to Lusebrink (1990), dot-to-dot drawings require greater amounts of eye-to-hand coordination than scribble drawings, and as a result, they are more likely than scribble drawings to evoke form perception. Adam's dot-to-dot image is displayed in Figure 3.1 and was called "The Fight." Adam explained that he frequently argued with kids at school because they broke the rules and he corrected them, or just because they were mean to him. The therapist introduced the concepts of cause and effect and thinking before acting. Later, Adam's mother and the therapist talked about reinforcing with Adam and his teacher these concepts as they applied to his behavior at home and school.

In the third session, Adam was reintroduced to the scribble drawing. The rationale was that since he was able to connect the dots and find an image in the second session, he might be able to create form out of the scribble, and move once more to the Perceptual dimension of the Expressive Therapies Continuum. This movement up the developmental hierarchy would indicate a more mature level of functioning than demonstrated in the previous sessions. Adam had no difficultly making a scribble, but did not find an image in the scribble the first or second time that one was created. The therapist made scribbles and found images in an attempt to demonstrate how it could be done, and this helped Adam identify forms in subsequent sessions. One of the images that he discussed was a lone duck, and this image helped Adam identify how he was frequently alone

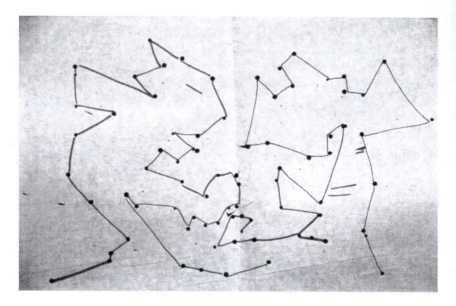

Figure 3.1 "The Fight": Dot-to-dot drawing shows movement from the Kinesthetic component to the Perceptual component.

and that he would like to have more friends. At about this time, Adam was invited by the school counselor to join a "friendship group," which taught social skills to a mixed group of undersocialized boys.

Perceptual Functioning

At the fourth session, Adam was asked to focus on form by making an *abstract family collage* in which each family member was represented by a separate form and perhaps by a different color. The resulting collage showed tiny figures separated by large amounts of white space, but Adam was unable to comment about the collage or the experience of making it. However, Adam's mother viewed the collage and stated that if this was Adam's perception of the family, it made her sad. She said that at times having such a challenging child did cause distance among family members due to the number of arguments and conflicts caused by his impulsive acting out. Adam's mother concluded the session by saying that she would like to learn more about parenting a child with attention-deficit/hyperactivity disorder and she was given appropriate resources.

Perceptual to Affective Functioning

The fourth, fifth, and sixth sessions were spent making collages of faces representing various emotions. Adam chose faces with an assortment of emotional expressions and glued them to a white background paper. At first, the goal of the session was to help Adam identify emotions and name them. The Perceptual component of the Expressive Therapies Continuum was engaged by this activity because the focus was on formal elements of visual expression, and how the various emotions expressed themselves with different arrangements of eyebrows, eyes, and mouths. The activity moved to the Affective component when Adam was asked to identify how and when he experienced each of the emotions. In addition, he was asked to draw with markers a picture that expressed how he experienced each of the emotions he identified. These images were rudimentary forms, such as a teardrop for sadness and a smiley face for happiness, yet Adam was able to participate meaningfully on the Perceptual/Affective level of the Expressive Therapies Continuum.

With each step up the developmental hierarchy of the Expressive Therapies Continuum, a door was opened to new ways of functioning. Adam no longer had to remain functioning solely with the Kinesthetic dimension. In fact, Adam was given a homework assignment to reinforce his new abilities. He was asked to use his new skill of identifying and drawing emotions to draw in a notebook rather than act out an emotion at least one time during the week. Adam's mother at first reminded him about the notebook and helped him find and use it. Later in the week, he was able to draw rather than act out in school two times.

Cognitive Functioning

By the sixth art therapy session Adam was attending one time per week for a longer duration. The Cognitive dimension of the Expressive Therapies Continuum was entered by making another collage of faces, and then *thinking through* what sort of action might have caused the person in the picture to feel the way he or she did, and to predict what would happen in response to feeling that way. Adam competently performed this function and then was asked to apply the skill to thinking about his own emotions and behavior. He was asked to contemplate and discuss what caused him to feel certain emotions and what would he do in response to feeling that way. Again, Adam could participate meaningfully in the session. His mother was asked to continue the discussion at home and to point out cause-and-effect relationships between emotions and actions whenever possible. Adam was being asked to reflect on his own behavior and at times to stop and think before he acted.

Cognitive to Symbolic Functioning

In the seventh session Adam was invited to make a free drawing. The resulting image is shown in Figure 3.2; Adam called it "Race Course Stoplights." He explained that in a race like the Indianapolis 500 there were many stoplights to alert the drivers to begin the race, slow down for caution, and stop the race. The metaphor was used to reinforce with Adam his need to do the same things in his own life. Stoplights were created out of construction paper: one with a red light, one with a yellow light, and one with a green light. Adam explained to his mother how he wanted her to help

Figure 3.2 "Racecourse Stoplights": Free drawing showing functioning on the Symbolic level.

him use the stoplights to remind him to control his behavior. Adam was given the homework assignment to create another set of stoplights to use at school and to explain them to his teacher and ask for her help.

Symbolic Functioning

Perhaps because he had experienced previous successful cognitive functioning, Adam demonstrated by his quick understanding of the stoplight metaphor that he was also able to function at the Symbolic component of the Expressive Therapies Continuum. In the next session, Adam was introduced to the story *The Tortoise and the Hare*. The art therapist read the story and Adam was asked to draw a picture of his favorite part. Adam drew a picture of the tortoise crossing the finish line first, and there ensued a discussion of "slow and steady wins the race." The therapist shared with Adam's mother the content of the session and asked her to support her son in a homework assignment. She was asked to help Adam go to the local library and locate other versions of the story *The Tortoise and the Hare*. The art therapist informed Adam's mother of one version written with a southwestern theme called *The Tortoise and the Jackrabbit* (Lowell and Harris, 1994); the children's librarian could help them find others.

Reinforcing Cognitive Functioning

Finding the books at the library and checking them out was a project that required many steps and skills. Adam's mother was informed of the importance of allowing Adam to carry out the necessary steps independently as one part of a continuing effort to develop cognitive skills. In addition, Adam's mother was asked to read the books with Adam and to help him understand how various versions of the story could refer not only to different settings for the story, but also to different aspects of his life. Adam was to write down "slow and steady wins the race" on a 3-by-5-inch card and carry it with him to remind him to slow down his actions.

Conclusion

The final therapy session was used to review the homework and to draw another picture of "slow and steady wins the race." In addition, Adam and his mother reviewed his progress in therapy and stated that they believed that he would not need to come to art therapy on a weekly basis. His mother was encouraged to keep up the work with the stoplights as needed, and to increase the types of tasks that Adam could do with multiple steps and complicated instructions (Cognitive component of the ETC). A birdhouse construction kit was recommended as a first project. It was agreed that Adam would come for a follow-up session in one month.

At the follow-up session, Adam brought with him his completed birdhouse and his father, who helped him make it. It was the first time Adam's father had accompanied him to a session, and he detailed the progress that Adam was making using all of the tools that he had learned in art therapy. These included drawing his emotions, using the stoplight, and referencing the slow and steady reminders. All were pleased with Adam's increased control over his behaviors and reduced impulsive acting out. By this time in therapy, Adam had increased capacity for processing information with all levels of the Expressive Therapies Continuum. He was able to function in a more well-rounded way and continue to benefit from services provided by the school and a private psychologist.

Summary

Action, movement, and rhythm characterize the Kinesthetic component of the Expressive Therapies Continuum. Media often are used as passive facilitators of action as energy is released through vigorous or calming actions. Table 3.1 details the various kinesthetic activities discussed in this chapter. As is summarized in Table 3.1, the healing function of the Kinesthetic component has to do with finding an inner rhythm and the release of energy. The emergent function of this dimension is the perception of form or emotion that evolves from movement and action. The kinesthetic sense can be one of the most neglected, and it was shown how obstacles to kinesthetic functioning can occur. Overuse of kinesthetic activity can be used as a defense or disorder. Either alteration of functioning can be the target of art therapy. The case example in this chapter demonstrated a step-by-step approach to opening blocked functions while reducing overemphasis on Kinesthetic component processing.

TABLE 3.1   Examples of Kinesthetic Experiences and Associated Healing and Emergent Functions

Kinesthetic Activity	Materials	Healing Function	Emergent Function
Pounding, pushing, rolling clay	Clay, Play-Doh, plasticene	Release of energy or tension	Perception of form; relaxation
Kneading dough	Water, yeast, flour; or water, salt, flour	Finding inner rhythm	Increased well-being
Forming clay to music	Clay, Play-Doh, plasticene; classical music	Finding inner rhythm	Perception of form; relaxation
Painting to music	Premixed tempera or watercolor paint; classical music	Finding or matching inner rhythm	Perception of form; relaxation
Stone sculpture	Relatively soft stone; carving tools	Release of energy or tension	Emerging form; increased arousal followed by relaxation
Wood sculpture	Wood; carving tools	Release of energy or tension	Emerging form; increased arousal followed by relaxation
Tapping nails into Styrofoam	Thin ½-inch nails, small hammer, Styrofoam block	Discover internal rhythm	Emerging emotion
Tearing paper	Newsprint	Release of tension or energy	Decreased tension; relaxation
Family sculpture	Clay; group members to pose as family members	Increased kinesthetic awareness	Increased emotional awareness
Self-sculpture or self-portrait	Clay; paper and drawing materials (posing)	Increased kinesthetic awareness	Increased emotional awareness
Clay throwing	Balls of clay; protected wall	Increased kinesthetic awareness	Expression of emotion

4

Sensory Component of the Expressive Therapies Continuum

Introduction to the Sensory Component

The Kinesthetic/Sensory level might be considered an exploratory level along the range of experiences represented by the Expressive Therapies Continuum. As was discussed in Chapter 3, one goal of the Kinesthetic component is to release energy through the use of physical actions and movement, often through exploration with art media. The Sensory dimension of this level focuses on both the internal and external sensations that are experienced through interaction with various media (Lusebrink, 1990). In its purest form, the Sensory component of the Expressive Therapies Continuum refers to information processing that involves only sensation without cognitive overlay.

The Sensory component includes information from visual, auditory, gustatory, olfactory, and tactile channels. Together with the Kinesthetic component, the Sensory component of the ETC represents the simplest form of information gathering and processing. Sensory information processing abilities develop very early in life, as infants, at first passively and then increasingly more actively, take in information through sensory means and sensory motor feedback loops (Piaget, 1969). Because infants and very young children process information without words through sensory channels, early experiences are stored on the right side of the brain (Riley, 2004; Schore, 2002). These right-brain memories, including early childhood trauma, are most effectively accessed through sensual nonverbal expressive art therapy experiences (Klorer, 2003; Malchiodi, 2003a).

There is a venerable tradition in the fields of philosophy and psychology of the importance of sensation in influencing thought and behavior. It has long been held, and continues to be the focus of scientific attention, that sensation forms the basis of emotion and cognition (Damasio, 1994; Plutchik, 2003). Under normal circumstances, persons receive input from sensory channels, and this sensory information serves as the basis for day-to-day decision-making processes (Siegel & Hartzell, 2003). According to Siegel and Hartzell, infants live in a "sea of sensations" (p. 226). As children grow up, left-hemisphere, language-dominated processing of information becomes more prevalent, making the constant stream of sensory input seem irrelevant. However, sensations form the basis of mental activity, and achieving a meaningful sense of self depends in part on the ability to decipher this ambiguous and sometimes confusing flow of sensory input (Marshall & Magoun, 1998).

Karges (1999) suggests that people who are able to sharpen their ordinary senses into "super senses" (p. 12) and employ sensory information rapidly, deeply, and without conscious thought are those that are described as having extrasensory perception or good intuition. This sort of afferent information is utilized in a purely sensory fashion, without cognition superimposed in the form of overt decision making. Malcolm Gladwell (2005) seems to be discussing the same type of phenomenon in his book *Blink*. What Gladwell termed the "adaptive unconscious" is described "as a kind of giant computer that quickly and quietly processes a lot of the data we need in order to keep functioning as human beings" (p. 11). The data the author is referring to are the second-to-second sensory input that we are constantly bombarded with from internal and external sensory sources.

Many art therapy experiences involve sensory input: clients handle materials and sense their tactile qualities, or view them and take in their visual characteristics. But this attendant sensory stimulation is not what is meant by focusing on the Sensory component of the Expressive Therapies Continuum. When the Sensory dimension is the central focus of therapy, the sensory aspects of an experience are emphasized for their healing and emergent qualities. Sensory experiences can involve quietly stroking wet clay with closed eyes (Lusebrink, 1990; Sholt & Gavron, 2006). Keeping the eyes closed helps clients focus on the tactile component of the clay, and perhaps more easily resist the urge to create form. Mixing paint while focusing only on the blending of colors can be a pure sensory experience. Scented paints or markers increase stimulation by involving more than one sensory channel. Engaging as many channels as possible beyond the visual sense is imperative for making learning salient for all children (Lowenfeld, 1952), but especially for children with learning or physical disabilities (Anderson, 1992). The Slingerland multisensory structured language approach is an example in which auditory, visual, and tactile channels are simultaneously involved in order to promote language learning in children with dyslexia (Slingerland Institute for Literacy, 2007).

In order to heighten the sensory qualities of art experiences, mediators often are reduced or eliminated. Finger painting is a more tactile and sensual experience than painting with a brush. Dropping paint or ink onto wet paper and allowing it to merge and blend can be a more visually sensual experience than one in which the client attempts to impose form on color with a paintbrush. Clay work is encouraged without the use of tools for cutting and scoring. Working with just the hands emphasizes the earthy, tactile, and haptic qualities of the material. The word *haptic* comes from the Greek word *hapthai*, meaning "pertaining to the sense of touch" (DK, 2003). The interaction between kinesthetic and tactile sensations gives rise to haptic information (Arnheim, 1992). Haptic information apprises people about the shapes, weight, contours, outlines, and relief qualities of the surface of objects (Lusebrink, 2004). For the visually impaired, learning Braille requires receiving and processing information through the haptic sense (Anderson, 1992).

Developmental Hierarchy

As was mentioned above, at the sensorimotor stage of development, infants exist in a sea of sensations, and these sensations form the basis of their early emotions and memories. Most memories of experiences occurring before the age of three or four years are preverbal, and thus are encoded as sensations (Riley, 2004; Schore, 2002). Whether pleasant and soothing or harsh and negative, early sensual experiences inform the infant's sense of security and provide the basis for emotional language (Siegel & Hartzell, 2003). Sensations continue to have an evocative relationship with emotions, as will be discussed later in this chapter.

As was discussed in Chapter 1, when toddlers first use art materials, they are not necessarily interested in the outcome or producing an image. Toddlers often are absorbed in the sensory and motor aspects of the art experience. As mentioned in the last chapter, very young children will use art materials for their action potentials, and also will become caught up in the sensory qualities of art materials. Often this preoccupation with the textures, sounds, and smells of art making is the principal quality of the art experience for them.

Art making continues to excite the senses, and this sensory stimulation often is the primary goal for art therapy with the elderly (Jensen, 1997; Kahn-Denis, 1997), and for children with sensory integration difficulties and disorders along the autistic spectrum (Gabriels, 2003; Iarocci & McDonald, 2006). Due to their close association with and ability to evoke affect, sensory experiences are used therapeutically to elicit emotions in people who have difficulty accessing, labeling, and expressing their feelings (Lacroix, Peterson, & Verrier, 2001; Meijer-Degen & Lansen, 2006).

Healing Dimension of the Sensory Component

The healing dimension of the Sensory component is slow sensual experience (Lusebrink, 1990). Emotions and thoughts are eased through the Sensory level: The mind can relax, allowing physical sensations to dominate consciousness. The focused state of attention achieved with sensory stimulation can allow clients to become more aware of internal sensations (Lusebrink, 1990). This type of experience includes the quieting of external stimulation in order to increase awareness of internal calm. Marianne McGriffin (2002) wrote about the healing touch of clay: "A calm pervaded my body as I relaxed into the ambiance of the smooth, cool, yielding yet resisting texture of the clay" (p. xi).

Sensory experiences can be used in an entirely different manner to help a child with sensory processing disorder (SPD) achieve a focused state of attention (Exkorn, 2005; Miller, 2006). Sensory processing disorder describes a condition in which sensory signals are not organized into appropriate behaviors. In response to sensory stimuli or lack of it, the SPD child's responses seem over- or underreactive; daily routines and activities are disrupted as a result (Miller, 2006). According to Miller, there are three broad subtypes of sensory processing disorder, and each one responds best to increasing or decreasing sensory stimulation so that the right amount of stimulation occurs in each situation. Thus, the sensory stimulation available from art activities such as finger painting or clay work can be part of the "complete sensory diet" (Miller, 2006, p. 193) needed to help calm and focus a child with sensory processing disorder. At the same time, art therapy can provide occasions to explore the social and emotional characteristics of the child's internal experience (Kearns, 2004).

Additionally, sensory stimulation can bypass impaired brain areas to reconstitute memories that are subsequently available for visual and cognitive use (Lusebrink, 2004). Working with Alzheimer's patients on the

Sensory level can help them regain lost memories and other vital cognitive functions (Jensen, 1997; Kahn-Denis, 1997).

Examples of Sensory Experiences

Sensory art experiences are those in which stimulation of the senses is the primary goal. Anderson (1992) wrote about the use of various sensual experiences with physically disabled children, and about how incorporating stimulation of many senses was one way of helping them focus on the immediate occurrence. She indicated that hearing and visually impaired children work best with multiple sensual experiences, and especially the tactile stimulation arising from three-dimensional work with clay. Anderson explained two different types of tactile stimulation:

> Synthetic touch, which is one's direct tactile experience of the world through experiences with items that are small enough to be held in one's hand or enclosed in both hands, and analytic touch, which is the tactile experience of parts of objects too large to be held in the hand or hands and the mind attempts to form some sort of composite. (p. 81)

The author mentioned that visually impaired children learn best through tactile experiences because they lack visual input that provides, for sighted persons, an integrated concept of an object. Anderson noted that the tactile information, available through synthetic or analytic touch, could provide integrated concepts of objects for visually impaired persons. As was defined above, the haptic sense is that which focuses on contours, outlines, and the surface qualities of an object, and according to Lusebrink (2004), it is the most important aspect of tactile information used in art therapy.

Clients' experiences of external reality can be enriched through sensory exploration of simple objects with eyes closed; this tactile exploration can be supplemented with the awareness of other sensations, such as olfactory or auditory, that are perceived during the exploration. A subsequent portrayal of the experience, possibly through media involving tactile or fluid components such as pastels, oil pastels, or watercolor crayons could help heighten awareness of the richness of the exploration. If appropriate, a similar sensory exploration can involve a guided experience outdoors with a subsequent representation of the experience. An interesting variation of these experiences is to record the differences in the representations of an object before and after the sensory exploration reflecting the increased richness of the percepts. Figure 4.1 demonstrates an eight-year-old girl's depiction

Figure 4.1 Sensory exploration drawings: pictures drawn before (left) and after (right) sensory exploration of pinecones with eyes closed.

of a pinecone before and after sensory exploration of the object. The two representations show notable differences. Prior to the sensory exploration the girl drew sharp, pointy edges and concentrated the drawing on the contour of the pinecone. After sensory exploration, the pinecone does not have sharp edges, but rather the rounded ones that she encountered when handling it. In addition, the drawing shows greater depth and dimension. Clearly, tactile exploration of the pinecone with eyes closed made its true features stand out for the artist.

Media Experiences That Enhance Sensory Functioning

A warm-up experience and introduction to art expression using the Sensory component of the Expressive Therapies Continuum can begin with a sheet of finger paint paper. With eyes closed, clients can be asked to touch and explore the smooth surface of the glossy paper and to become increasingly aware of the slow rhythm of the hand moving over the surface of the paper. This experience allows for increasing awareness and matching of internal sensations. These sensations can be expressed in visual form by adding finger paint to the movement of the hand. The

Sensory dimension of this art experience can be amplified by continuing to focus on sensory awareness while finger painting on additional sheets of paper. In this manner, the quantity-determined characteristics of the experience could be explored with eyes open. Through this exploration, clients might find that larger or smaller quantities of paint allow for greater or lesser sensuous responding. Also during this experience, clients can become mindful of inner rhythm changes until a still point is reached (V. B. Lusebrink, personal communication, February 18, 2007).

In a simple warm-up experience focused on sensory input, adult clients can be asked to deliberately focus on pressure, temperature, and sensations that usually are below the level of conscious awareness (Gonick-Barris, 1976). With eyes closed they can be encouraged to feel the sensations of their backs and buttocks on the chair, the feeling of their feet on the floor, sensations from their clothing, and to note the hum of the air conditioner or furnace. These sensations can be depicted through art as a way to help increase awareness of the constant stream of sensory input that influences existence.

Although experimenting with mixing colors can be a visually stimulating exploration involving the use of a paintbrush, generally eliminating the use of mediators increases the sensory aspects of expressive experiences. Thus, as was mentioned above, finger painting usually is a more sensual experience than painting with a brush. Sumptuous "finger paint" involving multiple sensory channels can be made of colored and scented shaving cream or colored and flavored whipped cream. The sensual aspects of clay work can be facilitated by warming the clay to make it more pliable and inviting than the usual cold, hard clay (Landgarten, 1981). Other sensory experiences involve scented markers and paints, spices, found objects such as pinecones, leaves, and flowers, and work with texturally rich, stimulating fabrics (Landgarten, 1981; Wadeson, 2000).

Media that stimulate two senses at the same time can be particularly engaging with physically disabled children as mentioned above, or with the elderly, who may experience reduced sensory abilities such as impaired visual acuity, and perhaps lessened interest in their environment as a result of vision loss (Landgarten, 1981; Wald, 2003). Wadeson (2000) wrote that residents in assisted living communities have few opportunities for changing environments. Therefore, a principal goal of art therapy programs in those settings is to promote sensory stimulation in order to improve quality of life. Deborah Del Signore (as cited in Wadeson, 2000) provided varied sensory experiences to the elderly through art therapy groups.

These experiences included potpourri collage, silkscreen painting using fabric softener sheets, edible still-life pictures, and art responses to specific evocative aromas such as tea, mint leaves, and candy. Residents who were at first reluctant or skeptical about the art therapy group eventually began to value it highly for the richly stimulating experiences that it provided.

Reflective Distance With the Sensory Component

In general, reflective distance with the Sensory component of the Expressive Therapies Continuum is low. Clients usually will be highly involved in the sensual experience, making reflection about it difficult and even undesirable. Perhaps what is most advantageous about an experience on the Sensory dimension is the ability to lose oneself, and focus wholly on sensation. *Mindfulness* is a term from clinical psychology that has become increasing influential in a number of areas of psychology in recent years (Germer, Siegel, & Fulton, 2005; Hanh, 1999; Kabat-Zinn, 2005; Smith, 2005). Mindfulness encourages an exclusive focus on present sensation. The idea behind mindfulness and stress management is to allow sensory (and emotional) input to come and go without thought or judgment attached to it. In this way, clients do not become caught up in thinking about or evaluating minute-to-minute sensory input that in the past caused increased anxiety or tension. In addition, patients can be fully present in the moment when they are focused on pure sensation (Hanh, 1999; Smith, 2005).

Questions and Discussion That Promote Sensory Information Processing

In order to enhance the sensory qualities of a media experience, the therapist would help the client focus on the sensual aspects of it. Questions such as "What do you smell?" "What do you see?" or "What do you see happening where the paints begin to make contact?" and "How does the clay feel in your hands?" help clients focus on sensory input. Questions and comments such as "What do you sense as you begin to stroke the clay?" or "Focus on the sensations as you begin to handle the fabric" would help clients focus on internal sensations evoked by the external sensory stimuli. Directing a client to "Try to focus on the sound and sight, while at the same time bringing the color in line with the music" would help a client integrate information from more than one sensory channel. If clients are not using visual information, they can be encouraged to close their eyes as one way to help them focus on the sensual experience (Lusebrink, 1990).

Emergent Function of the Sensory Component

As was discussed in Chapter 3, the emergent function of a component on the Expressive Therapies Continuum refers to an experience that is generated from or arises out of the current mode of information processing. A higher level of functioning generally emerges from the current experience, permitting more sophisticated information processing to occur. Sensory stimulation represents one way to focus attention, and the external focus on sensory stimuli can allow an interior shift that increases attention to internal sensations or emotions (Kagin & Lusebrink, 1978b; Lusebrink, 1990). Therefore, the emergent function of a sensory activity often is an affective experience.

Tactile stimulation can provide the most straightforward example of how focusing on an external sensation can lead to the realization of an internal state or emotion. Lusebrink (1990) gave the example of having clients stroke wet clay with eyes closed, and explained how this act evokes an internal experience of love or sadness. A strikingly similar example was provided by Sholt and Gavron (2006). They related the experience of an adolescent girl who immersed herself in the sensory experience of stroking soft, wet clay, and subsequently modeled a figure that was able to express her love for and sadness about being raised by a depressed mother. As will be seen in the case example at the end of this chapter, tactile stimulation is not always soothing. Work with clay, plasticene, glue, or other tacky substances can evoke disgust and attention to other negative affective states.

That which emerges from an experience with the Sensory component does not have to be emotional; it can be a form. According to Lusebrink (V. B. Lusebrink, personal communication, February 18, 2007), in order to facilitate image formation for mentally retarded individuals, exploration of simple objects with eyes open (rather than closed, as discussed above) can lead to increased motivation for an art experience. The tactile and haptic information gained through sensory exploration elaborates the figurative aspects of the object taken in visually. Figurative information, along with operative aspects, aids in the formation of symbolic representation. Thus, the tactile and haptic information added to the visual input makes the object more salient for a mentally retarded client, and increases interest in using art materials.

When Work With the Sensory Component Is Indicated

The Sensory level of the Expressive Therapies Continuum can be the starting place for therapeutic work when a sensory experience evokes emotions or reconstitutes memory, when a slow sensual experience eases cognitions and emotions, or when a vigorous sensual experience helps clients focus attention for future effort. Work on the Sensory dimension can help a child with autism who is overwhelmed by typical sensory input (Evans & Dubowski, 2001). Sensory involvement is indicated when a person is so caught up with cognition that he or she has lost the ability to feel sensations and emotions. The inclusion of nonthreatening sensory art experiences with chronic schizophrenic patients helps them to reconstitute their involvement with their environment, as suggested by Denner (cited in Lusebrink, 1990). A sequence of art experiences, starting with simple hand movements and drawings of various lines, can be expanded into tactile explorations and paintings of simple, nonthreatening objects such as flowers in a vase.

Traumatic experiences are not entirely cognitive events, but rather, include a large Sensory component (Riley, 2004; Steele, 2003). For example, in the case of a car accident, auditory channels are stimulated with the sound of the crash; the tactile sense is involved by the impact of the crash and resulting pain. Olfactory stimulation comes from the smell of burning rubber or dust from the airbag deployment. Visual sensations include images before, during, and after the crash. Because of the significant sensory elements in traumatic experiences, effective therapy for trauma resolution includes visual and sensory experiences (Johnson, 2000; Steele, 2003). Therapists must be careful in any therapeutic exploration to empower, not retraumatize, the individual with stimulating exposure techniques (Steele, 2003).

Therapeutic work with the Sensory component of the Expressive Therapies Continuum can be the focus of therapeutic experiences for physically disabled children and Alzheimer's patients (Anderson, 1992; Jensen, 1997; Wadeson, 2000). Jensen (1997) described a multisensory approach with Alzheimer's patients using music, movement, and visual art making. The goal of the multisensory work was to stimulate remote memory and provide patients with a link to past identity. Jensen added that stimulating sight, sound, and smell calls up emotions from the past, thus identifying or capitalizing on the emergent function of the Sensory level of the ETC. In a similar vein, Kahn-Denis (1997) recommended working with specific personal sensory stimuli in order to connect a person to his or her own individual past. Stewart (2004), working with Alzheimer's patients, noted that even when their diminishing cognitive abilities caused them to lose motivation for art therapy, the sensuous textures and colors of the art materials could still draw them into an expressive experience. As was mentioned previously, sensory experiences may help increase awareness of the symbolic aspects of artistic expressions and experiences. "Faded" metaphors (Wright, 1976) and symbols, which have become detached from their affective charge, can be enriched or enlivened through exploration of metaphorical and symbolic images with an emphasis on the Sensory level.

Overcoming Blocks to Sensory Functioning

Individuals can be so cognitively oriented that they are out of touch with their bodies and the natural wisdom gathered through internal and external sensations. One might see an outright rejection of the body or expressed feelings of hatred for the body, as seen in eating disorders (Bruch, 1973). It has been my experience that people suffering from eating disorders express this bodily rejection by reporting that they "do not feel comfortable in their own skin." In addition, they state that they do not believe themselves capable of living with their bodily sensations, often feeling confused or overwhelmed by them. Further, persons with eating disorders often claim they do not recognize physical sensations such as hunger and satiety cues; they eat when and what they think they should eat, rather than eating based on those cues. In cases such as this, increasing sensory functioning and reorienting a client to the significance of gaining information from the senses can be one goal for art therapy.

As was mentioned earlier, geriatric patients can experience the opposite of the sensory overload characteristic of eating disordered patients. Geriatric patients can experience a type of sensory deprivation due to reduced opportunities for experiences outside of nursing homes and other long-term-care facilities (Jensen, 1997; Wadeson, 2000). Art therapy can provide many and varied sensory experiences accompanied by significant increases in quality of life, as well as improvements in cognitive and social functioning (Jensen, 1997; Kahn-Denis, 1997, Wadeson, 2000). Jensen (1997) reported approaching dementia patients through many sensory channels because primary sensory functioning often remains intact in Alzheimer's patients. Stimulating the senses through music, movement, and art often improved memory functioning.

Children with sensory processing disorder have been described as not taking in and processing information equally from all senses, especially tactile, auditory, and vestibular senses, and therefore as being less able to organize sensory information into appropriate thoughts and actions (Exkorn, 2005). Children with a subtype of sensory processing disorder called *sensory modulation disorder–underresponsive type* have been hypothesized to have an underresponsive autonomic nervous system that can be activated by intense or vigorous sensory activity (Miller, 2006). Art therapy using activities on the Sensory dimension of the Expressive Therapies Continuum could be one way to help activate an underresponsive child. Finger painting with bright colors, and perhaps even scented paint, on 3- or 4-foot pieces of paper could be an intensely stimulating sensory experience that helps "feed" the underresponsive child.

Balancing Excessive Sensory Information Processing

Atypical sensory behaviors are seen throughout the developmental course in persons with autism, and are generally viewed as aiding in managing sensory input from the environment (Iarocci & McDonald, 2006). For example, the stereotypical movements, repetitive behavior, and self-stimulatory behavior seen in children with autism have been conceptualized as defenses against sensory stimulation that are perceived as overwhelming or even painful (Evans & Dubowski, 2001). Self-stimulatory behavior can occur in any sensory channel: auditory, visual, tactile, vestibular, gustatory, or olfactory. This behavior may be focused primarily in one sensory modality (e.g., visual—staring at an object or flicking fingers in front of the face), or it may cross modalities (e.g., licking body parts or objects and spinning) (Exkorn, 2005). According to Exkorn, self-stimulatory behaviors provide autistic children with a sense of control over their level of sensory stimulation or serve to reduce the intensity of environmental stimulation.

Art therapy using the Sensory component of the Expressive Therapies Continuum can be used with autistic children in therapeutic ways. Rather than allowing the autistic child to shut out unpleasant or overwhelming sensory stimuli, Evans and Dubowski (2001) attempted to help the child connect "unconscious non-physical sensory experience to physical sensory conscious activity" (p. 65). The authors state that making sensory stimuli salient with thick tempera paint and large brushes helped increase the autistic child's awareness of the physical and emotional boundaries of the art therapy session. One of their stated goals for art therapy was that through making these boundaries prominent, they helped the autistic child make an emotional connection with the art therapist in the present moment.

Meeting the autistic child at his or her level is a way to engage the child in the process of therapy. The sensory-engaged child could become so caught up in smelling the paint that he or she would probably progress no further. However, drawn into the experience of painting, the autistic child can begin to create form. Beginning at the scribble stage and experimenting with the sensations involved in painting, the autistic child can be gradually helped up the developmental hierarchy not only toward more sophisticated representations or schema, but to a more sophisticated level of self-perception and perhaps interpersonal interaction (Henley, 1991; Osborne, 2003).

In a related vein, Elaine Aron (1996) has written about what she termed the highly sensitive person. In her definition, Aron stated that the highly sensitive person is more susceptible to sensory stimulation than is the normal person. She claimed that what is moderately arousing stimulation for the majority of people will be overly arousing for the highly sensitive person. Both positive and negative environmental stimuli: Sound, aromas and flavors, lights, beauty, and tactile stimulation will all be more deeply processed (Aron, 1996; Zeff, 2004). According to Aron (1996), the heightened sensitivity that she is writing about is not the same thing as shyness or introversion. She made clear that she was writing about a nervous system condition in which persons take in greater amounts of sensory information, process sensory stimulation more deeply, and take longer to recover from intense sensory stimulation.

Aron (1996) described a vicious cycle that highly sensitive persons find themselves in when they experience arousal. First, they look around for a source of the arousal and put a name to it in order to react to potential danger. Often a person calls unexplained arousal *fear*, not realizing that his or her heart may be beating hard from the sheer effort of processing extra sensory stimulation. In addition, other people, having noticed the highly sensitive person's obvious arousal, assume he or she is afraid. Once labeled fear, arousal can contribute to avoidance of "feared" stimuli or situations. When a person retreats from a feared stimulus instead of remaining in its presence, habituation does not occur, and arousal continues. A more active approach to overstimulation can be to use art media and expression to define and contain unwanted arousal. Activities on the Perceptual dimension can provide containment by emphasizing the formal elements of visual expression.

Case Example

Introduction

Belinda was a 25-year-old single Caucasian woman who had obtained a master's degree in business administration. She was diagnosed with anorexia nervosa after graduating from her master's degree program, when faced with the prospect of leaving home for the first time. Belinda entered an intensive outpatient treatment program for eating disorders, begging for help with her eating and weight issues. She talked at great length about her struggles with caloric restriction, excessive exercise, and weight. She wrote out elaborate diet plans that demonstrated that she ate in response to the time of day and what she thought she should eat. Belinda denied ever feeling hungry and stated that she never felt full. She did not trust her body, which sometimes "took on a life of its own" when she engaged in occasional eating binges that felt completely out of her control.

Cognitive Functioning

During her first week in art therapy Belinda attempted to engage the art therapist in discussions about her weight, diet plan, and exercise regimen; she required frequent redirection to the art tasks. Belinda's initial drawings were small, light, wispy drawings done in pencil. The drawings were characterized by many small, isolated figures seemingly drawn independent of, rather than in relation to, one another. In response to the art therapist's suggestion to incorporate color into her images, the next phase of drawings completed during her second week of art therapy was done in blue ballpoint pen. The inclusion of this mild form of color seemed to provoke another change in the drawings. Rather than the previous small, separate figures, the images now took on the form of diagrams that seemed to relate a story. Belinda herself could not perceive the story in her diagrams; she stated that she was developing a drawing from the first image that came into her mind. The sequence of drawings merely represented the progression of images taking on the shape she desired. All drawings were done hurriedly, using only 10 to 15 minutes of the allotted 45 minutes of the art therapy sessions.

It was apparent to the art therapist from her use of pencil, ballpoint pen, line drawings, and diagrams that Belinda was processing information predominantly with the Cognitive component of the Expressive Therapies Continuum. Her description of eating in response to what she thought she should eat, rather than in response to bodily cues of hunger and satiety, also suggested a cognitive approach to eating decisions. In a collaborative consultation, Belinda and her art therapist decided that one goal of art therapy would be to help Belinda begin to value sensory information. By using art therapy to focus on what she identified through sensory channels, Belinda would begin to value internal and external sensory stimuli. She could then add sensory information to cognitive input for use in making decisions. This therapeutic change involving sensory information processing was explained as an attempt at reducing overreliance on cognitive processing. It was further elaborated as a relatively nonthreatening precursor to accessing important bodily information such as hunger and satiety cues, and a step in the direction of Belinda's relearning to experience her emotions.

Movement to the Sensory Component

At the beginning of her third week in art therapy, Belinda was asked to choose materials that would lend themselves to a focus on sensation—physical sensation through touching with her hands was suggested as perhaps the fastest way to accomplish this. Speed was a concern because Belinda was participating in an intensive outpatient treatment program with managed care concerns limiting the length of stay. Belinda chose to work with dryer lint of various colors. She spent time handling the lint and describing the sensations: "soft, fuzzy, and crumbly. It's not as sweet as I thought it would be, holding this stuff." After spending some time just handling the lint, Belinda glued it to a circular form as instructed by the art therapist. She separated the lint by colors and glued them, separated by pipe cleaners, in a spiral fashion to the circular form. At the end of the session, Belinda complained about how messy and dirty the task was.

Movement From Sensory to Perceptual/Affective Level

Still focused on the Sensory component, in the next session Belinda spent some time stroking wet clay. Again, she was dissatisfied with how dirty the task was, and she asked if she could switch to plasticene, which she noticed sitting next to the clay. The plasticene was cold and hard, and Belinda had

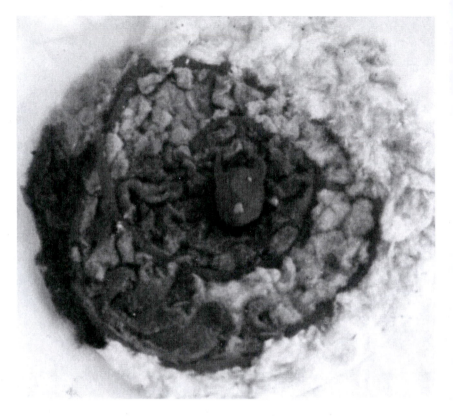

Figure 4.2   Dryer lint and devil: Sensory experiences evoke affective expression.

to spend some time warming it up in her hands in order to make it pliable. She was encouraged to just work with the substance and focus on the physical sensations that arose as she handled it. Belinda noted that she was becoming irritable and annoyed with the task. She did not want to continue just holding the plasticene; she wanted to make something out of it. Belinda used red plasticene to make the small sculpture displayed in Figure 4.2. It was a small head with horns; she worked in minute detail to add yellow eyes and a yellow tongue.

Conclusion

When she was finished, Belinda cried for the first time in art therapy. She explained her reaction by saying that she had made a devil's head and that it belonged inside the lint circle that she made in the previous session.

Belinda repeated that the lint was dirty and not what she expected when she first imagined handling it. The dirty lint brought to mind thoughts that she was not supposed to talk about personal matters, even in her treatment program. She had always been admonished not to "air her dirty laundry" in public. It was Belinda's perception that in her family of origin, it was important to look good and act as if everything was fine regardless of how badly she felt. The devil's face completed the image because she wanted to talk and felt as though the "devil was making (her) do it" against her parents' wishes. From this point forward, Belinda began a different level of participation in her intensive outpatient treatment program. In addition, she made sure that her parents were involved in the process of her recovery.

Belinda began her treatment program processing information predominantly cognitively: she talked, she discussed, and she argued. She was out of touch with physical sensations and emotions. At the outset of art therapy, she chose pencil and ballpoint pen with which to render small, unconnected figures. Working together, Belinda and the art therapist decided that helping Belinda access sensory information processing would benefit her by both beginning the process of trusting her body again (e.g., the connection between physical sensation and acknowledgment of hunger) and introducing her to her emotions. Lusebrink (1990) has written that changing levels of the Expressive Therapies Continuum can lead to increased connections among levels and improved and expanded possibilities for information processing. In Belinda's case, it seemed that changing to the Sensory component of the ETC helped her form an internal image of frustration and express emotions related to it. She began to participate in art therapy and the rest of her treatment program in honest and emotionally communicative ways that did not seem possible to her before.

Summary

Work on the Sensory component of the Expressive Therapies Continuum allows clients to explore the sensory qualities of art materials. Through this tactile, visual, auditory, and sometimes gustatory exploration, clients can be encouraged to focus on inner sensations. The healing function of the Sensory component includes the development of slow rhythm and an awareness of internal sensations. The formation of an internal image can emerge from a sensory experience as it did for Belinda. Interestingly, for Belinda, the internal image provoked by unpleasant sensory input was negative. But the experience had healing qualities nonetheless. In addition to the emergence of an internal image, Belinda's sensory experience also evoked affect. Again, perhaps because the sensory experience was negative (the lint and clay were perceived as dirty; working with the placticene was irritating), the resulting affect was negative. However, changing levels of the ETC allowed the expression of affect that had not been experienced previously.

Sensory stimulation can be organizing for children with autism or sensory processing disorder. It can provide a way for those who are over- or underresponsive to sensory stimulation to organize their responses into appropriate behaviors. Sensory stimulation can help reconstitute memory and cognitive functioning in persons with Alzheimer's disease. Rich sensory experiences can increase the quality of life and active engagement of persons living in assisted care facilities with little opportunity for varied experiences. Finally, art expression, especially using the Perceptual component of the ETC, can provide a container for highly sensitive persons who need a way to express and contain overwhelming external and internal sensory stimulation.

TABLE 4.1   Examples of Sensory Experiences and Associated Healing and Emergent Functions

Sensory Activity	Materials	Healing Function	Emergent Function
Stroking wet clay	Clay	Focusing on internal sensations; matching internal and external experiences	Emergence of emotion such as sadness, perhaps disgust if clay is perceived as dirty
Mixing paint while focusing on the blending of colors	Watercolor or tempera paint; wet watercolor paper	Focus on external sensation to match internal; soothing	Emergence of emotion or perhaps form
Finger painting	Finger paint; slick finger paint paper	Matching internal state with external sensation; focusing, calming	Emergence of a state of calm, focused attention
Finger paint with scented shaving cream or flavored whipped cream	Shaving cream, flavored whipped cream; heavy paper or cardboard; individual cutting boards	Absorption in the task by involving more than one sensory channel; focusing attention; calming the mind	Emergence of a state of calm, focused attention; mind can relax
Potpourri collage	Potpourri; craft glue; heavy paper or cardboard	Absorption in the task by involving vision and olfactory senses; increased stimulation and well-being	Emergence of calm; personal memory might be stimulated
Art responses to specific aromas	Essential oils, spices, potpourri, perfume	Sensual responding	Stimulation of many senses and personal memories
Painting to music	Paint supplies; vaious music CDs	Music connects client to present or past; reconstitution of memory	Emergence of emotion
Exploration of finger paint paper with hand	Finger paint paper; finger paint	Awareness of internal sensations	Matching of internal sensations and internal rhythms until a still point is reached
Sensory exploration with eyes closed	Explore objects placed in hands with eyes closed	Enhances awareness of other senses	Increased depth and dimension to experiences

5

Perceptual Component of the Expressive Therapies Continuum

Introduction to the Perceptual Component

The Perceptual component represents one pole of the next level of the Expressive Therapies Continuum—the Perceptual/Affective level. The Perceptual component deals with the figurative aspects of mental imagery and emphasizes the formal elements of visual expression. Information processing occurs in a more sophisticated manner at the Perceptual/Affective level; it requires that clients use visual imagery to represent their internal experiences. In a sense, clients working therapeutically on the Perceptual dimension must learn a new visual language, the foundations of which are line, color, form, size, direction, and other visual elements. Work with the Perceptual component requires that clients use both this visual language and their accustomed verbal language in a parallel fashion to differentiate and describe their inner worlds.

In the case of the Perceptual/Affective level, it was explained that at first affective involvement energizes and gives motivation to perceptual work, which involves the often difficult translation of mental activity into concrete expression through art materials and visual language. Later, too much emotional involvement blocks the ability to function in a perceptual fashion; emotion changes experience and distorts form quality and its expression (Kagin & Lusebrink, 1978b). A person can be so emotional that he or she is unable to see clearly or use perceptual abilities effectively. Alternatively, the focus on form demanded by perceptual experiences can be used therapeutically to "contain" affect and provide a safe setting for expression. At the extreme polarity of the Perceptual component, rigid repetition of forms or overuse of geometrical forms characterizes visual expressions (Lusebrink, 1991b).

In perceptual experiences, the focus is on the formal elements of visual expression such as line and shape, as well as the structural qualities of the media involved (Kagin & Lusebrink, 1978b; Lusebrink, 1990). Lusebrink (1991b) writes, "The differentiation of form is used to define an appropriate schematic representation of inner and outer experiences" (p. 399). Focus on the structure of images means highlighting the formal elements of visual expression, or inherent form qualities, of mental images as they emerge from the background. According to Kagin and Lusebrink (1978b), media used in perceptual experiences have *form potential* or the ability to evoke form when handled or used for expression. Media with a great deal of form potential are such things as metal, wood, and tile.

The structural qualities of media with a high degree of form potential such as mosaic or wood can be transferred to individuals through a process called *isomorphism*. Previously mentioned in Chapter 3, the principal of isomorphism is taken from Gestalt psychology and refers to the correspondence between an external state and its internal manifestation, or vice versa (Arnheim, 1966; Cohen, 1983; Lusebrink, 1991b). Consequently, working with highly structured media or creating structured perceptual images allows the individual to internalize a sense of structure, which often has a calming effect (Lusebrink, 1990).

Developmental Hierarchy

Structure becomes important to children after the sensorimotor phase of childhood. Following the sensorimotor phase, children enter a stage of cognitive development in which they use concrete objects in their play to assimilate and accommodate their growing sense of the world (Piaget, 1962). Their artistic productions become dependent on schemas or graphic shortcuts to represent the world. In using schemas, the child creates forms with which to process information from the world. Cognitively, these schemas are the child's first belief systems (Rich & Devitis, 1996); graphically, this stage is characterized by visual schemas or familiar symbols. Elements of familiar objects such as people, trees, and houses typically are represented by geometric forms that lose their meaning outside of the context of the original drawing (Arnheim, 1969; Lowenfeld & Brittain, 1987). A triangle can represent a nose, but outside of the context of the drawing, it is merely a triangle.

Reliance on graphic shortcuts becomes a way for children to relate information quickly and easily. In fact, children who are good at using schemas do it repeatedly in attempting to master their material. Eventually children who find it pleasant and easy to represent information schematically begin to use art as a way to communicate important information. They can even begin to consider themselves "artistic," with attendant increases in self-esteem as they receive praise from peers and adults for their abilities. In addition, they are likely to attempt drawing unfamiliar objects, basing new drawings on existing familiar schemas (Thomas & Silk, 1990). Children who do not master the use of schemas usually abandon drawing in childhood.

As was mentioned earlier, the emphasis on form or structure characteristic of the Perceptual component of the Expressive Therapies Continuum can help contain affect. Alternatively, in this bipolar relationship, affect can modify form (Lusebrink, 1991a). For children in the schematic stage of graphic development, deviations from the typical schemas, or form distortions, give clues to the emotional importance of a subject (Lowenfeld & Brittain, 1987). For example, the inclusion of very large hands can demonstrate that a child has been the recipient of physically aggressive treatment or has treated others aggressively (Koppitz, 1968). Adults also consciously or unconsciously distort form to denote the emotional importance of a visual element (Arnheim, 1966; Furth, 1988).

The Importance of Good Gestalts

In the early part of the 20th century Gestalt psychologists studied the physiological and psychological aspects of perception. These early psychologists demonstrated that the brain possesses self-organizing abilities that cause people to be attracted to pleasing forms or good gestalts (Arnheim 1966, 1969). Good gestalts have characteristics such as regularity, stability, and wholeness (Feldman, 1972). Children's preferences for certain shapes such as the mandala demonstrate their search for order, harmony, and balance in their drawings (Kellogg, 1970; Thomas & Silk, 1990).

Feldman (1972) wrote that when presented with a visual stimulus, people attempt to bring about a good gestalt or "pattern of maximum efficiency" (p. 364) that is characterized by regularity, symmetry, and simplicity. Kellogg (1970) developed the idea of a "primary visual order" (p. 61), which she described as an ability that exists in all persons allowing them to see and depict images that are symmetrical, balanced, and regular without necessarily understanding the abstract concepts underlying them. She stated that these pleasing formations do not need drawn pictures, and they need not provide emotional release except in the sense that the images themselves "nourish the human spirit" (p. 61).

The architect Gyorgy Doczi (1981), in his wide-ranging book *The Power of Limits: Proportional Harmonies in Nature, Art and Architecture*, described our attraction to forms that are regular, symmetrical, and whole. Doczi wrote that there exists a uniquely reciprocal relationship between two unequal parts to a whole; this relationship forms the visually pleasing "golden section" (p. 2). Arnheim (1969) suggested that the golden section is so satisfying and ever-present because it "may successfully combine unbreakable unity with lively tension" (p. 103). Doczi (1981) explained that the term *golden section* derives from the uniqueness as well as the distinctive value attributed to this proportional relationship found in nature, art, and architecture. Doczi gave examples of this pleasant proportional relationship in flowers, seashells, temples, and the human body. According to Doczi, the ubiquitous nature of the golden section demonstrates our attraction to proportional harmony and good gestalts. For him, the value of the golden section is that it provides form and limits to which humans respond harmoniously. Doczi wrote

> Perhaps one of the ways leading to the wisdom of maturity is the pathway of proportions, of shared limitations, which we need to find beneath the weeds and underbrush that have overgrown it. Proportions are shared limitations. As relationships they teach us the mana of sharing. As limitations they open doors toward the limitless. This is the power of limits. (p. 139)

Healing Function of the Perceptual Component

The healing quality of the Perceptual component of the Expressive Therapies Continuum has to do with the power of limits. Increasing structural awareness, as happens in perceptual expression, also has been said to impose order on chaos (Ulman, 1975a). This statement usually has been taken to mean the imposition of limits, boundaries, or structure on the turmoil of confusing thoughts and emotions. Thus, the healing power of a perceptual orientation has to do with the organization of stimuli and the formulation of good gestalts. Through the principle of isomorphism, the pleasing arrangement of external stimuli can be translated into a satisfying internal state. For instance, the coloring of predrawn mandala pictures has been demonstrated to reduce anxiety (Curry & Kasser, 2005; Henderson, Rosen, & Mascaro, 2007). Also, healing is the awareness of boundaries and the focus on boundaries, physical properties, and the formal elements of the image. Increasing awareness of the formal elements of visual expression or the structural qualities of an image can safely hold or contain the emotional characteristics of an experience (Kagin & Lusebrink, 1978b; Lusebrink, 1991b).

Because of the bipolar nature of the Perceptual/Affective level of the Expressive Therapies Continuum, as perceptual involvement increases, affective involvement decreases and eventually is blocked. This relationship can be used in a therapeutic manner to help clients impose limits on overwhelming emotion by deliberately using highly structured materials or by intentionally focusing on the perceptual or form qualities of the expressive experience. Elizabeth Layton was a self-taught artist who claimed that she cured herself of depression by drawing. When explaining her experience to reporter Don Lambert (Lambert, 1995), she made it clear that drawing helped relieve her lifelong symptoms of depression. Layton created extremely detailed, *blind or semiblind contour drawings*. In this sort of drawing, the artist remains intently focused on the edge or contour of the subject and draws it without looking at the paper. While the artist is drawing, the image is not named and internal dialogue is discouraged. A keen focus remains at all times on the lines being created, not their meaning or the emotions associated with them (Edwards, 1989).

With dedicated attention to line in her many contour drawings, Layton focused on the perceptual qualities of the expressive experience. The medium that she used, colored pencils, was restrictive and amplified the structural qualities of the experience. This intense focus on the perceptual had the unexpected associated benefit of containing affect. Mrs. Layton noticed, within a few months of beginning drawing, that her depression was lifting (Lambert, 1995). Her biographer reinforced the idea that affect was effectively contained by adding: "The drawing, along with the particular feelings it represented, could then be put away. Even when the drawing was revisited the feelings stayed with it rather than triggering a depression within the artist" (p.14).

Examples of Perceptual Experiences

Perceptual experiences are a developmental sequel to the actions and sensations of the Kinesthetic/Sensory level of the Expressive Therapies Continuum (Kagin & Lusebrink, 1978b). As children become more capable of using forms for self-expression, the scribbles that characterized the earlier stage of graphic functioning now become the schemas for increasingly sophisticated graphic expression in this new stage (Kellogg, 1970). The repeated creation of regular configurations helps children develop schemas to describe their experiences and their world (Lowenfeld, 1952).

As was discussed above, experiences involving the Perceptual component of the Expressive Therapies Continuum are those that emphasize the formation of representational images through form and boundaries, pattern, or color elements (Lusebrink, 1990). The focus on formal elements of visual expression can be developed as a language that benefits therapeutic progress. For example, allowing adolescent clients to describe images exclusively in terms of their formal elements may permit them to disclose important information without talking directly about embarrassing or problematic topics (Riley, 1999). An adolescent girl suffering from depression made a series of three abstract images that included a square black shape that she described simply as "a box." In the fourth session she was asked, "What would the box look like it if was opened up?" She created the mixed media image displayed in Figure 5.1 and several more like it over the next sessions. In time, she was able to articulate that the box contained her anger that she did not believe her parents wanted to witness, but which had threatened to overwhelm her unless she kept it contained. The visual image of her emotion being released from the box allowed the girl to realize it would not overwhelm her if allowed expression.

Rhyne (1973) believed that the way in which people organized stimuli visually through art was an indication of the way in which they organized their lives. She had clients make drawings or doodles of their immediate perceptions and, in discussing these simple line drawings, brought people into increased awareness of their current thoughts and feelings, and of how they lived their lives. For Rhyne, awareness did not necessarily have to be translated into words; the experience could be wholly effective remaining on the Perceptual level. She wrote, "Without pushing for interpretations, we explore the dimensions of the drawing and elaborate its impact through active present experiencing" (Rhyne, 1987, p. 173). The perceptual focusing on external objects may enhance clients' abilities to interact with the external environment (Lusebrink, 1990).

Media Experiences That Enhance Perceptual Functioning

Media properties and the structural qualities of media were introduced in Chapter 2; their role in promoting functioning with the Perceptual

Figure 5.1   An adolescent girl's perceptual representation of her anger being "let out of the box."

component will be further elaborated in this chapter. Boundaries and containment are among the first considerations when beginning to work with the Perceptual dimension. The paper given to or chosen by clients creates the first boundaries for an expressive experience. Larger paper can contain more images, emotions, and thoughts. Smaller paper necessarily contains fewer of these same elements, so the choice of a smaller paper may be one of the first ways in which an expressive experience can be contained. Other natural containers can include trays, boxes, or frames that mark off space and contain it (Landgarten, 1981; Lusebrink, 1990).

When materials are boundary determined as mentioned in Chapter 2, the physical properties of the materials themselves limit expressive possibilities. Materials such as wood, metal, and tile have firm external boundaries, which limit or contain the emotional release experienced when working with them in a perceptual manner. The external limits inherent in resistant materials usually provide a safe and nonthreatening experience for clients

(Kagin & Lusebrink, 1978b). If materials are quantity determined, like paint, then limiting the quantity of paint can limit the expressive potential of the experience. However, emotionally fragile clients still may feel apprehensive with quantity-determined materials when first using them.

Reflective Distance With the Perceptual Component

Reflective distance with the Perceptual component of the Expressive Therapies Continuum increases from the Kinesthetic/Sensory level. On the Kinesthetic/Sensory level, reflective distance is low because clients are caught up in the physical aspects of the expressive experience and often unable to distance themselves from it. With the Perceptual dimension, reflective distance can vary depending upon whether the client is actively immersed in creating an image or evaluating the quality of representation. The Perceptual component, with its emphasis on structural elements and form, necessarily requires some distancing in order to evaluate how well the form is being represented. Therefore, perceptual work usually is characterized by fluctuation between immersion in the creative process and evaluative distance.

This alternation between immersion and reflection can be incorporated into the therapeutic goals for experiential art. Clients can learn through their experiences working on the Perceptual dimension that they have the ability to step back during an experience and view it objectively. Often the goals of cognitive therapy are first to help the client become an objective observer of his or her thoughts, and second to change automatic negative thoughts (Beck, 1995). Along similar lines, cognitive restructuring through art has been used in the short-term resolution of trauma with children. Children first picture the traumatic scene and later add images of themselves using new coping skills or attitudes learned through therapy (Steele, 2003). This type of therapeutic approach requires immersion into the traumatic memories and reflection about new and healthier thoughts and behaviors in the past and in the present.

Questions and Discussion That Promote
Perceptual Information Processing

Functioning with the Perceptual component of the Expressive Therapies Continuum can be stimulated by asking clients to describe in concrete terms their perceptions of the formal elements of their images (Lusebrink, 1990).

Clients should be asked to focus on the lines and forms themselves, not on what they planned to create when they began the experience, and not about the symbolism that can exist in the finished product. The focus remains on the structure, construction, and perhaps the deconstruction of the images. The therapist would engage in conversations about the structural qualities of the image by making comments and asking questions such as "Tell me about that shape" and "In what order were the lines added?" The deconstruction of an image can be queried by asking: "How would the picture look if that shape was taken away?" or "Let's look at the image without those lines."

Mala Betensky (1995) developed a phenomenological approach to art therapy that focused on what she termed "intentional looking" at the art product. Betensky's multistep approach is greatly simplified here, but one important aspect of the process was that after images were completed, Betensky had clients hang them on a wall, gain some physical distance from them, and respond to the question "What do you see?" (p. 17). Descriptions focused on the structural elements of the image, their relationship to one another, and their relationship to the overall image. Betensky asked that her clients forget what their images were supposed to mean and focus instead on how they looked.

Other questions that can lead to information processing with the Perceptual component are: "How does that look to you?" or "Describe the lines and shapes that you see." A client can be asked to represent a therapeutic issue and then to imagine a significant change to that issue by responding to the question "What would that look like?" or "How would you like it to look?" To maintain focus on the Perceptual dimension, the emphasis would be on how the new situation would look, not on what it would mean.

For example, a nine-year-old girl who refused to go to school was asked to draw her classroom. The drawing included so many chaotic, scribbled lines that it was difficult to perceive anything from the image. Next, the girl was asked: "How would you like it to look?" The resulting drawing provided a stark contrast to the first: It was orderly and neat. These two drawings provided the first steps toward change. The child was able to see what she perceived the problem to be and then, with the help of her therapist and parents, to develop some steps towards making it look the way she wanted.

Emergent Function of the Perceptual Component

As can be seen from the previous example, stimuli can be organized into perceptions that inform change. Therapeutic work with the Perceptual component can enhance clients' abilities to see things more clearly. The ability to perceive things clearly can promote the capacity to verbally label experiences and think about them differently. Thus, increased cognitive functioning and self-understanding can emerge from an experience with the Perceptual dimension (Lusebrink, 1990). The *changing point of view* experience is a perceptual experience that asks clients to vary their typical way of viewing a situation (Lusebrink, 1990). In this experience, clients are asked to represent a problem. A second image is requested in which clients take an extreme close-up view of one small portion of the original image. Finally, a third image demonstrating a bird's-eye view of the first picture is created. These three different views of the same issue can show clients that how they view a situation dramatically affects the way they think and feel about it.

For instance, a 15-year-old Hispanic boy was asked to draw an image of his difficulties with his parents. He drew a tree with limbs stretched to the edges of the paper. The close-up view was a picture of a bird's nest in the branches, and finally, the distant view showed him that the tree existed in a forest of other similar trees. The use of the visual language required by the perceptual work helped move the experience to the Cognitive/Symbolic level of the Expressive Therapies Continuum. The young man was able to talk about his experience of being part of a nurturing family (bird's nest), but also part of a larger community that did not include his parents (forest). He explained that the tree drawing with the branches spreading out so far in both directions represented himself trying to be part of his family and part of his community of friends. The drawings helped him better understand that his difficulties with his parents had to do with the natural process of separation from parents and the individuation of self. In addition, the process of separation was complicated by being part of the Hispanic culture.

When Work With the Perceptual Component Is Indicated

Our ability to perceive certain images develops over time and with experience. Therefore, our experiences predispose us to perceive particular stimuli in specific ways. In fact, people can become such experts at visual perception that they seem to possess superhuman abilities (Arnheim, 1969). For example, a skilled ultrasound technician can perceive a tumor or a fetus in a sonogram image, whereas the untrained eye sees a fog of confusing gray masses. Bird watchers can sharpen their perception to the point where they easily perceive various species of birds when the amateur eye cannot distinguish a bird from the tree in which it is sitting. In addition, perception and survival are inexorably linked, such that the better a species is at perceiving danger, the better its chances of survival (Arnheim, 1969). Experiences can shape perceptions such that people become adept at perceiving threats, especially if these experiences included trauma.

Therapeutic work with the Perceptual dimension can help clients begin to perceive themselves and their world differently. Rather than automatically perceiving a threat, clients can be retrained to perceive the world more objectively. Work on the Perceptual level of the Expressive Therapies Continuum can help people develop this perceptual objectivity. In addition, it has the added advantage of making the perceived change concrete in the form of an image. What can be perceived in an image can perhaps be more easily managed in real life. In addition, the manipulation of images can be the first step toward influencing, controlling, or changing various factors in life (Hinz, 2006).

Other people are notoriously difficult to change or control. Nonetheless, clients often enter therapy with the expressed purpose of helping change another person. This goal is prevalent in couples and family therapy where clients would be better served by being taught that they can change only their own behaviors, thoughts, and feelings. Relationships are most fulfilling when people do not struggle for control, but rather can see issues, ideas, and values from their family member's point of view. As was discussed in the first chapter, people in relationships can develop the ability to perceive representational diversity (Siegel & Hartzell, 2003), which means that two views of the same object or issue are possible. One art therapy technique that can help couples (parent and child, husband and wife, therapist and client) begin to see one another's point of view is a *nonverbal communication* experience. In this expressive exercise, a dyad uses drawing materials to communicate a message without words; the idea must be perceived through the images alone. This technique can be used in families where the ability to perceive another's viewpoint can be developed along with empathic understanding (Hinz, 2006). These and other perceptual experiences used with couples and families will be explored in depth in Chapter 12.

As was mentioned above, the *cognitive restructuring* approach to trauma uses the manipulation of images as the first indication that responses to trauma can change (Steele, 2003). Clients can be encouraged to represent themselves in their images as responding to the traumatic situations with new attitudes and skills. Depending upon the age and cognitive abilities of the clients, this approach can be a step-by-step, fully guided art approach similar to imagery rescripting (Smucker, Dancu, & Foa, 2002), or a more open-ended approach where the client is asked to depict a different reaction to the trauma using the new knowledge and skills that he or she now possesses (Steele, 2003).

Working on the Perceptual component of the Expressive Therapies Continuum can give clients with dementia or with psychosis a visual focus for reorienting to the reality of their external environment (Wald, 2003). Therapeutic work on the Perceptual level with persons suffering from schizophrenia would include having them make representational drawings of topics from real life. This sort of perceptual work can help them increase and maintain contact with the external reality of their environment (Lusebrink, 1990).

McNiff (2004) wrote about his experiences with a schizophrenic man named Anthony who engaged in drawing the objects around him with increasing detail. In the author's opinion, involvement with the physical matter in his external world increased Anthony's perceptual awareness of all things and grounded his experience in external reality. After numerous perceptual expressions of objects Anthony moved on to represent the people around him. With increased perceptual awareness, he gained greater autonomy in other areas of his life and eventually left the hospital after years of institutionalization.

Overcoming Blocks to Perceptual Functioning

Blocks to the use of perceptual information processing can be seen in the overly emotional client, one who is so caught up in the experience of affect that she or he is unable to view himself or his situation clearly. Due to the bipolar nature of the Perceptual/Affective level, being mired in powerful emotions will block the ability to perceive. Additionally, overuse of kinesthetic activity can be a defense against moving to the Perceptual dimension (Lusebrink, 1990). Clients can be so involved with movement that they are unable to perceive form.

As was mentioned above, because of the way the nervous system organizes psychological energies during the perceptual process, people impose wholeness upon perceived images even when presented with interrupted outlines (Arnheim, 1966). If visual forms are unstable or incomplete, the human organism completes them through a process called closure. Closure is required to form a good gestalt because the organism cannot tolerate instability in its perception (Feldman, 1972). Intolerance of unstable or incomplete forms can be used therapeutically as one way to introduce inexperienced or reluctant clients to perceptual information processing. Henley (1991) used unfinished images or sculptures as one way to invite clients with little experience in functioning perceptually into the world of form and structure. He described a closure experience where clients were given a paper containing the beginning of a form and encouraged to develop it and to close it. He theorized that the push to form good gestalts (regular, symmetrical, and whole) contributed to a desire among clients to complete an interrupted picture or incomplete sculpture.

Balancing Excessive Perceptual Functioning

Children and adults sometimes seem to be stuck in the repetitive and inflexible use of schematic representations. Images used in this way can be thought of as defenses against unwanted thoughts or emotions (Henley, 1989; Kramer, 1975a; Lusebrink, 1990). Lusebrink wrote that repetitive geometrical forms can be used as a way of warding off repressed anger or anxiety. For Lowenfeld (1952), repetitious pattern making demonstrated a form of escape indicative of extreme cognitive inflexibility. In every era, there are characters from television shows such as Ninja turtles, Pokemon, and Sponge Bob that children repetitively copy without change and without tremendous emotional involvement. The repetition of these stereo-typical drawings may ward off the emotional upheaval that real creative work may cause (Kramer, 1971). The drawings of persons suffering from obsessive-compulsive disorder demonstrate the extreme use of form to ward off anxiety with images characterized by perseveration and repetition of form (Lusebrink, 1990).

Eating disordered men and women often initially respond in therapy with stereotypical images (Lubbers, 1991; Makin, 2000). It has been my experience that the initial images of women with eating disorders often include hearts, flowers, and rainbows. These stereotypical images serve to maintain the pretense that no problem exists. Just as the body in the anorexic or binge eater demonstrates that a problem actually does exist, so does the stereotypical image. The first images of bottles or drug para-phernalia drawn by persons with substance use disorders also seem to be defensive images rather than symbols. These drawings are indicative of functioning with the Perceptual component and often are made with the intent to glorify the substance or at least maintain a defensive stance about it. Dickman, Dunn, and Wolf (1996) found that images of drugs or drug paraphernalia, lack of human figures, and a majority of geometric forms in posttreatment drawings were significant predictors of relapse after chemical dependency treatment. It can be hypothesized that these graphic indicators demonstrated that clients were still functioning predominantly with the Perceptual component of the Expressive Therapies Continuum, not flexibly with all components.

When clients present repetitive, stereotypical images it is recommended that therapists accept them in a noncritical fashion just as they would any other image (Henley, 1989; Kramer, 1971). Kramer warns that therapists should not move clients, especially children, away from comforting images too quickly. She explained that conventional or stereotypical productions sometimes represent a needed defense against internal chaos and confusion. In order to help clients break out of stereotypical presentations, therapists can begin at the level of information processing where the client is comfortable. With each accepted image, the therapist can look for any slight deviation in the artwork and ask clients to expand on that deviation in a subsequent image (Henley, 1989). For example, if one flower were a different size or color than the others, the client could be asked to draw another image of the different flower. In this manner, the client's own comfort level with deviation is honored and forms the basis for the next step in therapy that can allow more personal information to be revealed through the art.

Henley also recommended that therapists use a sensory awareness technique described by Lowenfeld (as cited in Henley, 1989) in which clients are made aware of the real sensory qualities of their experiences through art and nature. By increasing sensory input through multiple sensory channels and asking clients to respond to them in art, clients can be made aware of what exists beyond the comfort of their usual stereotypical images. This experience is similar to the sensory exploration exercise described in Chapter 4 in the example of the pinecone drawings. The first drawing can be seen as a stereotype of a pinecone, uninformed by all of the actual sensory possibilities of the concrete object. After sensory exploration, the pinecone drawing contained much more depth and possibility.

Case Example

Introduction

Carla was a 38-year-old married African American woman suffering from major depressive disorder and binge eating disorder. She had two teenaged children and worked outside the home as a legal assistant. Carla had been seeing a psychiatrist and licensed clinical social worker for approximately three months. She was prescribed antidepressant medication and had participated in several insight-oriented treatment sessions. The social worker consulted an art therapist when she felt that she was not helping Carla understand or change some of the core beliefs that were maintaining her binge eating disorder. These beliefs were thought to be related to a history of childhood physical abuse.

Assessment of Functional Level

In order to gain an impression of the client's preferred level of the Expressive Therapies Continuum, the art therapist invited Carla to use any of the various art materials available in order to create an image. Carla chose watercolor paints and made an abstract landscape image. She held her image as she talked about it and the paint ran down the page. When she quickly righted the image, wet rivulets of paint ran off the paper. Carla cried quietly for a few minutes and crumpled the paper up in disgust. She was asked to allow the art therapist to keep the image, and she agreed.

In the second session, Carla again was invited to use any material that she wished and was asked to make a self-portrait. Carla chose a medium-sized piece of white paper, wet it, crumpled it up, and painted with tempera paints on the wet irregular surface. She called the resulting image, displayed on the left in Figure 5.2, a self-portrait. She said that it looked like her because it was "fat and ugly." She created a second, similar self-portrait, also shown in Figure 5.2 (right), in the third art therapy session. In these succeeding sessions, Carla worked quietly and methodically, moving the paint around the paper in a contemplative fashion without exerting a great deal of energy. She was tearful at times, but responded to questions asked of her, disclosing details of her life history and the development and maintenance of her disorders.

During each of the first three sessions, after the paintings were completed, Carla related historical information and was queried about automatic negative thoughts and significant core beliefs that maintained depressive thinking, binge eating, and a desperately low sense of self-esteem. It became clear that Carla, who was raised by alcoholic and physically abusive parents, had a negative view of herself, the world, and the future. In these initial sessions she also received psychoeducational information about binge eating disorder.

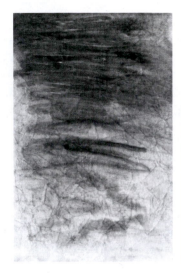

Figure 5.2   Information processing with the Affective component shows affect distorts form.

Expressive indicators and graphic elements from Carla's final art products are summarized in Table 5.1. These indicators—preferred media, manner of interaction with the media, stylistic features from the finished product, and client verbal communication style—indicate a preference for the Affective component. In the first three sessions, Carla chose to work with paint, which, being a fluid medium, would increase emotional flow and suggest functioning with the Affective component of the Expressive Therapies Continuum. She worked in a listless manner, pushing the paint around the paper without expending much energy. In addition, she crumpled the paper prior to working on it, perhaps in an imitation of her first image in art therapy that she intended to destroy. The lack of energy and mildly destructive tendencies are characteristic of depression, and again indicative of functioning with the Affective component.

Carla's images are relatively formless, large, and dark. The use of dark colors has been associated with the diagnosis of major depressive disorder (Gantt & Tabone, 1998; Wadeson, 1980). In addition, a low level of implied energy and lack of attention to details also were found to be characteristic of the drawings of depressed persons (Gantt & Tabone, 1998). The lack of form, but inclusion of color, is indicative of the Affective dimension. Thus, the stylistic features and expressive elements of the drawings themselves demonstrated a preference for processing information with the Affective component. Finally, Carla's communication style during the art process and

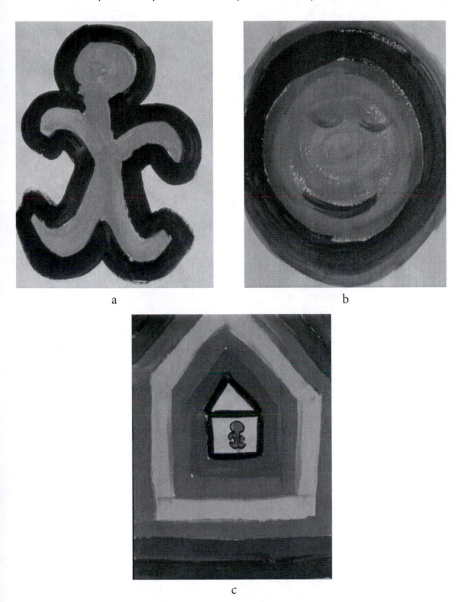

a   b

c

Figure 5.3 Changing point of view—a: original image, b: close-up view, c: bird's eye view.

in other parts of the therapy experience demonstrated depressive characteristics: she was tearful, quiet, and spoke mainly to answer the questions asked. In summary, features of the person, process, and product demonstrated that Carla's preferred method of functioning and expression was affective.

TABLE 5.1   Example of Art Assessment Demonstrating Preferred ETC Component Process

Assessment Element	Results From Assessment of Carla
Preferred media	Watercolor paint; tempera paint
Manner of interaction with media	Listless, lack of energy, mildly destructive
Stylistic or expressive elements of final art product	Abstract, formless, lack of details; dark colors
Verbal communication	Quiet, tearful, answered question when asked, did not volunteer information

Functioning With the Perceptual Component

After determining the preferred component of the Expressive Therapies Continuum, the therapist worked with Carla to establish treatment goals for therapy. Together, client and therapist determined that it would be beneficial for Carla to achieve a different view of herself and her circumstances, one that was more realistic and less negative. Secondly, they determined that Carla would like to reduce the frequency of binge eating and find healthier ways to express emotions and meet needs. Finally, therapist and client wanted to work together to improve Carla's communication skills with her husband, children, and coworkers.

In order to address the first treatment goal, Carla was asked to paint another *self-portrait* with more form to it. This request was made in order to help Carla begin to move toward the Perceptual component. It was hypothesized that moving Carla toward the Perceptual component of the Perceptual/Affective level would help contain her emotion and perhaps allow her to gain a different view of herself and her life situation. In addition, what could emerge from a different viewpoint can be a new level of self-understanding or empathy.

Carla was asked to carry out the *changing point of view* art experience. Carla used tempera paint on 12-by-18-inch white paper for all three images. Her three paintings are displayed in Figure 5.3. She first created the self-portrait in Figure 5.3a and was asked to describe it in terms of its formal artistic elements. Carla said of the image, "It is fat, it is looming, and it is large. It fills the page. It is green and black, and it has the appearance of a gingerbread man. I don't like it; it is fat." Carla was reminded to refrain from making comments except about the formal artistic characteristics, such as line, shape, and color. She did not add more. Carla described the close-up view (Figure 5.3b) as details of her face. She said of the second image: "It is round, it is rounded, lines are curving; it is green and smiling."

Finally, Carla described Figure 5.3c (the bird's eye view) as follows: "It is a square and a rectangle, and a rainbow. There are many colors here—red, orange, yellow, green, blue, purple. That is a little person inside a house with a rainbow all around it."

Movement to the Cognitive/Symbolic Level

Carla clearly wanted to talk about the Symbolic components of her images. She was excited and energized for the first time in therapy. Carla stated that she was not aware of a reason for choosing the color green for her figures. Green was not a color used in her previous images, which were predominantly red, white, and blue. However, she said that her association with green was growth, and she added that she felt as though she was growing in the process of creating these images. Carla was surprised that the close-up image displayed a smiling face. She claimed that this countenance showed her that a positive attitude was possible; she could view herself as beautiful and not as fat.

Carla was bemused by the third image as well, but eager to explain that she could get her needs filled and express important issues at home. She said that she realized she had a wonderful home that included her husband and two daughters, who cared very much about her. Carla explained that she seemed to be telling herself that she was safe at home; she could get what she needed without always turning to food. Carla mentioned that for the first time she understood that she did not have to act like a down-trodden victim, but could reach out to others.

Alternating Between the Perceptual and Cognitive Levels

Carla continued in therapy with an emphasis on strengthening her new view of herself and increasing assertiveness and other communication skills. She continued to make self-portraits and to get as much information as she could describing their formal elements on the Perceptual dimension, before moving on to discussions using the Cognitive component. In one exercise, Carla made *inner-outer self-portraits*, which included three images: (1) how I see myself, (2) how others see me, and (3) how I feel right now (Lusebrink, 1990). This experience allowed Carla to see herself from a different perspective and to visualize and express how others (husband, daughters, and coworkers) might see her. Finally, Carla expressed feelings about the two portraits and the discrepancies between them in the third image. This art experience helped Carla to further explore her role as victim and survivor of childhood physical abuse.

Summary

The Perceptual component of the Expressive Therapies Continuum focuses on helping clients use a visual language as a parallel process to their verbal communications to differentiate and depict their internal experiences, thoughts, and emotions. Experiences with this dimension are immersed in the formal elements of images and the structural qualities of media used. People are attracted to patterns and images that are simple, regular, and balanced. Through the process called isomorphism, these qualities of images and art experiences can be internalized during creative expression on the Perceptual dimension.

Perceptual experiences encourage clients to concentrate on a visual language defined by formal visual elements such as line, shape, size, and color to communicate in a relatively objective fashion. Clients are encouraged to view themselves and others in a new light, to see people or situations from another person's perspective, and to change lifelong ways of perceiving the self and the world. The role of perceptual experiences in therapeutic work with couples and families will be further explored in Chapter 12. What can emerge from perceptual experiences are a new degree of self-understanding and the development of new levels of empathy for the self and others. Examples of the perceptually oriented art experiences discussed in the chapter are included in Table 5.2. This summary table also includes information about the healing and emergent functions that can be evoked by each experience.

TABLE 5.2   Examples of Perceptual Experiences and Associated Healing and Emergent Functions

Perceptual Activity	Materials and Procedure	Healing Function	Emergent Function
The closure game	Drawing media—incomplete drawing Sculpting materials—half-formed sculpture	Organizing and closing form; forming good gestalts; internalizing structure	Symbol formation can occur; cognitive processes and learning how to begin
Doodles of present perceptions	Watercolor markers and paper	Organization of thoughts and feelings; schematic representations of feelings	Clarity of thought about emotions
Drawings from reality	Paper and pencil or pen	Perceptual focus on external objects enhances interaction with external environment	Increased reality testing or improved cognitive functioning
Blind or semiblind contour drawings	Pencils, colored pencils, pens, and drawing paper; following contour of object with eyes, drawing it without looking at paper	Focus on line and contour, organization, containment of affect	Thoughts about self and experiences
Nonverbal communication	Partners, drawing materials, large paper; communication through image only	Increases representational diversity, ability to perceive another's point of view	May increase empathic understanding
Changing point of view	Drawing or painting materials, paper Three views depicted: (1) therapeutic issue, (2) close-up view, (3) bird's-eye view	Clients can see that the view they take of an issue affects their experience of it	Increased self-understanding or self-awareness
Inner-outer self portraits	Drawing or painting materials, paper Three depictions: (1) how I see myself, (2) how others see me, (3) how I feel right now	Compare and contrast inner and outer self-portraits; express feelings about similarities or discrepancies in third image	Clients enlarge view of themselves in relation to others, explore social roles and feelings about self or persona

6

Affective Component of the Expressive Therapies Continuum

Introduction to the Affective Component

Affect is a word used to describe the multidimensional construct of emotional states that include cognitive, experiential, and neurophysiological input (Taylor, Bagby, & Parker, 1997). The Affective component of the Expressive Therapies Continuum describes the emotion aroused in the individual, and accessed and expressed by him or her through interaction with art media (Kagin & Lusebrink, 1978b). The Affective component is opposite the Perceptual component on the Perceptual/Affective level of the ETC. Whereas therapeutic work with the Perceptual component is concerned with structure and the containment of emotion, work on the Affective component allows for and amplifies the expression of feelings. The use of art materials in general, and the artistic process itself, may arouse affect, and therefore many expressive experiences include emotion; the creator's emotion imbues artistic images with a dynamic quality (Lusebrink, 1990). However, when working with the Affective component of the ETC, therapists support a more direct expression of feelings by giving explicit directives that help clients access emotions, by offering fluid media, and by encouraging the use of vivid colors.

Disturbances of affect regulation and expression are the chief symptoms, or associated features, of the majority of DSM-IV diagnostic categories (American Psychiatric Association, 2000; Taylor et al., 1997). Therapists often create therapeutic goals and treatment plans that include helping clients work on the Affective component. Such goals include using art media and expressive experiences to access and identify emotions, to discriminate among them, and to express emotions appropriately. Art has been demonstrated both to help manage anxiety (Curry & Kasser, 2005) and to improve mood (De Petrillo & Winner, 2005). It is imperative that therapists help clients learn the benefits of developing a repertoire of skills to assist in managing emotions in healthy ways.

Emotions can become problematic when they are experienced by clients as overwhelming (Linehan, Bohus, & Lynch, 2007), when substances are used to manage emotions (Hinz, 2006; Sher & Grekin, 2007), or when emotions are not expressed at all, as in the case of alexithymia (Meijer-Degen & Lansen, 2006). Therapists must be prepared to help their clients understand the function and necessity of emotions in order to begin what probably will impress some clients as an impossible task: deciphering the complex, confusing, and chaotic information available as affective input, as well as determining and executing appropriate affective output. As was mentioned in Chapter 5, a structured approach can be a palatable introduction to affective material as the schematic representation of emotion through color, line, and form might be perceived as a nonthreatening starting point.

In conjunction with the use of art, clients may require psychoeducational information about the nature and purpose of emotions. This type of basic information can render the subject matter safe when previously clients have perceived it as dangerous. Clients can be taught that emotions are basic to human experience, and there seem to be 6 to 12 primary emotions "hardwired" into the human brain, such as interest, joy, disgust, sadnesss, anger, fear, shame, and surprise. These emotions are not taught; infants and elders alike express them, and they are recognized across cultures (Ekman, 2003; Taylor et al., 1997). Emotions are elemental to human experience because they are signals about inner experiences and events in one's surroundings: Emotions indicate that people must act on something in their environment (Ekman, 2003). The classic example of an emotional signal is that of fear. Fear signals imminent threat; in response to threat, fear prepares individuals to fight or flee. Other emotions also are signals; happiness and sadness invite caring and participation, anger and disgust motivate action. Clients benefit from understanding that emotions are merely signals and, like other signals, they are temporary. Emotions usually are experienced intensely, but temporarily, before the individual returns to an internal homeostatic balance. Emotions perform their signaling function and then subside. Clients can be taught that they can experience their emotions like waves that rise, peak, crest, and recede

(Linehan, 1993), and that they can use expressive art experiences to help facilitate the peaceful experiencing of their emotions. Clients with eating disorders frequently have experienced their emotions as threatening and have used food to avoid feeling them and self-induced vomiting to purge them. Through art therapy they can learn to "purge on paper" and ultimately to express emotions directly (Hinz, 2006).

Developmental Hierarchy

The Expressive Therapies Continuum is arranged in a hierarchical manner from the simplest Kinesthetic/Sensory processing to the most complex Cognitive/Symbolic use of imagery formation. The development of children's graphic abilities seems to parallel this hierarchical arrangement. In the last chapter, it was explained that as children develop, the Perceptual component of the ETC is embodied in the schematic representations that typify early to middle childhood drawings. Continuing through the developmental hierarchy of graphic expression, elementary school-aged children are capable of making fully formed images. They have moved away from the schematic representations that characterized earlier stages of drawing, and have moved to a realistic stage. This phase of graphic development is supported by increased attention to detail with special consideration to the clothing, hairstyle, and facial features that create individual identity (Lowenfeld & Brittain, 1987). Young adolescents move into the naturalistic phase of graphic development. More importance is given to the correspondence of drawings with nature or objects in the external world. Identity formation or self-definition is one important task of adolescence that can be supported by creative art expression (Carolan, 2007; Linesch, 1988).

Adolescents have not yet developed full control over their emotions and can use art to provide a socially acceptable release for the intensity of feeling they are experiencing at this age. Emotions and moods can be conveyed in the art of young adolescents through exaggeration, emphasis, or distortion of forms or the nontraditional use of color (Lowenfeld & Brittain, 1987). It is interesting to note that many types of modern art make use of form distortions and the unorthodox use of color to express emotion (Arnheim, 1969; Feldman, 1972). Similar to adolescent art and modern art, form distortions, vivid colors, and unconventional color use characterize the Affective dimension of the Expressive Therapies Continuum. With this component, art processes and products can effectively express a wide range of emotion.

Healing Function of the Affective Component

The healing function of the Affective component of the Expressive Therapies Continuum is increased awareness of appropriate affect (Lusebrink, 1990). Art expression can be a means of facing emotions previously conceived of as daunting or dangerous. Creativity can be an authentic companion on a difficult journey to reclaim appropriate emotional expression (Arnheim, 1992; Swados, 2005). Elizabeth Swados chose to write and illustrate *My Depression: A Picture Book* rather than act out upon suicidal urges. Clients will learn through their direct experiences with the Affective component that the expression of emotions is not only acceptable, but that it is stress reducing and life enhancing as well. When clients are at a loss for words, sometimes art can be a way to invite the expression of emotion. The image in Figure 6.1, made by an adolescent girl, demonstrates the expression in line, shape, and color of a previously unspeakable emotion. The verbal discussion of the emotion depicted was a much less important aspect of

Figure 6.1   Art expression with the Affective component: The use of art can aid the expression of emotion.

the therapeutic session than the actual expression itself. The client experienced great relief after making a picture to express the affective state she previously never felt free to openly share.

Examples of Affective Experiences

As was briefly mentioned above, activities with the Affective component of the Expressive Therapies Continuum often include the use of fluid media and vivid colors in order to facilitate the experience and expression of emotion (Lusebrink, 1990). Color has long been associated with emotional expression (Birren, 1988; Feldman, 1972). According to Feldman, abstract expressionist painters strove to develop a color language for emotional expression; they wanted to use color rather than content or form as the primary communicator of affective states. Advertisers use the power of color associations in order to manipulate consumer preferences for products (Callejas, Acosta, & Lupianez, 2007; Lee & Lee, 2006). Line quality also has been associated with the expression of feelings (Betensky, 1995; Martin, 2003). Therapists can direct the use of both line and color to aid clients in conveying their emotions in art therapy.

A warm-up exercise to help clients get in touch with feelings and begin to express emotions through artistic means is drawing or painting to music. In order to emphasize the different types of emotions that can be felt, various kinds of music can be played to capture different moods (Lusebrink, 1990). The object of this type of warm-up exercise is to paint unconsciously, without overthinking the event, so that an affective experience, not a cognitive one, arises from the occurrence. In recent years, an expressive painting movement has evolved designed around the theme of painting in order to express emotion rather than with an eye to the finished product (Cassou & Cubley, 1995; Goldstein, 1999).

Kinesthetic/Sensory art experiences can be used as a catalyst for the Affective component. Beginning with the Sensory component, clients first can be immersed in the sensual aspects of the media experience. After focusing on external impressions, they can be guided to attend to internal sensations and moved up the developmental hierarchy of the Expressive Therapies Continuum by then focusing on emotions evoked. Sensory experiences can be used to suggest peace, calm, sadness, disgust, and a whole host of other feeling states. Kinesthetic experiences that require vigorous movement can call up strong emotions. Pounding clay, tearing paper, hammering nails, chiseling stone, and crayon resist are kinesthetic activities that can evoke excitement or anger.

Crayon resist entails covering a sheet of paper with colored crayon, and then again with black crayon; this concentrated kinesthetic effort can be arousing without being emotionally threatening. Kinesthetic arousal can begin to loosen obstacles keeping emotions under control and out of awareness. Colors emerging from scratching back through the dark background with fingernails or sticks can provide a contained representation of the threatening emotions or content. Using watercolor paint on wet paper can be a method of emotional release (Lusebrink, 1990). The difficulty of controlling the paint as the colors run and bleed can be used to reflect frustration with control issues in life or can be expressive of other emotions. Therapists can subtly guide color choices and placement if necessary to ensure that resulting paintings are not characterized by muddy colors and dissatisfaction.

Media Experiences That Enhance Affective Functioning

Media properties were introduced in Chapter 2, and the relationship between media properties and affective experience was demonstrated in Figure 2.1. To reiterate, the more fluid the media, the more likely an expressive experience is to evoke emotion. The use of paint and other fluid media such as chalk pastels or water-soluble oil pastels greatly enhances affective expression. Fluid media are fast; they easily flow out of their containers or off their mediators and quickly fill the page. There is little time to think about fluid expression as it is occurring. Kramer (1975b) described children who draw very well, but whose artistic abilities regress with the use of paint. In her estimation, the emotionally evocative qualities of paint cause this type of artistic regression. She stated that children who regress while using paint likely depend on intellect to control or repress affect, but lose that control when handling paint, perhaps becoming flooded with affect. These words by Kramer remind us that the use of art media to evoke emotion is not always a benign experience and must be carefully monitored and controlled. The framework of the ETC demonstrates that adding a focus on form or structure can keep clients' experiences with paint from becoming nontherapeutically regressive.

There is a long-standing historical association with the evocation of affect and the use of color (Birren, 1988; Hammer, 1997). For example, in the field of psychological assessment, the Rorschach Inkblot Test is a method of personality assessment in which persons respond to indefinite images. Interpretation of the Rorschach Inkblot Test distinguishes the use of form from the use of color in organizing the ambiguous stimuli. If color is the predominant organizing factor, clients are viewed as excessively emotional or as having a tendency to act out emotions (Exner, 1993). The chromatic House-Tree-Person Test is another personality measure developed to study the effects of emotional evocation on the projective process. It was assumed that emotion was suggested by color, and that the use of color would probe underneath defenses to emotional material that was likely avoided in achromatic House-Tree-Person drawings (Hammer, 1997). Finally, the Luscher Color Test is a personality test based on physiological and psychological responses to color. The test records color preferences and purports to uncover associated personality traits and life stressors. Although it is no longer widely used in the United States, both mental health workers and physicians use the Luscher Color Test in Europe. An active website exists where materials pertaining to the test are available: http://www.luscher-color.com (Luscher, 1969, 2006).

The body's physiological response to color was the basis for color therapy, which was developed in the United States in the late 1800s by Edwin Babbitt (Birren, 1988). Color therapy grew out of research into the responses of plants, animals, and humans to surface exposure of various hues. Although color therapy has had many detractors, research into the physiological and psychological aspects of color continues today, and different colors are used for their arousing (red) or calming (blue) effects (Birren, 1988; Elliot & Maier, 2007; Elliot, Maier, Moller, Friedman, & Meinhardt, 2007; Hoss, 2005). One type of color therapy still in use today is the painting therapy associated with the Waldorf School of Education and Anthroposophy (Hauschka; 1985; Trostli, 1998). In anthroposophic painting, therapy colors are chosen and therapeutically applied according to their objective physiological and psychological effects on the soul-spirit (Hauschka, 1985). Blue is associated with inward absorption and red with outward revelation (Trostli, 1998).

In popular Western culture, color is used to describe emotions: one is described as "blue" to indicate sadness, or "green with envy." Red has been associated with passion, including passionate love or uncontrollable rage. Yellow is viewed as an aggressive color, and green as a calm one (Hammer, 1997). However, many color associations are personal and related to past events in clients' lives (Lowenfeld & Brittain, 1987). In addition, colors also occur in contexts or in relationships—in art and in life—that influence their emotional values (Callejas et al., 2007; Feldman, 1972). Finally, colors evoke physiological responses, and they have cultural associations that impact their use and meanings (Hoss, 2005). Therefore, therapists cannot assume color associations; clients *must* provide information about color choices, meanings, and relationships.

In summary, having many vibrantly colored art media and fluid media available for client use can help stimulate affective responding. However, materials should not be limited just to those that are considered fluid. Clients' needs for materials evolve from their needs for emotional expression and can develop from functioning at the Kinesthetic/Sensory level of the Expressive Therapies Continuum. Virtually any type of material can be used in ways that evoke affective responding. In general, an effective therapeutic approach involves allowing the client free choice of materials and subject matter. Freedom of choice, in content especially, has been demonstrated to encourage more meaningful artistic production than the prescription of topics for depiction (Ellenbecker, 2003).

Reflective Distance With the Affective Component

The expression of emotions through affective processes and images reduces reflective distance (Lusebrink, 1991b). When caught up in emotional expression, clients do not necessarily have the ability to gain distance from the art process or product in order to reflect on or think about what is occurring. Extreme emotional involvement is manifested through distorted form or lack of form in an image, as was demonstrated in Chapter 5, Figure 5.2. Also at the extreme affective pole of the Perceptual/Affective level, clients experience overwhelming affect or the projection of affect onto the environment, both of which can reduce the capacity to experience any degree of reflective distance (Lusebrink, 1990). In fact, helping clients reduce or eliminate reflective distance can be one goal of the art experience. Regression to a more primitive state and a crude manner of self-expression may free individuals from immobilizing inhibitions (Kramer, 1971; Lusebrink, 1990).

There are times when the expression of emotion without reflection is desirable. A client might not know what he or she is feeling and just need to release emotion without first thinking. However, most of the time a modicum of reflective distance is necessary in order for clients to move forward in therapy. Without some reflection, clients can become mired in rumination about a subject, lacking the ability to transform expression into action. For emotionally fragile clients especially, aiding the ability to establish reflective distance and use art to communicate rather than just to purge feelings is extremely therapeutic (Levens, 1990).

Questions and Discussion That Promote Affective Information Processing

Questions and discussions that can elicit and emphasize affective functioning have to do with feelings. Very basically, the therapist can ask clients how they are feeling as they work with a medium, focusing on the medium being experienced, especially if it is more fluid than clients are used to handling. The invitation to "describe what you are feeling" is the most elemental one to begin processing with the Affective component. This question implies that clients will experience emotion during or after the creative process. It encourages elaboration rather than a yes or no answer, which can be given in response to a question such as "Did you feel angry?" or a comment such as "You looked sad." When clients are just beginning to experience their emotions it can be better not to label them with words at all. These labels might have pejorative connotations and shut down communication. Rather, it can further the therapeutic discussion to simply ask clients to describe the sensations, perceptions, and actions involved in creating the image and the resulting feeling state. Other affect-oriented questions and comments include: "How would it feel to be in this picture?" and "Talk about the emotions expressed in this image."

In order to invite information processing with the Affective component of the Expressive Therapies Continuum, it is important to listen carefully to the words clients use to describe their emotional states. Clients unfamiliar with expressing emotions often respond to queries about feelings with statements of their opinions, with criticisms, or with explanations. In attempting to respond to an inquiry about the emotion expressed in an image, a client might respond, "I feel like it expresses my mother's alcoholism." The fact that the statement includes the word *feel* can influence people to believe that it is a statement about feelings. Therapists must listen carefully and help redirect descriptions back to the Affective component by using comments such as "That sounds like what you *think*; please think carefully about what you *feel*. Feelings are angry, afraid, happy, or sad." The tendency to describe thoughts with the statement "I feel like ..." reinforces the necessity of educational information about the purpose and function of emotions.

Emergent Function of the Affective Component

The emergent function of the Affective component of the Expressive Therapies Continuum is the recognition and verbal labeling of feelings and possibly the internalization of affective and symbolic images (Lusebrink, 1990). As was mentioned earlier in this chapter, many clients come to therapy without an awareness of what they are feeling and lacking the ability to discuss their own emotions or other emotional topics. Careful work on the Perceptual/Affective level of the Expressive Therapies Continuum aids in helping clients recognize their emotions, discriminate among them, and express them appropriately. Without an emotional vocabulary or the ability to recognize and verbally label emotions, further discussion of them would be impossible. With a strong emotional vocabulary, clients can gain reflective distance from their emotional experiences, talk about them, and learn from them.

Affective experiences with a significant perceptual element can provide a nonthreatening introduction to the experience of emotions. The focus on form, boundaries, and limits in perceptual experiences can provide a safe container for what otherwise threatens to overwhelm. One experience that can help clients begin to understand and reflect upon their affective experiences is *mood states/mind states* (Lusebrink, 1990). In this art exercise, clients can be asked to draw or paint 8 to 12 small paintings on 6-by-9-inch papers. Therapists can provide a list of basic mood states/mind states, or therapist and client can together generate a list. Some basic emotional states are anxiety, anger, calm, contentment, curiosity, disgust, excitement, fear, happiness, sadness, surprise, and thoughtfulness. Keeping the paintings small is one way to contain the expression of affect. In addition, therapists can chose more resistive drawing materials for containment or more fluid materials for increased expression.

Mood states/mind states paintings are created and labeled on the reverse side so that no verbal label is visible when the image is viewed. Later in the session or in a subsequent session, clients are asked to sort their small mood state/mind state pictures into piles based on the formal elements of visual expression. From the groupings created based on line, shape, and color, clients begin to understand that certain emotions were confused in their families of origin and in their current lives. Many emotions have a similar physiological substrate: heart rate and blood pressure increase, muscles tense, and perspiration begins (Ekman, 2003; Plutchik, 2003). If children were expected not to display anger in their families, as adults they also could confuse and suppress excitement or anxiety due to the underlying physiological similarity of the three emotions. Two paintings from one woman's experience with the mood states/mind states experience are displayed in Figure 6.2. In sorting her pictures, this client realized that anger, pictured at the top, was confused with excitement, shown at the bottom. The mood states/mind states experience was the first step toward untangling emotional confusion and developing an accurate emotional vocabulary.

In a follow-up activity, clients can be asked to focus on *four primary emotions* and the experience of making those emotions as distinct from one another as possible. A 12-by-18-inch paper can be folded twice to produce four 6-by-9-inch compartments. Again, using small, contained expressions, clients can be asked to create images that uniquely describe four primary emotions: anger, fear, happiness, and sadness. An example of the four primary emotions activity is shown in Figure 6.3. In this experience, it is important to emphasize that the pictures should be as different from one another as possible in their use of line, color, and form. Clients can be instructed to remember a time when they were certain each emotion was being experienced, and then to reexperience that feeling and create a distinctive image of it using a variety of artistic elements. This focus on the individual elements of each affective state can help reeducate clients about the various and different affective and cognitive aspects of each of the four primary emotions depicted.

In a different activity, clients can be encouraged to gain reflective distance and think about feelings in a cause-and-effect fashion. This technique, introduced in Chapter 3, can be used with children, adolescents, or adults. Beginning on the perceptual pole of the Perceptual/Affective level, clients are asked to identify faces from magazine images and to create a *collage of various emotional expressions*. Following the creation of this collage, they can be asked to write on the collage what they believe were the antecedents to the expressions, and what they think the consequences will be. This activity reinforces the idea of emotions as signals, as well as the concept of choice in responding to them.

Overcoming Blocks to Affective Information Processing

Inhibited emotional processing is characteristic of certain DSM-IV diagnoses such as posttraumatic stress disorder, obsessive-compulsive disorder, somatoform disorders, and substance abuse disorders, among others. Inhibited emotional processing can manifest itself either in the

Figure 6.2   Mood states/mind states activity demonstrates how emotions with similar physiological substrates are confused with one another. Anger (top) is confused with excitement (bottom).

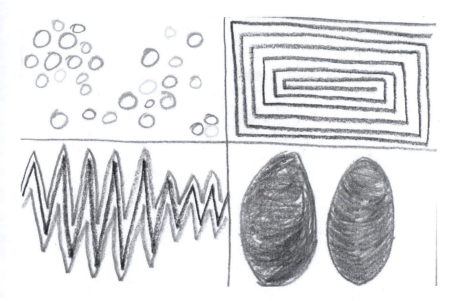

Figure 6.3 Four primary emotions activity helps discriminate emotions. Beginning in the upper left and continuing clockwise, the emotions depicted are: happy, anxious, sad, angry.

expressive style of the individual or in the types of images used. The working through of affective blocking may be one of the therapist's primary tasks in using art in the therapeutic process (Collie, Backos, Malchiodi, & Spiegel, 2006; Hanes, 2007; Kagin & Lusebrink, 1978b; Lubbers, 1991). As was mentioned in Chapter 4, working with the Sensory component of the Expressive Therapies Continuum may evoke information processing with the Affective component. In using sensory-rich media or materials, attention is focused on the affect-producing qualities of the media. Focusing on irritating or disgusting sensations or calm or soothing ones can be an entrée into emotional experience for those to whom emotional responding previously has been elusive.

Difficulties with affect regulation, characterized by inhibited emotional processing, have been associated with the development of somatoform disorders (Taylor et al., 1997; Waller, 2006). Clients with somatic illness may be suffering from overwhelming emotion that finds expression through subjective health complaints. These bodily symptoms may function as both a defense against perceived unmanageable emotions and a means to communicate them (Lacroix, Peterson, & Verrier, 2001). One goal of art therapy with somaticizing clients is to give voice to suppressed affect.

When emotional conflicts can be expressed through created images, clients can experience less pressure to express conflicts through somatic means (Lacroix et al., 2001). Clients suffering from somatic disorders can benefit from the *body map of feelings* exercise in which they associate four basic emotions (anger, fear, happiness, and sadness) with separate colors and then use colored markers to fill in parts of the body where the various feelings are experienced. This exercise can represent the first time that the relationship between emotions and physical symptoms is discovered (Hinz, 2006).

Alexithymia is a condition in which people do not consciously experience emotions, nor do they have words to describe emotions (Meijer-Degen & Lansen, 2006; Taylor et al., 1997). Alexithymia is an extreme condition related to our societal value of rational thought over emotional responding (Greenspan, 2004). In effect, most people in our American culture are socialized to suppress their feelings and present a stoic facade. This stoicism is especially true for men who have been described as suffering from "normative male alexithymia" (Levant, 2003), effectively devoid of knowledge of or language to express their emotions verbally or visually (Trombetta, 2007). Art therapy has been used effectively to help clients suffering from alexithymia recognize and name emotional reactions as well as to regularly express feelings (Hinz, 2006; Meijer-Degen & Lansen, 2006). After learning to identify and name emotions in the types of experiences described above, clients can be taught that art provides safe expression at any time (Hinz, 2006). Clients can use a small notebook and colored markers to express affect that previously would have been concealed. Figure 6.4 is an example of using such a journal. Following successful safe expression in journal form, clients can be encouraged to branch out to larger formats or different forms of affective expression. The ultimate goal of such art therapy experiences is to increase clients' level of emotional intelligence or their ability to understand, express, and regulate their own and other people's feelings, as well as to use emotions as guides for behavior (Ekman, 2003; Taylor et al., 1997).

Balancing Overuse of Affective Functioning

Overuse of affective functioning refers to the extreme reliance on or exclusive use of affective information processing strategies. When the Affective component of the Expressive Therapies Continuum is overused, form is distorted or not involved with images. In addition, affect is perceived as

Figure 6.4   Art expression with the Affective component: Journaling contains emotional expression.

overwhelming or projected onto the environment, and emotions are acted out aggressively or destructively (Cooper & Milton, 2003; Lusebrink, 1990). Overuse of affective processes can be seen in severe mood disorders, anxiety disorders, and borderline personality disorder.

Art is a tool that can be used when emotions are experienced as over-whelming or when they are projected onto the environment in the form of aggressive or destructive acting out. Rather than engaging in self-injurious behavior, clients can be taught to use art as a way of expressing their psychic pain; art affords a concrete alternative to acting out intolerable affect. In addition, by using art to express distressing emotions, acceptance of aggressive feelings can develop over time, also decreasing clients' tendency to be overwhelmed by previously unacceptable affect (Cooper & Milton, 2003). As was stated previously, for clients suffering from bulimia nervosa, feelings that previously would have been purged through self-induced vomiting can be purged on paper (Hinz, 2006; Levens, 1995). Clients can develop a higher level of tolerance for previously overwhelming emotions through the repeated use of art to express troublesome feelings. In addition, it is therapeutically beneficial for acting-out clients to learn to use art as a means to communicate with others, rather than just as a means of pouring out intolerable emotions (Levens, 1995). According to Levens, when art *communicates* emotional experiences rather than simply purging them, the potential for therapeutic growth is greatly enhanced.

Case Example

Introduction

Dan was a 27-year-old, single, Chinese American emergency room nurse at a suburban hospital. Dan heard about art therapy through a stress management program put on at the hospital. He said that he never would have referred himself for art therapy, but his supervisor at work told him that he must "do something" to alleviate the problems that he was having missing work. Dan stated that he missed an average of one shift per week due to headache, backache, and stomach upset. He reported that he often had informally consulted the emergency room physicians about his symptoms, and that he had visited his family physician on several occasions without significant relief from pain. Dan said he had never been formally diagnosed, but he believed that he suffered from irritable bowel syndrome, migraine headaches, possible duodenal ulcer, and chronic lower back pain. He was rarely prescribed medications, but took many over-the-counter remedies for his numerous ailments. Dan claimed that he loved his job because emergency room work involved constant challenge, thinking on one's feet, and adrenaline rushes. He stated that between working 12-hour shifts and illness he did not have time for a social life. Dan saw his parents and sibling (he had one younger sister who was attending graduate school nearby) for weekly Sunday dinners.

Assessment of Functional Level

In the first three art therapy sessions, Dan was presented with a wide assortment of art materials and was encouraged to use whatever media with which he felt comfortable. He reported that he loved cartooning, and in the first three sessions and several others, Dan used paper and a fine-tipped permanent marker to produce cartoons demonstrating concerns from his past and present life. Dan showed himself as a child growing up in an upper-class, half-Chinese community in southern California. Academic excellence, musical performance, and Chinese language and culture were important to his parents, who were recent immigrants from

Taiwan when Dan was born. Dan used these cartoons to show the pressure he felt while growing up to excel scholastically and to make his parents proud by learning and living Chinese cultural traditions. He disclosed through drawing that his parents were deeply disappointed by his decision to become a nurse rather than a doctor. Dan explained that by the time he graduated from high school he was already so burned out from academic pressure that it was all he could do to make it through four years of college. Dan laughingly related that he did not live up to the Chinese student stereotype. When asked how he felt about his parents' disappointment Dan replied, "It's okay, no problem." He used the same response when asked about any potentially emotional subject.

From his use of fine-tipped marker and his comfort with the detailed planning and execution of the fine line drawings required in cartooning, it was apparent that Dan was processing visual/artistic information primarily with the Cognitive component of the Expressive Therapies Continuum. His matter-of-fact telling of poignant stories from his childhood and his insistence that things were "okay, no problem" added to the impression that cognitive information processing strategies were dominant. The art therapist hypothesized that a mixture of cultural, gender, and personality factors combined to suppress Dan's emotional responses. Additionally, it was hypothesized that suppressed emotion was at least partially responsible for some of the unresolved physical symptoms that plagued him. Gentle guidance toward the Affective component of the ETC was the determined course of therapeutic movement.

Beginning at the Cognitive Level

As has been mentioned, affective responding can be stimulated by the use of brightly colored media and fluid materials. However, with all of these materials available and not chosen by Dan, it was hypothesized that a jump to brightly colored or fluid media would be too great a shift at first. Instead, color was introduced in the form of collage images. Collage provided a controlled, cognitive experience; however, the topic addressed through collage was the identification of moods and emotions. Dan had a difficult time at first finding a variety of images. The first collage created contained all smiling faces. When asked to discuss his collage, Dan insisted that advertisers only used photographs of happy people because other emotions would not sell products. Although Dan was not asked why he only included pictures of happy faces, his response indicated he

Figure 6.5 Collage of various emotions.

understood that he had only used happy faces and hinted that he knew he had avoided other emotions.

Figure 6.5 shows Dan's second collage of faces with a variety of emotions included. He engaged in a discussion of the collage that included naming the emotions he believed to be present in the picture, and imagining what he thought led up to each emotion depicted and what would result from it. Dan was encouraged to use a journal to practice making various emotional expressions in cartoon form to emphasize the learning taking place in therapy, and he did this with pleasure. He made and discussed two similar collages in subsequent sessions.

Affective Responding

After success with the collage, the therapist asked Dan to experiment with chalk pastels. It was conjectured that the movement to this more fluid and brightly colored medium would stimulate functioning with the Affective component of the Expressive Therapies Continuum. Dan was hesitant with the pastels at first, attempting to use them to produce the same type of accurate line drawings featured in his cartoons. The art therapist

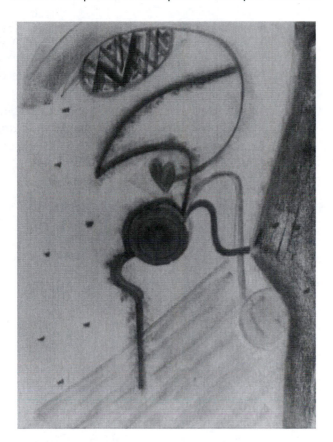

Figure 6.6   Art expression with the Affective component: free art expression leading to realization of relationship between stress and physical symptoms.

demonstrated different ways of using the pastels and encouraged Dan to experiment with them. When he was more comfortable using the pastels, Dan was encouraged to make a free drawing with the new medium. He took the rest of the session to produce the drawing displayed in Figure 6.6. The therapist kept the drawing in the office, but Dan was encouraged to think about it and talk about it at the next meeting. Dan reported that he could hardly think of anything else over the course of the week between sessions. He said that the drawing was an "epiphany" for him, revealing how he took in toxic stimuli and stress from his work environment and, because he did not express those feelings, they went into his body and caused physical symptoms such as headaches and stomach aches. He said that he knew that the stress of holding in his feelings about the pressures at work was making him sick.

During the next few sessions, Dan worked with pastels to create images providing different outlets for environmental stressors. He developed drawings showing many different routes and outlets that provided him with great feelings of satisfaction. Dan mentioned that since beginning art therapy sessions he had experienced fewer aches and pains, and that his symptoms had not been so bad that he missed work due to illness. He felt that art therapy could be a continued emotional outlet to improve the quality of his life. Future sessions focused on cultural and gender influences on the expression of emotion, and supported further emotional expression in art and in life.

Summary

The Affective component of the Expressive Therapies Continuum is concerned with the emotions evoked through participation with art media and the formation of images. Affective information processing can be blocked and unavailable for use, as in the case of alexithymia, somatoform disorder, and other psychiatric disorders. In these cases, affective information is not available for labeling, processing, or reacting to life situations. On the other hand, affect can be experienced as overwhelming, and affective responding overused, as in the case of mood disorders and aggressive or destructive acting out. The healing function of the Affective component of the Expressive Therapies Continuum is the increased awareness of appropriate affect and support for the constructive expression of affective impulses. Clients can be taught that art provides a method of communicating feelings without experiencing the threat of emotional devastation or self-destruction. Art therapy can be used to teach an emotional language. Art experiences can teach clients to name their emotions, discriminate among them, and express them safely.

The emergent function of the Affective component of the Expressive Therapies Continuum is the ability to gain enough reflective distance from an emotional experience to label it, think about it, and learn from it. The internalization of emotional and personal symbols may also result. Affective responding often elicits functioning on the Cognitive/Symbolic level of the ETC. Affective functioning is encouraged by brightly colored materials and fluid media. The affective activities and art experiences discussed in this chapter are displayed in Table 6.1 along with materials and instructions used. Also included in Table 6.1 are the healing and emergent functions expected as a result of participation in each of the affective experiences.

TABLE 6.1   Examples of Affective Experiences and Associated Healing and Emergent Functions

Affective Activity	Materials and Procedure	Healing Function	Emergent Function
Painting to music	Various types of music on CD; drawing materials	Capture a feeling or mood evoked by music in visual form	Ability to identify and label emotions
Mood states/ mind states	Drawing or painting materials; see detailed instructions in chapter	Safe expression of affect through schematic representation of emotion	Ability to label future emotions; development of verbal vocabulary for feeling states
Four primary emotions	Drawing or painting media, one 12-by-18-inch paper folded twice to make four 6-by-9-inch squares; emotions depicted: angry, fearful, happy, sad	Safe affective expression through schematic representation of emotion	Ability to distinguish among emotions; further development of emotional vocabulary
Collage of faces	Magazines, paper, glue; identify various emotional expressions; add cause-and-effect labeling	Identification of emotions	Reinforces emotions as signals and choice in responding to emotions
Abstract emotion	Drawing or painting materials; client uses line, color, form to depict a feeling state	Nonthreatening emotional expression	Emotion can be expressed in a safe manner; reflective distance can allow discussion
Body map of feelings	Outline of body, markers; clients color body where they feel four basic emotions: anger, sadness, fear, happiness	Awareness that affective states can be related to somatic symptoms	Development of affective expression to reduce physical symptoms

7

Cognitive Component of the Expressive Therapies Continuum

Introduction to the Cognitive Component

Complex thought processes are functions taking place via the Cognitive component of the Expressive Therapies Continuum. These processes include abstract concept formation, analytical and logical thought processes, reality-directed information processing, cognitive maps, and the use of verbal self-instructions in the performance of complex tasks (Kagin & Lusebrink, 1978b; Lusebrink, 1990, 1991b). Problem solving using art media is an important part of the Cognitive dimension and one way in which this component is used therapeutically. Other important activities representing functioning with the Cognitive component include the ability to classify media along various physical properties, recognition of interrelated objects, and the ability to sequence events in time (Kagin & Lusebrink, 1978b).

Many art experiences require a minimal amount of cognitive input. It has been proposed that young children's cognitive abilities and problem-solving skills can be improved by engaging in drawing because drawing incorporates large amounts of planning and decision making. For example, a child must decide where to begin, which direction to take the drawing, and how big to make it in relation to the space available. In addition, the child must consider what shapes to draw first and how to relate them to one another. Finally, the addition of details to the drawing must be planned (Thomas & Silk, 1990). However, this type of associated thought is not the totality of cognitive activity intended with a focus on the Cognitive component of the Expressive Therapies Continuum. The Cognitive component includes thought processes that are intentional and deliberate, requiring a conscious effort at planning, decision making, sequencing, and problem solving (Lusebrink, 1991b).

Exploration of media properties and their internalization contribute to understanding the actions necessary to manipulate art materials successfully (Lusebrink, 1990). Information about media properties is internalized in the form of mental images that can be manipulated to allow thinking through possible results before trying them. Thus, the Cognitive component of the Expressive Therapies Continuum is qualitatively different from the previously discussed components and levels of the ETC because it involves the use of mental images of past experiences and future actions (Lusebrink, 1990).

Developmental Hierarchy

In early childhood, between the ages of 4 and 6 years, children realize that other people can have different ideas and beliefs from their own. Later in development, adolescent thinking broadens to include the ability to evaluate events from another point of view (Singer, 2006). "Executive functioning," defined as the ability to plan a course of action and regulate behavior, continues to develop during the adolescent years (Cozolino, 2002; Donders, 2002). The Cognitive component of the Expressive Therapies Continuum is markedly different from the previously discussed components because it depends upon a capacity for abstract thinking and often requires the use of language in order to express complex thoughts, ideas, and values (Kagin & Lusebrink, 1978b). In a similar manner, adolescent cognition requires more abstraction and is freed from the concrete experiences and schemas characterizing earlier developmental stages. Prior to adolescence, children's cognition is based on concrete experiences, with the child unable to comprehend similarities among seemingly different objects or events.

During adolescence several factors converge to make abstract thought possible. Attention span lengthens, autonomy (including autonomous thinking) increases, the adolescent's knowledge base is enlarged through formal schooling and greater life experience, problem-solving strategies become more effective, and young people are capable of metacognition, or thinking about their own cognitive processes (Arnett, 2006). Adolescents gain the ability to think about concepts without the necessity of actually seeing a physical representation of the fact, event, or thing they are addressing; abstract thought becomes a reality in what has been called the formal operational stage of cognitive development (Piaget, 1969).

A minority of adolescents can think about the past as well as plan for the future; they can profit from their experiences to moderate their behavior, including artistic processes. Only one-third of high school graduates in developed nations demonstrate the ability to use formal operational thought, and many never obtain the ability even in adulthood (Arnett, 2006). Research has demonstrated, however, that formal operational thought processes can be taught with some success (Vandendorpe, 1990). Art therapy activities using the Cognitive dimension of the Expressive Therapies Continuum also can be used to promote formal operational thought in adolescents.

Cognitive functioning, including memory and executive functioning, decreases with increasing age in healthy elderly people across cultures (Kramer et al., 2007; Lin, Chan, Zheng, Yang, & Wang, 2007). Cognitive processes that develop throughout childhood and adolescence tend to devolve parallel with the decreasing brain mass and reduced cerebral vascularization accompanying old age (Kramer et al., 2007). Accelerated cognitive deficits are characteristic of disorders common in elderly populations, such as Alzheimer's disease and delirium (Silveri, Reali, Jenner, & Puopolo, 2007; Stewart, 2006; Wald, 1984, 2003). Art therapy with the Cognitive component often is considered in the treatment of the elderly in order to heighten mental functioning (Wald, 1984, 2003). Cognitively oriented activities can provide a visual focus for reality orientation and build compensatory skills to counteract naturally occurring cognitive deficits such as short-term memory loss, word retrieval difficulties, and decreased processing speed (Landgarten, 1981; Wald, 2003).

Healing Function of the Cognitive Component

The healing dimension of the Cognitive Component of the Expressive Therapies Continuum is the ability to generalize from one concrete experience to other situations. Cognitive problem-solving skills also begin to emerge and are emphasized on this level (Lusebrink, 1990). As was shown in Chapter 3, clients who are overly kinesthetically involved, such as those with attention-deficit/hyperactivity disorder (AD/HD), can benefit greatly from increasing cognitive control over behavior. Teaching and reinforcing cognitive skills such as cause-and-effect thinking, planning a course of action, and reflecting on behavior can help clients who are overly affectively involved and who experience their emotions as potentially overwhelming. Silverman (1991), in explaining her work with borderline personality disorder clients, wrote: "Because they have difficulty in both thinking and talking, they become overstimulated and overwhelmed and are not able to encode and order their thoughts effectively. The concrete, graphic representation of images and emotions makes it easier to label internal states, rather than drifting in a world of sensation-dominated impulses" (p. 107).

Self-care is a multifaceted cognitive function involving reality testing, judgment, control, and synthesis. It is one of the cognitive operations previously referred to as executive functioning (Taylor, Bagby, & Parker, 1997). Many clients enter therapy with extreme self-care deficits. They do not have knowledge about self-care, including not knowing what their needs are or how to distinguish between a need and a desire. They lack the ability to organize their thoughts and feelings about self-care, or they lack the judgment necessary to prioritize their needs. Some clients do not feel that they have the ability to delay gratification of needs in order to apply healthy coping skills. These deficits can be approached therapeutically with art therapy on the Cognitive dimension.

The healing function of any ETC component represents optimal intrapersonal functioning, and with the Cognitive dimension, the healing quality involved helps individuals apply knowledge gained from one concrete experience to other areas of their lives without necessarily having other real-life occurrences. Clients learn to relate lessons learned from one experience to other areas of their lives. A two-year-old child may learn from the harsh experience of touching a lit burner that the stove will burn. However, he or she will not be able to apply this knowledge to other hot things, such as lightbulbs, without additional direct experiences. Adolescents, on the other hand, have the ability to understand that hot items can burn and do not need to touch other hot surfaces to find out if each one actually does so.

Art therapy with the Cognitive component can be one way in which clients learn to generalize beyond concrete experiences. An image can form the basis of an abstract principle to which other ideas are related. In addition, art therapy can aid in reframing problematic abstract thoughts such as the core beliefs related to psychological problems (Singer, 2006; Steele, 2003). For example, a young man who had been sexually abused as a child developed the core belief "I am helpless." Consequently, he acted helpless and his life spun out of control in a sequence of abusive sexual encounters fueled by substance use. Working on the Cognitive dimension of the Expressive Therapies Continuum, this young man began creating images depicting the emerging belief "I am powerful." Discussions reinforced

Figure 7.1   "I am Powerful": cognitive art experience demonstrating assertiveness.

appropriate powerful behaviors such as assertiveness skills, as shown in the image displayed in Figure 7.1.

Examples of Cognitive Experiences

A warm-up activity on the Cognitive level may improve visual-spatial understanding in learning disabled and mentally retarded individuals. This activity would focus on observing, depicting, and naming relationships among objects such as left/right, above/below, and front/back. Another activity that can be used to increase cognitive functioning for mentally retarded, learning disabled, or autistic youth involves sorting, matching, and gluing precut shapes to papers containing corresponding predrawn outlines. The complexity of the task can be manipulated to match the individual client's developmental and functional levels so that increasingly complex concepts of space, order, and group are presented and mastered (Gabriels, 2003; Silver, 1987).

Listening to and following directions about using art media is a cognitive task that emphasizes social and communication skills. The visual character of art media and art tasks can augment the social and communicative learning aspects of art therapy for children who have autistic spectrum disorders, including Asperger's disorder (Gabriels, 2003). Interestingly, the presence of a tangible product can enhance understanding of abstract concepts that previously may not have been well understood. Roth (1987) provided the example of a delinquent adolescent boy who, after participating in art therapy in which he constructed two- and three-dimensional houses, was better able to appreciate the physical and emotional devastation caused by his previous fire-setting behavior.

Cognitive activities also include *predictive drawing, drawing from observation, and drawing from imagination using stimulus drawings* (Silver, 2002). According to Silver, presenting individuals with predetermined stimuli for use in drawings liberates them from the sometimes crippling effects of too much choice. In the *stimulus drawing technique*, clients choose 2 or 3 of 50 small stimulus drawings and combine them in an image that depicts something happening between the objects in the drawing. This task requires the cognitive skills of selecting, combining, projecting, representing, and describing (Silver, 2002).

Creating a *topic-directed collage* and identifying the images with words or elaborating on the images with verbal messages also requires clients to select, combine, represent, and describe (Landgarten, 1981). These higher-order cognitive processes can be capitalized upon in order to help clients think through life choices and core beliefs. Collage images that require comparisons, such as *pro and con collages* (Horay, 2006; Linesch, 1988), also are cognitive activities requiring complex thought and action, and have been used to increase predictive capabilities.

According to Lusebrink (1990), highly structured art therapy tasks are hallmarks of the Cognitive dimension. As was explained in Chapter 2, highly structured experiences involve a number of different steps for successful completion. This high level of structure requires thought, memory, and planning for effective execution and leads to increased cognitive functioning. One example of a highly structured task is *drawing a floor plan* of a childhood home. This activity can be used with incest survivors as one way to contain the affect associated with the highly emotional aspects of beginning therapy. The complex cognitive processes involved in remembering, visualizing, planning, and executing the floor plan drawing help ensure that emotional energy is safely contained.

A *lifeline* is another cognitively oriented activity that can help clients structure past experiences, begin to relate past experiences to present behavior, and plan for the future. In the lifeline activity, clients use a large piece of paper and drawing materials to construct a line that represents their life from birth to the present moment (Martin, 2003). Life events determine the direction, quality, and course of the line, such that the ups and downs, and twists and turns of the line are correlated with developmental milestones and other life experiences. In order to complete this activity, clients must think through and evaluate the events of their lives, represent their lives in an abstract manner, and describe their complex thought processes.

Cognitive maps are mental representations of the relative positions and other features of places or objects in daily life that can be used to augment navigational skills and reinforce visual–spatial relationships (Redish, 1999). Cognitive maps can portray relationships between self and the world, self and the community, and the interior landscape of the person (Harmon, 2004). Clients who present with self-care deficits can use cognitive maps to organize and prioritize feelings and needs. Maps have been used to explore the world of dreams as schemas for understanding internal relationships between self and body as well as external relationships between self and world (Signell, 1990).

Janie Rhyne (1973) created the *problem-solving collage*, in which clients are asked to define a problem as specifically as possible. Various aspects of the problem are assigned colors or simple shapes. Without further reference to these building blocks, an image is created that forms or contains the solution to the problem. Often the image solution that arises from this experience is not a new concept, but rather one that has been in mind but not acknowledged as a viable option. Hinz (2006) gave the example of a female attorney who was struggling with the issue of returning to work following the birth of her first child. The image that arose from the problem-solving collage was that of a sunrise or sunset. The image reinforced for the young woman that she did not want her baby to be in child care from sun up to sun down, and that she would work part-time in order to accomplish the goal of having her baby in day care for a limited period. Working part-time was not a new idea, but rather one that was strengthened and validated through the problem-solving exercise.

Media Experiences to Enhance Cognitive Functioning

As was mentioned in Chapter 2, resistive media, because of their inherent structure, are likely to bring about cognitive experiences. Resistive media, like any media, can be used in all manner of application. However, because of their higher structure and greater complexity (more steps and tools required for their successful implementation), they are more likely to evoke cognition than affect. Examples of highly structured media are wood and stone sculpture, mosaic tile work, clay work (either throwing onto a wheel or building by hand), and collage.

Collage, as was stated earlier, is considered a cognitive activity because it requires clients to select, categorize, combine, and explain concepts through visual means. Because collage uses images created by others, it can be less intimidating than drawing or painting for clients who are unused to artistic tasks (Landgarten, 1993). By using ready-made images, clients are one step removed from the experience when choosing and combining images, not actively creating them. Collage work often involves words and verbal explanations, which also increases cognitive involvement in the task.

As was mentioned above, increasing the number of steps a person must work through to achieve a completed product greatly enhances cognitive functioning. A multistep task requires that many operations are kept in mind and followed in a specific order. Activating working memory and sequencing skills as well as the operations necessary for successful completion ensures that a task utilizes the Cognitive component, and at the same time increases the reflective distance involved.

Reflective Distance With the Cognitive Component

To reiterate, reflective distance refers to the time span between an impulse or stimulus and the individual's reaction to it (Lusebrink, 1991b). Because clients are using internal representations of operations and task instructions, the reflective distance using the Cognitive component is significantly increased over previous components of the Expressive Therapies Continuum

Figure 7.2   Abstract images can create increased reflective distance and lessen affective involvement in the artistic experience.

(Kagin & Lusebrink, 1978b). Clients can use internal representations of activities and tasks to significantly delay responses and plan coordinated action. At times, increased reflective distance is desired and even necessary in art therapy. Increased reflective distance can give clients the opportunity to consider various explanations for situations that previously caused immediate feelings and problematic reactions. It can help clients contemplate various meanings in the process of changing problematic beliefs. Increased reflective distance can provide clients with the opportunity to reinterpret childhood events. Clients can learn that although they cannot change their personal histories, they can change their interpretations of them. They can be encouraged to reflect on childhood events and the objective evidence about them, rather than on the emotions accompanying the memories.

Abstract representations also are likely to increase reflective distance and lessen affective involvement in the artistic experience (Kagin & Lusebrink, 1978b). Ideas and emotions expressed nonfiguratively require veiling in abstract terms, and therefore are more cognitively involved and can be somewhat less emotionally charged. For example, an abstract family collage, such as the one displayed in Figure 7.2, in which family members are portrayed via color and form using construction paper, can be less emotionally evocative than a family drawing in which family members are portrayed representationally (Kagin & Lusebrink, 1978b). By using color, form, size, and spatial relations, similarities and differences among family members can be examined beyond their physical characteristics. In this way, abstraction can increase clients' understanding of complex family dynamics based upon personality traits, values, and interests, and can be used in future family interactions.

Questions and Discussion That Promote Cognitive Information Processing

Any discussion that requires clients to think through a problem and its solution can increase cognitive functioning. Therapists can simply ask clients to talk about the necessary steps required to create the current artwork (Lusebrink, 1990). In this way, thoughts are structured in a logical sequence from start to finish. Cognitive processing of the experience can be developed by having clients elaborate on how they imagine modifying the steps that they went through would influence the finished product. This type of thinking and explaining requires abstraction beyond the concrete process and product.

Interaction on the Cognitive dimension of the Expressive Therapies Continuum frequently requires verbalization to convey the complexities of abstract thought. Intense discussions can result from cognitive experiences involving problem-solving skills and decision-making abilities. Therapists should avoid asking clients *why* they did a particular thing or portrayed something in a certain way; this type of question often leads to rationalization (Lusebrink, 1990). The *why* question invokes the need to explain oneself and engages individuals in defending their choices and behaviors, rather than deepening their understanding of them. Instead of asking *why*, art therapists can engage clients in discussions of their artwork by asking them to develop an idea, or to "say more about that" in reference to either a part of an image or its entirety.

The discussion of color can take on a cognitive direction when therapists ask clients if a particular color reminds them of anything, or under what circumstances they have seen a color like that before. Engaging memory and analytical functions helps move clients to the Cognitive component.

Emphasizing the relationships among component parts of an overall image evokes cognitive processes. Clients can be asked to talk about how the different parts of an image are connected to one another (Levens, 1990). Clients can discuss the concrete relationships pictured or think through relationships that are more abstract. For instance, noticing a comparatively isolated portion of an image, the therapist can ask: "How is this part of the image related to the whole?" or "How does this part fit into the whole picture?" Talking about the relationships strengthens abstract thinking abilities, and relating parts to the whole can give a more global and abstract view of a situation.

Finally, asking clients to create titles for their images increases cognitive functioning. The title of an image can distill the essence of a problematic situation in a way never before realized by the artist. A 28-year-old Caucasian woman joined a community college extension class on using art for self-expression. Among the first images that she created in class was a painting representing an aerial view of a hurricane. When asked to make a title for her image, she wrote, "I of the storm." When one of the class members asked why she used "I" instead of "Eye," the young woman immediately explained that the "I" was a mistake, and she should have written "Eye." However, upon further consideration, the young woman revealed that "I of the Storm" truly was a more accurate title, because it portrayed her as in the center of her angry alcoholic mother's rages—feeling forlorn and responsible. Thus, naming the image helped provide another layer to the complex expressive experience.

In summary, experiences that activate cognitive information processing are those that call for or emphasize planning, thinking through a complex process or sequence, problem solving, spatial relationships, and abstract thought. The types of media that complement and enhance cognitive functioning are those that have a high degree of inherent structure, such as mosaic tile, construction paper, and collage. Complex activities involving multiple steps to completion are those that require processing with the Cognitive component. The many steps require internal representation of materials and methods, which also increases the reflective distance of work with the Cognitive component. Questions and discussion that emphasize abstract concepts, steps in a process, or that require other types of higher-level thinking can increase cognitive information processing. Creating a title is a simple way to refine thinking and expand the cognitive features of an experience.

Emergent Function of the Cognitive Component

The emergent function of the Cognitive component of the Expressive Therapies Continuum is creative problem solving using verbal and imaginal interaction, including symbolic representation at the opposite end of the Cognitive/Symbolic level (Lusebrink, 1990). As patients think through the various aspects of a situation and construct images to represent their thoughts and feelings about it, new possibilities often become apparent. A structured example of this process is provided by the *problem-solving collage* created by Rhyne (1973), mentioned above. Rhyne used stickers of various shapes and colors to represent aspects of a problem situation. Tissue paper or craft paper also can be used to represent components of a dilemma. The paper can be torn to signify destruction of old ways of thinking in order to make way for the construction of new modes of thought.

Dorothy was a 64-year-old Caucasian woman who entered art therapy in distress over her future. She was attempting to plan for her approaching retirement and was struggling with the problem of how to care for her 85-year-old mother. The mother was becoming increasing frail but did not have any major health concerns; she lived in a different city from her daughter and would not consider moving from her home to an assisted living facility. Dorothy spent several sessions talking, discussing, and arguing about her rationale for wanting to move her mother into an assisted living facility. She talked so persistently that even when an art task was introduced, it was not completed. In the fourth session, Dorothy used a paper and pencil to create a written list of pros and cons of leaving her mother where she was and moving her to an assisted living facility.

Dorothy created the image shown in Figure 7.3 in the fifth session in response to the problem-solving collage instructions. She chose one color to represent each of five identified aspects of the problem situation and then, putting away the list of colors, cut corresponding colored tissue paper and used the pieces to make an image. After the collage was completed, Dorothy was asked to talk about how the image provided the solution to her dilemma. After extended contemplation, Dorothy said that she realized that she was "making a mountain out of a molehill" and creating stress for herself where none needed to exist.

Dorothy stated she realized that she thought her mother should move to an assisted living facility at the age of 85 years because her husband's mother had done so. She added that her mother-in-law was in poor health with complications from obesity, hypertension, and diabetes. By comparison, her mother was in good health and did not need the level of care that Dorothy was offering. She resolved that she would respect her mother's decision to stay in her own home, visit as often as she reasonably could, and not cause herself further worry.

Figure 7.3   "Mountain out of a Molehill": example of problem-solving collage.

Dorothy showed many qualities of obsessive-compulsive personality disorder. She preferred talking, rationalizing, and intellectualizing; she said the same things many times. She had greater access to her thoughts than to her feelings. In her usual mode of operation, Dorothy could only see the situation from her point of view. She mounted vigorous arguments, and intellectualized a great deal with no change in circumstances. Art therapy allowed Dorothy to evaluate the situation differently. It seemed that the addition of the visual input allowed her to reshuffle the same facts, but come to a different and peaceful resolution.

Another example of working with the Cognitive dimension that can bring about creative problem solving is an art therapy exercise where individuals or groups imagine *survival on an island*. Instructions for the project ask that clients imagine that they are on a ship that sinks and that they can only take three things with them in order to survive on an island. In a group, the task can be extended such that participants find themselves together on the island and must negotiate a common survival experience. Negotiation skills are an important element of cognitive functioning that many eating disordered and substance using clients are lacking (Taylor et al., 1997). The portion of the experience requiring negotiation can be conducted in various ways to highlight the roles of cooperation and individuation.

Performed individually, the survival experience can help clients identify positive personality traits and coping skills. What can emerge because of this endeavor is a new appreciation of inner resourcefulness. When used with eating disordered or substance abusing clients, this art experience can stress the differences between surviving and thriving. Substance use of any kind leads only to survival, whereas creative activity fuels the ability to grow and thrive. Clients will find not only an increased awareness of problem-solving skills emerging from this cognitive experience, but will come away with an appreciation of their own inner wisdom (Hinz, 2006).

Overcoming Blocks to Cognitive Functioning

Optimal functioning of each individual requires access to information processing at all levels and with all components of the Expressive Therapies Continuum. However, biological or environmental forces sometimes influence individuals such that functioning with one component is more difficult than with others. Neuropsychological research in trauma and trauma recovery has found that unresolved trauma leads to dysregulation of the emotional centers of the (right) brain, making them less amenable to regulation by the cognitive, rational centers of the (left) brain (Schore, 2002; Taylor et al., 1997). Posttraumatic stress disorder (PTSD) is a common diagnosis following child abuse or neglect and adult trauma. The effects of PTSD can have opposite manifestations: Sometimes clients are caught up in emotions, and other times they are avoidant of affect (Keane, Weathers, & Foa, 2000). Schore (2002) explains that

> PTSD patients, especially when stressed, show severe deficits in the preattentive reception and expression of facially expressed emotion, the processing of somatic information, the communication of emotional states, the maintaining of interactions with the social environment, the use of higher level more efficient defences, the capacity to access an empathic stance and a reflective function, and the psychobiological ability to regulate, either by autoregulation or interactive regulation, and thereby recover from stressful affective states. (p. 23)

From this description, it is obvious that all levels of the Expressive Therapies Continuum are impacted in the case of severe PTSD. Successful trauma recovery involves synthesizing experiences from the two hemispheres of the brain, so that they can work together effectively (Cozolino, 2002; Johnson, 2000; Riley, 2004).

Individuals who are not able to fully access their thinking brain and executive functioning become overly emotionally involved. Difficulties with affect regulation can lead to self-medication with substances (alcohol, drugs, and food) or behaviors (gambling, acting out, or sexual activity) to attain a desired outcome. Overly emotional clients who find it difficult to tolerate anger or anxiety may take heroin or opiates to achieve inner calm (Taylor et al., 1997). In treatment, they can experience art as a positive approach to soothing emotions, as discussed in Chapter 6. For example, coloring mandalas has been shown to significantly reduce anxiety (Curry & Kasser, 2005). It is hypothesized that the focus on the perceptual aspects of the activity contains affect and allows cognitive skills to emerge from the experience. In addition, anger can be released through clay work (Sholt & Gavron, 2006). The kinesthetic properties of the experience can be guided to allow the expression of pent-up anger to emerge. In this way, art becomes an appropriate affective outlet.

As was discussed in Chapter 6, it is desirable to guide overly emotional clients to increased cognitive control over their emotions and behaviors. Working toward optimal functioning on the Cognitive level enhances self-care, problem-solving, and decision-making skills, increasing clients' behavioral repertoire and providing freedom of choice in responding to stressful situations.

Balancing Overuse of Cognitive Functioning

Clients who are overly reliant on cognitive functioning use rational thought to the exclusion of other modes of information processing. These clients have been termed alexithymic due to their lack of ability to identify and express emotions. Excessive use of the Cognitive component can be indicated in art therapy by insistence on rigid structure and concrete images, inability to generalize, progressive analysis of details, loss of personal meaning, and abstraction as a means of emotional distancing (Lusebrink, 1990). Persons who abuse substances often use complex intellectualization, accompanied by abstract rationalization, as a defense against realizing the long-term price paid for intoxication. Alexithymic clients at times use stimulants such as cocaine and amphetamines or eat large amounts of food to relieve feelings of boredom and emptiness (Taylor et al., 1997). Art therapy is a way to help these clients develop an emotional language to identify, express, and soothe emotions. Art can help clients struggling with feelings of emptiness and boredom fill themselves with meaning rather than substances.

Aside from substance abuse disorder or eating disorders, persons who are overly dependent on cognitive information processing are likely to be diagnosed with posttraumatic stress disorder. Treatment guidelines from the International Society for Traumatic Stress Studies indicate that creative therapies, including art therapy, will be especially helpful for clients who have difficulty finding words to express their emotions, and those who are highly intellectual and whose use of words obstructs access to their emotions (Johnson, 2000). Both descriptions point toward overuse of the Cognitive component. Cognitively oriented art therapy activities can provide a framework to approach traumatic memories without overwhelming emotion (Hinz & Ragsdell, 1991).

Patients with subjective health complaints are those who repeatedly seek medical treatment for physical symptoms but demonstrate little or no medical cause (Verkuil, Brosschot, & Thayer, 2007). These individuals frequently suffer from an inability to identify, discriminate, express, and soothe emotions. They have learned through early experiences to express emotions as physical symptoms (Taylor et al., 1997). Again, they have severely limited emotional vocabularies. Additionally, unresolved stress or lack of positive coping skills to deal with stress are related to many chronic health problems and delay recovery from illness (Ray, 2004). Art therapy utilizing cognitive strategies can be used with somaticizing clients, chronically ill clients, and for clients in need of increasing stress management skills. Therapeutic goals can include better matching of coping skills with environmental demands, educating clients about emotions, and providing outlets for unresolved stress or affect, as discussed in Chapter 6.

Persons who overuse the cognitive function may be diagnosed as obsessive-compulsive personality disorder or obsessive-compulsive disorder (OCD). Although OCD is an anxiety disorder, the anxiety often is not apparent. What is apparent are the repetitive, compulsive attempts to keep unwanted and intrusive anxiety-provoking thoughts at bay. Such behaviors include washing, checking, and hoarding. Persons with OCD and obsessive-compulsive personality disorder have been described as better able to access thoughts than emotions. They are often perceived as detail oriented, difficult to get along with, and rigid (American Psychological Association [APA], 2000). Art materials can be used in a rigid and repetitive manner without generalizing beyond the concrete task at hand. Art therapy can begin with work on the

Cognitive component, with the goal of moving to the Affective component in order to increase access to emotional information.

Case Example

Introduction

Brianna was a 10-year-old Caucasian girl diagnosed with obsessive-compulsive disorder who was fearful of dirt and germs, and engaged in repetitive hand-washing rituals. Her parents, who brought her to art therapy, wanted Brianna to express her thoughts and feelings about the disorder for which she was being newly medicated. Brianna responded to a request for a free drawing in the first art therapy session by stating that she did not know what media to use or what to draw. She did not react to gentle suggestions to draw whatever she liked or whatever came to mind. The art therapist decided to administer the Kinetic Family Drawing (KFD) assessment (Burns & Kaufman, 1972) and provided Brianna with an 8½-by-11-inch piece of paper and pencil. The KFD was chosen because the familiar subject matter and the controllable materials (pencil and small paper) would likely keep the experience on the familiar Cognitive level. However, making this drawing took an extremely long time, as Brianna agonized over how to position the figures and what activities to include. In hindsight, the Stimulus Drawing Test (Silver, 2002) might have been a better way to reduce the anxiety of a free art task because it provides stimulus pictures to choose from in making an image.

Assessment of Functional Level

Brianna demonstrated many qualities that identified her as functioning with the Cognitive component of the Expressive Therapies Continuum. After the initial session, she continued to choose the resistive medium and small paper likely to evoke cognitive functioning. Brianna repeated the same drawing, perseveratively following the example of the first session, for three subsequent sessions. She talked concretely about the clothing and activities of family members, and did not generalize to talking about their personality characteristics or other traits not evident from the drawings. Brianna was comfortable with the Cognitive component of the ETC, and on this level she could gain an understanding of her disorder. However, in order to express her feelings about the OCD, it would be necessary, over the course of therapy, to increase her comfort working with the Affective component.

Beginning With the Cognitive Component

As was stated above, following the completion of the first Kinetic Family Drawing, Brianna only wanted to make pictures of her family with pencil on 8½-by-11-inch paper, and continued to do so for three sessions. She twice stated it was the same picture she had drawn in the previous session. The experience of repeating the Kinetic Family Drawing was interpreted and discussed to help Brianna understand how the sameness of things helped her feel less anxious and conversely how change increased her level of anxiety. She admitted that she was anxious about coming to art therapy and seemed to understand how drawing the same image helped make her feel better.

Introduction to the Affective Component

In order to begin movement to the Affective component, colored media were gradually introduced. As was mentioned in Chapter 6, the addition of color can aid in accessing emotions. Colored but resistive media such as colored pencils were introduced first so that movement to the Affective component was gradual. When change in media or style is rushed or abrupt, clients can feel out of control and resist the experience through regression or refusal (Simon, 1992).

Brianna agreed to use colored pencils and later thin markers, crayons, and oil and chalk pastels to draw pictures of her family, and was helped to appreciate this progress. She was encouraged to expand the subject matter of her images in order to expand the content of her thoughts and connections between them. However, although she was given the option to draw whatever she liked, Brianna continued to depict only her family for many sessions.

Further Movement to the Affective Component

The addition of color was a small and manageable step toward the Affective component of the Expressive Therapies Continuum. Adding color was hypothesized to open Brianna up to the experience of emotion. However,

Brianna chose to stay with safe subject matter as she experimented with color and progressively more fluid media. With each small change in medium, Brianna was asked to rate her level of anxiety on a scale of 0 (no anxiety) to 10 (the most anxiety ever experienced). These numbers were used to help Brianna understand how the first experience with a new situation often was highly rated, and that continued exposure helped anxiety abate. Brianna noticed how the messy media, such as oil and chalk pastels, were associated with more anxiety than the nonmessy ones, and that they required more exposure to achieve calm use. She learned to be patient with herself and not as dependent on ritual (hand washing) to reduce anxiety.

Functioning With the Affective Component

One of the final steps in therapy was to use paint to make a picture of her family on a 12-by-18-inch piece of paper. Larger paper was chosen because, as was mentioned in Chapter 5, larger paper encourages greater expression. Paint was actually a less anxiety-provoking media than were others, because Brianna was able to use a brush and not dirty her hands. Brianna painted a picture of her family and was able to talk about everyone's favorite colors and what they signify. She was able to talk about herself as both similar to and different from her family members, and she was not overly judgmental about the OCD qualities that made her different.

Brianna indicated in the next session that she would like to paint a rainbow, and it is obvious from her picture in Figure 7.4 that this departure from the familiar subject matter caused a regression to compulsive behavior. She used a stiff brush to daub the paint into a rainbow shape rather than allowing the paint to flow freely. In the following sessions she was able to use the paint more freely and paint various subjects. The free use of paint seemed to allow new freedom of verbal expression as well. Brianna was more talkative about and accepting of the OCD. Overall, working on the Cognitive dimension helped Brianna understand her disorder, and movement to the Affective component helped her express her feelings about it.

Summary

The Cognitive component of the Expressive Therapies Continuum requires abstract thought, planning and sequencing, and problem solving. Working with the Cognitive component enhances the development of cognitive

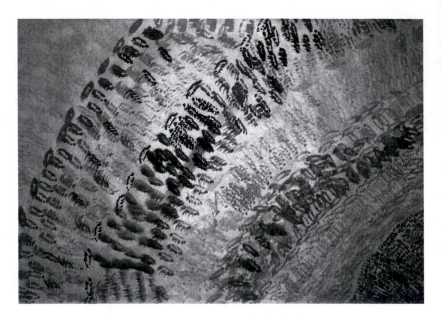

Figure 7.4 Painting by a 10-year-old girl suffering from obsessive-compulsive disorder shows regression to compulsive behavior with the use of paint.

skills. Media with inherent structure such as wood, mosaic tile, construction paper, and collage complement and enhance cognitive functioning. Examples of activities with the Cognitive component are highlighted in Table 7.1. These experiences include floor plan drawings, lifelines, cognitive maps, and the problem-solving collage. Complex experiences involving several steps require processing with the Cognitive component. Keeping multiple steps in mind involves mental representations of materials and methods that amplify the reflective distance of cognitive experiences.

Increasing reflective distance through questions and discussion can help clients analyze situations and come to new conclusions. The healing function of the Cognitive component is the ability to generalize from one concrete experience to other dissimilar situations. The function that can emerge from work with the Cognitive component is creative, imaginal problem solving, including the creative use of symbols. Creative problem solving encourages contact with healing inner wisdom, increases self-acceptance, and promotes peaceful self-understanding. Overuse and underuse of cognitive processes can be therapeutically addressed with art therapy that begins with work concentrated at the Cognitive component. Optimal functioning with the Cognitive component enhances negotiation skills and self-care abilities; it fosters mature decision making and problem solving.

TABLE 7.1   Examples of Cognitive Experiences and Associated Healing and Emergent Functions

Cognitive Activity	Materials and Procedure	Healing Function	Emergent Function
Depict relationships among objects in external reality, such as above/below	Various shaped and colored objects	Understanding spatial relations and relationships among diverse objects	Develop concepts of space, order, and class
Listening to and following directions about using media	Any complex task or procedure requiring two or more steps	Holding information in working memory, planning/executing multiple steps	Increases cause-and-effect thinking
Topic-directed collage	Collage materials, paper, glue	Focus on topic and relations among component parts to whole topic	Problem-solving abilities emphasized
Pro and con collage (pros and cons of using and not using substances; Horay, 2006)	Collage materials, paper, glue; represent pros of using, cons of using; pros of not using, cons of not using substances	Thinking through a course of action; relating past and future behavior	Complex problem-solving ability; ability to think through action prior to using substances; increased decision making
Floor plan of childhood home	Drawing materials; relaxation/guided visualization to remember and draw childhood home	Ordering and containing of affect; plan and structure associated with previously emotional content	Increased problem-solving abilities; think through past events and relate them to present behavior
Lifeline or timeline	Begin at birth using line direction and quality to signify ups and downs of life	Sequencing of life events, development of cause-and-effect relationships	Increased problem-solving abilities; think through past events and relate them to present behavior
Abstract family collage	Construction paper, scissors, glue; family is portrayed via color, shape, and size	Traits abstractly represented; relationships beyond the physical can be realized	Increased awareness of family dynamics

continued

TABLE 7.1 (continued)   **Examples of Cognitive Experiences and Associated Healing and Emergent Functions**

Cognitive Activity	Materials and Procedure	Healing Function	Emergent Function
Survival on an island	Drawing materials to represent three things one would take following a shipwreck	Identifying positive coping skills; abstract problem solving	Increased awareness of inner resourcefulness and abilities

8

Symbolic Component of the Expressive Therapies Continuum

Introduction to the Symbolic Component

The Symbolic component is the opposite of the Cognitive component on the Cognitive/Symbolic level of the Expressive Therapies Continuum. Whereas the Cognitive component emphasizes facts and logical thought, the Symbolic component is concerned with intuition and idiosyncratic or mythic thought. As was mentioned in the first chapter, the two poles of each bipolar level of the ETC have a curvilinear relationship. Therefore, as cognitive information processing increases, symbolic functioning is at first enhanced and bolstered by cognitive input; a modicum of rational thought is required to understand the mystical. Intuitive problem solving, self-discovery, and self-acceptance characterize the creative transition level, where optimal levels of each component influence creative activity. However, when cognitive thought becomes dominant, symbolic information processing diminishes and ultimately is blocked. The logical, linear decision-making and problem-solving characteristics associated with the Cognitive component of the ETC are opposite of the holistic, numinous qualities of the Symbolic component.

The Symbolic component involves intuitive and self-oriented concept formation, metaphoric representation, synthetical thought, and the expression and resolution of symbols (Kagin & Lusebrink, 1978b; Lusebrink, 1990, 1991b). The term *symbolic information processing* used within the context of the Expressive Therapies Continuum refers to thought that is condensed, displaced, or not wholly known to the creator. Symbols are multidimensional and often contain repressed kinesthetic, sensory, and affective aspects as well as obvious visual images (Kagin & Lusebrink,

1978b). The psychoanalytic view would add that symbols contain both manifest (overt) and latent (hidden) content that allows material too threatening for the ego to grasp to be disguised and utilized (Levick, 1983; Lusebrink, 1990; Wilson, 1987). Symbols are used as defense mechanisms when specific objects and thoughts are represented by subjective graphic representations (Levick, 1983).

The multiple layers inherent in symbols allow them to be understood through all components of the ETC in an integrative fashion. Symbolic thought has the potential to expand self-knowledge beyond what is concretely known and immediately available to the individual. A symbol can act as a bridge between outer existence and inner meaning; it has the capacity to describe an individual in his entirety, which a cognitive verbal description cannot do (May, 1960). Symbols take into account duality and ambiguity, and can provide unity, where words often fall short. Symbolism has been associated with the sacred, religious transcendence and spiritual growth (Jung, 1964; May, 1960).

Developmental Hierarchy

A symbol is something that implies meaning greater than that which is immediately obvious and straightforward (Jung, 1964). Symbols go beyond signs that merely indicate; symbols represent, transcend, or transform meaning. A sign is a signal that something is directly forthcoming. A symbol does not have to refer to something in the present surroundings. It has been argued that the use of symbols is the characteristic ability that sets humans apart from and above other animals (Greenspan & Shanker, 2004; Langer, 1967). Langer believes that humans possess a need for symbolism that gives rise to everything that is referred to as higher-order life. Symbol making is an ongoing fundamental mental activity that is sometimes conscious and is at other times unconscious. It takes in more than what is commonly called thought and allows humans access to fantasies, values, and passions. Edinger (1973) goes so far as to say that a symbol is a living thing containing dynamic energy that captivates the individual and compels symbol resolution.

Langer (1967) points out that the human brain does not act as a mere transmitter of data. Information available from sensations and perceptions is constantly transformed into symbols, which are embryonic ideas. Communication difficulties can occur because there is no one-to-one correspondence between the input and output of sensory or perceptual data. Each brain transforms the information slightly differently into basic symbols. Speech is one way in which the brain transforms experiences; ritual and art are other symbolic transformations of experience. All symbolic processes facilitate the expression of ideas and feelings that words cannot adequately convey (Langer, 1967).

Symbolic thought is not present at birth, but begins relatively early in life with the development of mental representations and language (Greenspan & Shanker, 2004; Wilson, 1987). As was discussed in the previous chapter, about formal operational thought, some clients will not attain this level of cognitive ability. In a similar fashion, some clients may be most comfortable with tangible things in the outer world, and not as readily attuned to the mysterious symbolic processes of the inner world (Signell, 1990). However, in many cases, access to basic symbolic thought processes can be taught through the introduction of art and literary works containing symbolic nuances, through exposure to mythology, and by reexperiencing folklore. Clients can be helped to make crucial shifts toward symbolic functioning by participating with the art therapist in a joint picture (Levens, 1990), by illustrating scenes from their favorite fairy tales (Lusebrink, 1990), and by exploring their dreams (Signell, 1990).

Healing Function of the Symbolic Component

The healing dimension of the Symbolic component of the Expressive Therapies Continuum is the ability to realize personal meaning within the larger context of universal symbols (Kagin & Lusebrink, 1978b). Working with personal symbols also can help clients generalize from concrete individual experiences to abstract general qualities. Accordingly, through work with the Symbolic component, someone who has had many experiences caring for others can begin to consider herself a healer. Integration of this new aspect could promote a new self-definition and guide future personal growth.

Understanding of personal symbols has been called symbol resolution (Lusebrink, 1990). *Resolution* is a word with many meanings, and it is quite appropriate for the process of "unpacking" symbolic meaning. Resolution can mean a thing resolved or solved; separation into components; conversion into another form; or increments of focus (DK, 2003). All of these definitions describe the process of understanding symbols. The symbol must be understood as containing multiple layers of meaning. These multiple layers are what allow symbols to convey so much more than words. Increasing increments of focus can improve resolution by sharpening the understanding of symbol meaning. Separation into component parts and conversion into different forms may be necessary to deepen understanding. Self-discovery and personal insight occur while using symbolic processing as individuals interact with personal and universal meanings.

The healing power of symbols can be categorized as regressive or progressive (Lusebirnk, 1990; May, 1960). Regressive symbols tend to represent unconscious, archaic desires, needs, and urges. Regressive symbols help elucidate the origin of personal meaning. Working with regressive symbols can help clients work through childhood conflicts. In contrast, progressive symbols are related to future strivings and may reveal new goals and personal options. Working with progressive symbols reinforces forward momentum and new directions, and enhances psychological growth (May, 1960). Examination and exploration of both types of symbols is necessary for healing, as clients will discover the underpinnings of personal content as well as uncover new possibilities through an expanded view of the self. Symbols function as tools for finding solutions to problems on a higher level of integration.

Examples of Symbolic Experiences

Part of the multilayered nature of symbols is that they contain not just an outward appearance, but also an underlying emotional charge. These emotionally charged internal structures must be externalized in order to be resolved (Kagin & Lusebrink, 1978b). Keeping symbolic material inside, or repressing it, can permit affective stimulation to obscure personal meaning. Externalizing symbolic material in the form of an image in art therapy is the easiest way to help a client take the first step toward symbol resolution and personal growth. At the same time, a symbolic readiness, or an open attitude toward the wisdom of symbolic material, is necessary for successful symbolic information processing to occur. Symbolic functioning also depends upon clients' willingness and abilities to project personal beliefs onto inanimate or abstract entities, and then to describe these characteristics. Physical relaxation can enhance the flow of internal images (Kagin & Lusebrink, 1978b).

Many clients can benefit from education about universal symbols or characters such as the hero, trickster, and great mother (Jung, 1964), or the warrior, teacher, and healer (Arrien, 1993). The widespread appearance of these and other universal characters in myths, fairy tales, and folklore can be demonstrated and used as a foundation for work with the Symbolic component of the Expressive Therapies Continuum. After establishing some familiarity with symbolic language, a warm-up activity with the Symbolic component can involve the construction of a collage using archetypal images. In this sort of collage, clients would choose from pictures of animals, nature, and mythological creatures. Present-day images would not be included, and words would not be added. Clients can be encouraged to discover their own archetypal qualities realized through identification with the symbolic material.

Other activities using the Symbolic component would include the formation of a guided daydream, environmental awareness, self-symbol in clay, bridging the opposites, constructing a personal shield or coat of arms, and dream amplification or clarification. The *guided daydream* can be used to take clients on a symbolic journey—into a cave, to a water source, or up to a mountaintop, where they meet with archetypal characters and face situations that must be navigated, revealing their inner resources. After completing the guided imagery journey in imagination, clients can be asked to illustrate three scenes from it. Ideas and instructions for guided imagery are available from many sources, including Leviton and Leviton (2004), Lusk (1993), and Schwartz (1995).

The instructions for *environmental awareness* require that participants go outside and find an object that appeals to them. After the object is located, clients spend time with it and imagine a story about how it came to be in the place where it was found. Clients then paint an image of the object and write a story detailing its journey to the present location. Clients project their own life history onto the object and journey. This art experience can help them realize forgotten or denied inner resources and internalize these newly discovered positive attributes.

Self-symbol in clay requires that clients create an object they believe defines them or one aspect of themselves. With adults, directions for creating a self-symbol purposely are kept vague so that anything—strength or challenge—can be portrayed. Children may need more direction in order to benefit from the experience; they can be instructed to construct a self-symbol based on an animal. Discussion of self-symbols reveals ways in which clients reflect the qualities represented in them. Therapists should bear in mind that not all self-symbols are positive, and that negative traits also must be accepted and integrated. Clients frequently have difficulty admitting and accepting negative traits, emotions, and behaviors; often they attempt to repress or deny them. Denial uses tremendous psychic energy, which is then not available to support psychological growth. Therefore, acceptance, not denial, is essential for a peaceful existence.

Bridging the opposites is an exercise in which two symbols are made in clay representing two opposing parts of the personality. One of these symbols could be the self-symbol from the previous experience. The bridge represents a means for clients to bring together two conflicting qualities. Conflicting instincts within the client often are the cause of psychic difficulties, and a symbol can function as an intermediary between the contradictory forces (Cane, 1951). In this exercise, divergent traits are integrated in a way that demonstrates the complementary nature of opposing forces and the strength in wholeness of the personality. Constructing a *personal shield* or coat of arms is a way to emphasize personal strengths. This experience can be supported by information from heraldry and dictionaries of symbols. The finished product will be a symbolic representation of clients' hopes, wishes, and dreams about personal strengths and resources. In this experience, clients can generalize from specific experiences to unique desired qualities.

It was through the study of dreams that psychologists became interested in the importance of symbols in understanding the psyche (Freud, 1938; May, 1960). Symbols are the natural language of dreams (Jung, 1964; Langer, 1967). According to May (1960), all dream symbols have a conscious pole and an unconscious pole. Dreams offer solutions from the unconscious to problems or questions posed by the client's immediate conscious circumstances. The conscious pole of a dream is its foundation in present reality and usually should be considered in terms of the events, thoughts, and feelings of the previous day. The unconscious pole is the symbolic message of the dream typically presented in the form of images. An image can be a multifaceted integration of information from a variety of inputs: a dream message (Robbins & Sibley, 1976). Consequently, making a picture of the dream for *dream amplification* or clarification is one way to better understand its symbolic content. For example, Figure 8.1 is the drawn image from a dream related by a newly married, 30-year-old therapist beginning a new position in private practice. She explained the dream as follows:

> I have a daughter with multiple handicaps: All senses seem to be impaired. The main issue is separation/individuation. I feel society wants her to be independent from me too soon. There is a field trip involving a bus ride. I want to go along. In the back of my mind, I wonder if I am being overprotective.

Figure 8.1   Dream image shows emotional energy pulling client in many directions.

The new therapist explained that making an image of the dream helped her realize that the daughter was a representation of herself. She said that the multiple handicaps were represented by the different colors surrounding her, and that they looked like different types of emotional energy pulling her in different directions. She went on to say that separation/individuation seemed to be shown by the gesture in the drawing—a wave. She stated that she felt the important issue represented in the dream was her own separation from her child self (which she felt was impaired) and her evolution into an independent adult. The responsibilities of a new marriage and career position perhaps added to the feeling that she felt pressured to grow up too soon. Finally, the young woman related that this "field trip"—life— is scary sometimes; she wanted protection to be provided by her adult self or the mother in her.

Later in the same month, the therapist had another dream:

> I am a young girl with my mother. I am flopped down on a big beach ball on a beautiful grassy hill; it is a lovely spring day. I am aware that we are at my mother's place of work. She works with children. I think to myself, "She got this job because of me, because I am handicapped." In this dream I have two handicaps.

The reference to handicaps helped the young woman realize that this dream was related to the previous one. The image created, and displayed in Figure 8.2, facilitated a deeper understanding of that connection and the symbolic meaning of the dream. The same colors were used in the second image as in the first. The dreamer mentioned that this time, however, the colorful energy (emotions, she guessed) was contained in a very orderly fashion in the ball. The ball resembles a mandala, and as such, would represent a way to remediate disorganization, by reorganizing psychic energy. In Jung's (1969) words, "A circular image of this kind compensates the disorder ... through construction of a central point to which everything is related" (p. 388). Further, the dreamer was pictured on top of the ball, perhaps feeling more in control of the emotions related in the previous dream. The young therapist also noted that in this dream she was not alone, as she was pictured in the previous one, but accompanied by her mother (the protection desired in the previous dream). Finally, in this dream she had only two handicaps, not multiple ones, and she was playing and protected, not pulled apart as in the first dream. The young woman added as a postscript to this interpretation that the dream occurred after receiving notification that she passed a licensing examination and was feeling more comfortable in her new career position and marriage.

In each case the symbolic dream content, externalized in the form of an image, helped deepen understanding of the dream message. The dream provided an answer to present-day feelings and concerns that helped deepen self-understanding. All of the activities on the Symbolic dimension provide information that previously might not have been available

Figure 8.2 Second dream image shows emotional energy contained within a ball or mandala.

to the client in other forms. The healing function of the Symbolic component is reinforced through activities that assist clients in furthering self-understanding on a personal or universal level.

Media Experiences to Enhance Symbolic Functioning

As was previously mentioned, symbols generally are multidimensional; they frequently include kinesthetic, sensory, and affective facets that partially determine their formation, expression, and resolution. Depending on the level of the Expressive Therapies Continuum evoked, various media can have differing effects on symbol development, expression, and resolution. *Resistive media* encourage energy release, allow emotions to emerge, and can facilitate a deeper experience with symbol formation because they promote multidimensional experiences. In addition, using resistive media without mediators allows symbols to develop on many dimensions: kinesthetically, sensorially, and affectively as well as in the imagination. *Nonmediated experiences*, such as work with plasticine or clay, are kinesthetically charged and can allow the development and flow of energy and emotion. These kinesthetic, sensory, and affective underpinnings can greatly augment the personal meaning gleaned from symbol resolution.

Mediated materials and experiences allow clients to remain somewhat removed from the creative experience, and therefore are useful in elevating concrete personal symbols to cultural or universal levels (Lusebrink, 1990). Kagin & Lusebrink (1978b) explained, "organizing personal expression within the quadripartite division of a mandala form while using felt tip pens may condense the meaning of these expressions and put them in a more universal context" (p. 177). The use of the precise mediator of the fine-tipped pens as well as the contained mandala form would augment the cognitive, universal application of the experience.

Media that produce ambiguous forms can increase physiognomic thought processes (Kagin & Lusebrink, 1978b). Physiognomic thought is related to the divination of aspects and characteristics of inanimate or abstract entities that occurs when clients imbue an image with personal meaning and project upon it personal or universal qualities. Ambiguous forms can be produced by *sponge prints, scribble drawings, string paintings, blot paintings, and tissue paper collage*. The resulting indefinite images facilitate the formation of symbols and intuitive concepts (Kagin & Lusebrink, 1978b; Lusebrink, 1990; Sakaki, Ji, & Ramirez, 2007; Wallace, 1990). *Fluid media* often produce indistinct forms and lend themselves to enhancing physiognomic thought and symbol formation, as increasing increments of focus allow the vague forms to be refined into meaningful symbols.

Low-structured art tasks such as those described above (blot painting, sponge painting, etc.) entail few instructions and allow art experiences to take any direction. These types of experiences are likely to induce symbol formation. Another example of a low-structured task is a nontopical collage. Without a prescribed organizing theme, clients must depend on an internal, intuitive sense to help them organize the divergent stimuli of multiple images. Intuitive concept formation aids the expression and resolution of symbolic material.

Quantity-determined media facilitate symbolic expression because they stimulate divergent thought processes. As was explained in Chapter 2, quantity-determined media are only bound by the amount provided. With large amounts of material provided, more and more options diverge from the initial image, providing many opportunities for expression and projection. *Boundary-determined media* have physical properties that limit the scope of their expressive potential. These media stimulate the understanding of symbols through convergent creations where ideas must come together to describe the stimuli at hand. The structure of boundary-determined media also assists symbol resolution through the crystallization of concrete meanings on a personal level (Kagin & Lusebrink, 1978b).

In summary, many types of media can stimulate symbol formation, expression, and resolution. Fluid media and low-structured tasks produce divergent and ambiguous forms that provoke physiognomic thought and can be intuitively organized, enhancing symbol formation and expression. Resistive media support the multiple layers of symbolic expression and resolution. Quantity-determined and boundary-determined media work in opposite fashions to promote symbolic expression and resolution through divergent and convergent thought processes, respectively. Finally, nonmediated experiences are likely to produce personal symbolic resolution, while mediated experiences more frequently allow symbol resolution on cultural or universal levels.

Reflective Distance With the Symbolic Component

Reflective distance with the Symbolic component is dependent upon the type of symbol created and the symbolic experience involved. As has been mentioned previously, symbols can be either personal or universal, and often they carry both meanings. Further, the healing power of symbols can be categorized as regressive or progressive (Lusebirnk, 1990; May, 1960). Regressive symbols are related to the past, archaic events, and immature parts of the personality. In contrast, progressive symbols lead clients on a journey into the future. They point to and describe future possibilities, desired traits, and mature aspects of the self (May, 1960).

Reflective distance will vary from great (when responding to universal, cultural, and progressive symbols) to very little (with personal and regressive symbols). The affect associated with personal and regressive symbols reduces the reflective distance involved in the experience. In addition, the immature or negatively valued contents present at times in personal symbols make them more emotional, and reduce the reflective distance achievable in attempting their therapeutic resolution. Symbols as defense mechanisms help individuals avoid threatening content or overwhelming affect (Levick, 1983; Lusebrink, 1990).

The collective nature of universal or cultural symbols allows for greater reflective distance. Their more widespread applicability facilitates discussions of general relevance and often reduces personal impact. The future direction of progressive symbols eliminates the immediacy of the moment and allows for speculation about a different time. This increased interval between symbol production and action increases reflective distance as well, and frequently generates greater client-led discussion of therapeutic possibilities. Alternating interaction between the relatively modest reflective distance of personal symbols and the high degree of reflective distance of universal symbols can be a desired therapeutic tactic. Facilitating the fluctuation between emotional connection and cognitive reflection can support client acceptance and internalization of new personal knowledge.

Questions and Discussion That Promote Symbolic Information Processing

Therapeutic discussions of symbols likely are related to reflective distance, as mentioned above. In addition, the type of symbolic formation also will help determine the direction of questions and discussion in art therapy. In reference to regressive and personal symbols, discussion often will revolve around unique associations and private meanings. Questions such as "What does this symbolize or represent to you?" or "Do you have any personal associations to the content or symbol?" will evoke unique symbolic meaning. Other questions can encourage clients to delve more deeply into the symbolism of colors or shapes. For example, the art therapist can ask, "Does this shape have special significance to you?" or "What does the color red suggest to you?"

The discussion can be moved to a universal or cultural level by asking clients to reflect upon mythology, folklore, or religious symbolism. All interpretations potentially can provide new layers of meaning to personal symbols. In discussing the interpretation of dream symbolization, Jung (1964) wrote, "Learn as much as you can about symbolism; then forget it all when you are analyzing a dream" (p. 56). Jung claimed that he frequently reminded himself of this advice in order to stem the flow of his own associations and projections onto client material. The same advice can be applied to the interpretation of client symbolism in art therapy. Clients must be considered the foremost experts on their own images. It would be dangerous to overproject unintended universal meanings onto client creations. On the other hand, therapists do have specialized training and knowledge that can be relevant. Cautious mention of universal or cultural themes can potentially broaden client self-perceptions and aid in self-acceptance (Hinz, 2008; McConeghey, 2003).

Robbins and Sibley (1976) point out that a therapist who is comfortable with complexity and ambiguity nurtures creative thought. Symbols can contain the duality, intricacy, and entirety of an individual. The authors add that art therapists must be able to resist easy answers, and the premature closure of simple solutions to complex issues. When working with the Symbolic dimension, it is important to keep the discussion open and flowing as one way to embrace intricate issues and explore diverse possibilities. Finally, Robbins and Sibley state that creative growth occurs when artist and therapist rely on intuitive abilities, such as those that are employed when working with the Symbolic component.

At times in group art therapy situations, clients imitate the images of others. When this happens, it is important for therapists to remember that an image is a symbol, not a duplicate of the object or idea it represents (Langer, 1967). For this reason, even when a client copies another person's art, it still is infused to a greater or lesser degree with personal meaning. The underlying concept may have been determined by imitation, but personal details make the symbolic representation personal. Discussion in this case can center on how copying another person's image was a way to begin an unfamiliar art experience, and eventually the client can be gently encouraged to take ownership of the symbolic image and to develop its particular content and singular meaning.

Emergent Function of the Symbolic Component

The emergent function of the Symbolic component of the Expressive Therapies Continuum is the discovery of new, previously unknown, and unavailable facets of the self and the integration of this knowledge into a new sense of self. What emerges from work on the Symbolic component is a new awareness of and greater ability to access unique inner wisdom. Being able to use hitherto dormant qualities improves self-esteem and promotes personal freedom. Individuals realize through working with the Symbolic component that they are not dependent on the art therapist for meanings but can determine their own purpose and direction in life (Hinz, 2006).

Investigation of archetypal qualities is not always a sanguine process. Symbols of destruction at times must break up the status quo in order to permit new psychological growth (Edinger, 1973). Malevolent characteristics must be examined and accepted along with benevolent traits. Human suffering frequently is caused by the repression or rejection of shadow characteristics (Jung, 1964). Through work with the Symbolic component of the Expressive Therapies Continuum clients will learn that the rejection of negative characteristics requires more psychic energy than their acceptance, because rejection and repression cause more tension and stress.

Mask making can be used as a way for clients to become familiar with both positive and negative aspects of the self. Hinz (2006) presented an example of a structured mask-making experience in which clients were asked to construct two masks, one after identifying traits of three persons whom they despise, and one after thinking about the characteristics of three admired people. Interestingly, clients commonly have just as much difficulty internalizing the positive traits that they idealize in others as they do accepting reviled traits. Acceptance of both bad and good aspects of the self leads to internal peace. Mask making also can help clients recognize, appreciate, and internalize the masculine and feminine traits that contribute to a balanced sense of self.

As was mentioned earlier, creating a *self-symbol* is another method of helping clients get in touch with previously unknown or unacknowledged qualities. The instructions can be open-ended in order to give clients free reign of the symbolic world. If clients are at a loss, the therapist can provide a dictionary of symbols to stimulate ideas. Clients can be instructed to choose an animal that has some qualities that they value or respect. Often a discussion of these qualities will help clients embrace the admired traits in themselves. The creation of a *self-portrait* also can be a method for discovering and incorporating split-off or denied aspects of the self (Hanes, 2007; Muri, 2007).

Overcoming Blocks to Symbolic Functioning

Clients who have not gained the ability to move past concrete experiences and generalize beyond their own life events may not be able to profit from use of the Symbolic component of the Expressive Therapies Continuum. Often images produced by concretely oriented persons seem impoverished for lack of detail, color, and emotion and do not contain a great deal of material for projection and amplification. This type of person is rooted in immediate tangible experience and cannot see beyond the image presented on the paper to a larger or more abstract meaning. For example, clients diagnosed with mental retardation and those with disorders along the autistic spectrum may not be able to benefit from work with the Symbolic dimension.

Conversely, clients who are caught up in details and "factual evidence" also can have a difficult time benefiting from work with the Symbolic component. Persons who overuse cognitive processing may be able to generalize beyond the concrete experience at hand, but remain fixed in the particulars and fine points of their thoughts. Images considered within the context of cognitive processing remain at a fixed or prescribed level of meaning and do not take on personal or universal significance. Images are not lifted above their known factual aspects and do not take on mysterious or unknown qualities. Cognitively oriented persons, being persuaded by facts, frequently experience discomfort with activities requiring conjecture. This type of client certainly would not be comfortable working with the Symbolic component of the Expressive Therapies Continuum.

One way to develop clients' abilities to make use of Symbolic component processes is to have them illustrate three scenes from a favorite fairy tale (Lusebrink, 1990). Clients often call to mind a story that has figurative implications for their own lives, and so can be introduced to the Symbolic component in a way that is familiar and nonthreatening. The following is an example of how an adolescent girl and her mother were introduced to the Symbolic component with valuable therapeutic results.

Jessica was a 13-year-old girl who was adopted by her parents when she was 4½ years old. Jessica was raised for four years by her single, teenaged mother whose parental rights were terminated due to severe neglect and abuse. Four-year-old Jessica spent six months in a foster home prior to being adopted. At the time of the adoption, the family had an eight-year-old biological son. Jessica was referred for art therapy by her mother, who was concerned about a pattern of increasing conflict with family members, lying, and shoplifting. Assessment showed that Jessica had difficulty trusting people and communicating with them. These problems were especially pronounced in her relationship with her mother.

Mother and daughter were seen together in art therapy as a way to help increase the trust, bonding, and communication between them. During the art therapy sessions, Jessica wanted to talk about specific incidents and had difficulty generalizing beyond concrete examples. Her images consistently were devoid of details and color, and her descriptions of them were monosyllabic. In attempting to help Jessica identify emotions, the art therapist asked her to paint several specified emotions and to choose two that were not specified to illustrate. Jessica showed fear as a scene in which she was watching a frightening television show, demonstrating the concrete nature of her thought processes. The two feelings that she chose to illustrate were "hungry" and "tired," again showing her difficulty with the abstract concept of feeling states.

Overall, progress in art therapy was frustratingly slow. Many weekly sessions were characterized by the repeated relating of similar incidents demonstrating Jessica's lack of trust and communication, and reactive anger from her mother. The art therapist believed that movement to the Symbolic component of the Expressive Therapies Continuum would benefit the couple by taking them out of immediate heated concerns to a new generalized understanding of the deeper issues influencing the relationship. The therapist asked Jessica and her mother to depict three scenes from their favorite fairy tales. They did not consult one another, but worked independently and shared the results when they were finished.

Jessica painted three scenes from the story "Goldilocks and the Three Bears." It was obvious from her drawings that she saw herself as Goldilocks, the intruder into a previously happy family. Jessica's mother drew three scenes from "Cinderella." She saw herself as the fairy godmother taking Jessica/Cinderella out of a life of drudgery and providing her with a happily-ever-after life. Mother and daughter were both struck by the assumptions and miscommunication that characterized their stories. The processing of this information took the better part of two therapy sessions. Afterwards, Jessica and her mother were able to engage in much more honest communication about their different expectations of each other and made more rapid progress repairing their relationship.

Balancing Overuse of Symbolic Functioning

Excessive use of the Symbolic component can be indicated by the presence of too many symbols, the defensive use of symbols, and the overidentification with symbols (Edinger, 1973; Lusebrink, 1990). When everything has a special meaning, the symbolic significance of the world becomes too abstract to manage daily tasks effectively. Such can be seen in the case of schizophrenia, when symbolic perception of reality renders thought so idiosyncratic or strange that it is not related to reality, and therefore not practical. To a lesser degree, some clients engage in abstract and symbolic thought processes to such an extent that they lose personal or affective references (Lusebrink, 1990). Clients such as this are difficult to engage with because their thought processes can seem impenetrable: There are no personal, emotional, or practical hooks for others to connect with in conversation. Additionally, symbolic thought can be used defensively in an attempt to avoid contact with affect or personal meaning. Such clients regularly refer to themselves and the events in their lives in metaphorical terms that reduce the personal significance of their images.

Overuse of symbolic thought processes can interfere with progress in therapy due to an impaired ability of therapist and client to connect on a level that facilitates personal growth. Therapeutic progress is impeded by an insistence on idiosyncratic or incomprehensible content and language. Clients who overuse Symbolic component processes can be approached therapeutically in a variety of ways. The art therapist can attempt to explore and develop the emotions associated with symbols through movement to the Affective component. Concrete sensory or perceptual experiences can anchor the individual in the present. For example, the client can be asked to sensually explore an object and then draw it as was demonstrated in the sensory exploration drawing of the pinecone in Chapter 4. Drawing objects or scenes from the immediate surroundings can increase reality orientation to the present (Lusebrink, 1990).

As mentioned in Chapter 5, McNiff (2004) discussed the healing effects of drawing from life in the case of a chronic schizophrenic patient who was institutionalized for many years. The patient was uncommunicative and disinterested in most activities. When first introduced to art therapy, the patient drew only quick contour drawings from imagination for many months. McNiff reported how he finally held the patient's arm and helped him draw something different, and that this break from the usual began a period in which the patient began drawing the objects around him. He drew with great detail and became subtly more interested in his surroundings. Finally, the patient began drawing the people around him. McNiff stated that this grounding in immediate reality also allowed the patient to participate socially with those people in ways that he had previously not been capable.

According to psychoanalytic theory, frightening dream content is disguised so that it can be encountered without threat. In addition, through condensation, many ideas can be expressed through one image. In the process of displacement, an indifferent object is substituted for a threatening one (Freud, 1938). These same processes occur in the formation of visual symbols and can be used defensively in drawings through the repetition of fixed images (Levick, 1983; Lusebrink, 1990; Wilson, 1987). A defensive image can be worked through with repetitive confrontation of the same symbolic image, with the goal of eventually changing the emotional value of the image to its opposite (Lusebrink, 1990).

Overuse and underuse of the Symbolic component of the Expressive Therapies Continuum can be handled by beginning therapy where the client is currently most at ease taking in and processing information. After a comfortable rapport and working relationship has been formed, the art therapist can introduce tasks that either heighten or lessen Symbolic component processing, depending on the desired therapeutic direction. Symbolic processing can be lessened by focusing on sensory or perceptual tasks such as drawing from reality. Heightening symbolic capabilities can be achieved through the introduction of metaphor, myth, folklore, and fairy tale.

Case Example

Introduction

Mary was an elegant Caucasian woman in her early 50s who presented for art therapy due to difficulties with binge eating and depression related to a history of physical child abuse and abusive adult intimate relationships. Mary was finally in a healing and stable marriage; she was a devout Catholic who was active in a number of church ministries. She donated her time, abilities, and money to many worthy causes and helped numerous people through her work.

Mary's first several images in art therapy were diagrams such as the one shown in Figure 8.3 executed in ballpoint pen. She used these detailed illustrations to describe the development of her self-image.

Assessment of Functional Level

Allowed to decide her preferred medium, Mary chose ballpoint pen and small paper. She rendered detailed diagrams, much like maps of the psyche, descriptive of her self-evolution. Her speech was metaphorical:

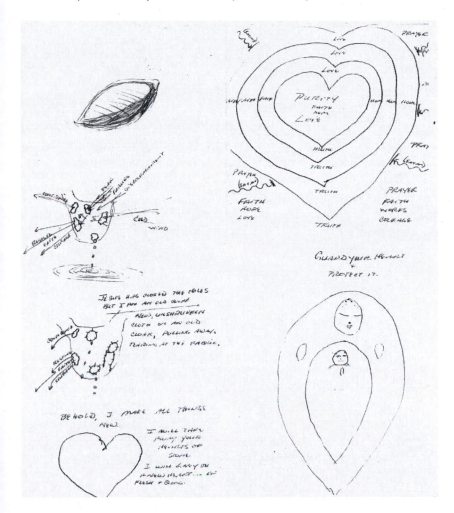

Figure 8.3   Achromatic, diagrammatic images demonstrate cognitive orientation.

full of descriptive figurative phrases and similes. Mary described herself as "full of holes," like the image in her first diagram. She said that at times she could feel the cold wind blow through her. She ate compulsively in an effort to plug up those holes.

At the beginning of therapy Mary seemed to be most comfortable functioning with the Cognitive component of the Expressive Therapies Continuum. She preferred the controlled medium of ballpoint pen, and she kept her drawings small. Stylistic elements from the completed expressions showed that the images were diagrams that functioned like cognitive maps, but they had metaphorical implications. Mary moved from the

Cognitive to the Symbolic component of the ETC when she used metaphorical descriptors in her images and spoken communication.

Formulation of Therapeutic Goals

One therapeutic goal Mary and the art therapist decided upon was to help her use art instead of food when she felt the urge to binge eat. Further, she and the therapist would attempt to discover what was preventing her from filling herself with God, which was Mary's expressed wish and ambition. Mary stated that she "wanted to get to heaven," and she felt that her binge eating was a gluttonous sin that would prevent her from reaching that goal.

Beginning With the Cognitive Component

Mary was encouraged to continue to explore and describe herself through the diagrams and cognitive maps with which she had demonstrated comfort and familiarity. It was hypothesized that there existed dark aspects and shadow characteristics with which Mary was unfamiliar, and which likely were propelling the binge eating and depression she described at the outset of therapy. The art therapist determined that these unfamiliar and potentially unwelcome aspects of the persona would be best confronted and accepted on the Symbolic level of the Expressive Therapies Continuum. Mary already had revealed some comfort with the Symbolic level through her use of metaphor.

Movement to the Symbolic Component

Through a series of *self-portraits*, Mary explored her sense of self from childhood through adulthood to the current time. The purpose of the self-portraits was to help Mary discover and integrate denied parts of herself—both positive and negative. Through this process, Mary discovered that she viewed herself as a "conduit." She explained that as a conduit she could do God's work, but not take the credit for it. She wanted all honor and glory to go to God. An unintended consequence of this self-image was that Mary did not hold anything inside herself. Everything slipped away— her good deeds, her piety, and even her physical nourishment. Another goal for therapy was added: that Mary would transform her self-image from conduit to container, so that she could internalize her fine qualities and accordingly be more equipped to combat depression.

Working principally with the Symbolic component, Mary continued making self-portraits: abstract and representational, attractive and repulsive. These views expanded her sense of self to incorporate old and new elements into a well-rounded, conscious self-perception. Through the creation of multiple self-portraits, Mary could accept that she was made up of a complex mixture of traits—not all saintly and not all demonic. The healing dimension of the Symbolic component was self-discovery; what emerged from this symbolically oriented art therapy process was a transformed self-image. A feeling of wholeness, and even holiness, replaced her experience of feeling full of holes. The last self-portrait was that of a "tarnished tabernacle," displayed in Figure 8.4. The tarnished tabernacle was not beautiful, but it was functional, in fine working condition. The image was at once holy and practical, tarnished and useful. The symbolic representation could describe much more than Mary was able to put into words. Mary no longer had to view herself as a conduit unable to contain anything positive; she was a sacred container. Work with the Symbolic component not only allowed Mary to transform her self-image; she also was more able to experience herself in her entirety, not fragmented, and forced into all good or all bad parts.

Including the Affective Component

By introducing first water-soluble oil pastels and later watercolor paints, an affective element was added to the therapeutic work that had engaged Mary for three months. Mary was encouraged to incorporate color into her images at the same time that she was learning to become more aware of what she was feeling during her urges to binge eat. She learned to use color to express the anger, fear, guilt, and sadness that she previously had repressed with food.

Summary

The Symbolic component of the Expressive Therapies Continuum is concerned with intuitive concept formation, idiosyncratic thought, and personal and universal symbols. Exploration of symbolic thought processes

Figure 8.4   Final image symbolically depicting change in self-image from conduit to container.

has the potential to expand clients' self-knowledge beyond that which is concretely known and immediately available. The healing dimension of the Symbolic component is the ability to realize personal meaning within the larger context of universal symbols. Examples of activities using the Symbolic component include collage construction using archetypal images, the formation of a self-symbol in clay or other medium, constructing a coat of arms, dream amplification, bridging the opposites, environmental awareness, guided day dream, and self-portraiture.

Overuse of the Symbolic component occurs when metaphorical thinking blocks the ability to ascribe personal meaning to events, images, and objects, or when everything takes on special symbolic significance, as is sometimes the case with schizophrenia. Blocks to the use of Symbolic component functioning occur when the ability for symbolic representation has not yet developed or when persons are so caught up with concrete facts that larger, nonprescribed, and individual symbolic meanings are obscured or lost. The emergent function of the Symbolic component of the Expressive Therapies Continuum is the discovery of new, previously unknown, and unavailable facets of the self and the integration of this information into a new sense of self. The emergent function of the symbolic component is detailed in Table 8.1 along with the healing functions of the various symbolic experiences discussed in this chapter.

TABLE 8.1   Symbolic Component Experiences and Associated Healing and Emergent Functions

Symbolic Activity	Materials and Procedure	Healing Function	Emergent Function
Collage of archetypal images	Precut images of animals, nature, mythological creatures; paper, glue; no words	Identification of internal archetypal qualities	Discovery of internal wisdom
Mask making	Hard cardboard, drawing materials and paint for decoration	Identification and integration of positive and negative parts of self; internalization of masculine and feminine	Internal strength gained from acceptance of parts of self; reduced repression of negative parts
Self-symbol in clay/bridging the opposite	Various colors of plasticene clay; clients create a symbol to represent self/parts of self	Integration of positive and negative aspects of the personality	Discovery or rediscovery of part of self
Guided daydream	Paper, drawing materials, guided imagery of a source, cave, or mountaintop encounter	Realization of internal wisdom and strengths projected onto characters in the story	Integration of new strengths
Environmental awareness	Found object, paper, paints, pens; make an image and write a story detailing the object's journey to present location	Identification of one's own journey	Realization of inner strengths and resources revealed through symbolic journey

continued

TABLE 8.1 (continued)   Symbolic Component Experiences and Associated Healing and Emergent Functions

Symbolic Activity	Materials and Procedure	Healing Function	Emergent Function
Personal coat of arms	Hard cardboard, books on heraldry and symbols, paint	Identification with personal strengths	Internalization of personal strengths; self-protection
Sponge printing or blot painting	Natural sponges, paint, water; sponge paint onto wet paper, fold for blot painting, unfold to reveal image	Ambiguous forms created that allow for projection of personal meaning	Intuitive concept formation
Self-portrait	Any materials; make an image of the self that can be abstract or representational	Reveals hidden parts of the self	Integration of all parts of self; peace instead of conflict due to repression

9

Creative Level of the Expressive Therapies Continuum

Introduction to the Creative Level

Creativity has been defined and studied from many points of view. It has been seen as a special form of intelligence, an ability developed through persistence and hard work, a genetically endowed talent, a unique personality trait, a response to psychopathology, or a mature defensive response to instinctual forces (Eysenck, 1995; Heilman, 2005; Panter, Panter, Virshup, & Virshup, 1995; Simonton, 2000). Creativity has been conceived of as the birthright of each human being. Because humans were created in the image of God, a divine and definitive creator, our basic human nature is believed to be creative (Azara, 2002; Fox, 2002). In fact, modern creativity research does not focus on creativity as a unique ability or skill, but rather as a typical way of thinking embedded in related cognitive processes, such as sustained attention, working memory, planning and temporal ordering, and decision making (Dietrich, 2004; Simonton, 2000). Recent creativity research has focused on the functional combination of convergent and divergent thinking such that during creative thought, theories are broadened and even overturned using divergent thinking, at the same time that innovative similarities are noted and capitalized upon through convergent thought (Heilman, 2005).

The Creative level of the Expressive Therapies Continuum, however, encompasses more than the use of cognitive processes; it refers to both the synthesizing and self-actualizing tendencies of the individual (Kagin & Lusebrink, 1978b). Synthesis takes into account at least three different types of fusion of information occurring during the artistic experience: the synthesis of inner experience and outer reality, the synthesis between the individual and the media utilized, and the synthesis between the different experiential and expressive components of the ETC (Kagin & Lusebrink, 1978b). Self-actualization refers to what Abraham Maslow (1970) saw as the individual's desire to become everything that she or he is capable of becoming—united and whole in a consistent self-perception. The person who has achieved this highest-level need presses toward the full use and exploitation of his or her talents, capabilities, and potentialities. Self-actualization is a person's desire for self-improvement, his or her drive to make actual what he or she is potentially. Research shows a connection between artistic expression and self-actualizing growth (Manheim, 1998; McNiff, 1977, 1981). Manheim (1998) discovered that participants in a sculpture class considered their lives enhanced and enriched by the artistic process, especially emotionally and spiritually.

The division of the Expressive Therapies Continuum into component parts can seem to promote a fragmented and reductionist view of people, but in reality, the opposite is true. Rather than analyze people in terms of separate aspects of experience and expression isolated from each other, the theory views individuals as organized whole persons, unique, and integrated. Cognitive, symbolic, affective, perceptual, sensual, and kinesthetic processes are conceptualized as working together to provide optimal experiences. The best expression of this integrated view of the person is found in an examination of the Creative level of the ETC. Creative information processing can occur at any level and with any component process. In addition, it can include functioning with all component processes in one event, or in a series of experiences.

Developmental Hierarchy

Investigations of creativity across the life span demonstrate a curvilinear relationship between age and creative functioning (Dietrich, 2004; Simonton, 2000). Creativity is natural in young children whose thought processes are characterized by magical thinking and whose behavior is marked by imaginative play (Lusebrink, 1990; Piaget, 1962). Creative productivity seems to increase through childhood and adolescence parallel with the maturation of the prefrontal cortex (Dietrich, 2004). Creativity reaches its highest point in adulthood with varying ages of peak ability, depending upon the creative domain under consideration (Simonton, 2000). Creative functioning appears to fall off with old age as the brain loses cognitive flexibility and shows declines in working memory and other executive functions (Dietrich, 2004; Kramer et al., 2007; Lin et al., 2007). The aging brain seems to decline in its ability to make novel connections, which is one of the hallmarks of creative functioning (Dietrich, 2004). Art therapy experiences can enhance creativity in the elderly by facilitating novel connections and supporting increases in executive functioning (Jensen, 1997; Kahn-Denis, 1997; Landgarten, 1981; Wald, 2003).

As was mentioned in Chapter 4, one of the goals of art therapy with elderly populations is to increase sensory stimulation in order to preserve and inspire creative information processing. Sensory stimulation can elicit long-term memory and facilitate new connections (Landgarten, 1981; Wald, 2003). Other art approaches encourage increasing respect for the wisdom of older adults and allowing their natural wisdom to generate creative processes and products. In addition, creativity is augmented with elderly participants by using materials that maximize strengths and minimize deficits (Stewart, 2006). For example, collage images that are precut reduce negative feelings about loss of fine motor skills (Wald, 2003).

Healing Function of the Creative Level

The healing dimension of the Creative level of the Expressive Therapies Continuum has been defined as inventive and resourceful interaction with the environment leading to creative self-actualizing experiences. Creative expression through art media involves the whole individual, and therefore has a healing influence on the person through self-actualizing growth (Lusebrink, 1990). Art therapy can support self-actualization by providing experiences that model, teach, and support spontaneity and openness in expression as well as courageousness in confrontations with the unknown.

May (1975) wrote that the creative process is an authentic encounter with reality that allows the individual to actualize potentials not previously known or understood. According to Maslow (1970), only 1% of the population will ever attain the goal of self-actualization. Possible reasons for nonattainment include that people often are blind to their own potentials, and individuals can fear their own abilities. In addition, society places demands or stereotypical expectations on individuals that stifle potential. Finally, lower-level safety needs often restrain individuals and render them unwilling to take the risks required for psychological growth and self-actualization (Hjelle & Ziegler, 1981; Maslow, 1982).

Therapeutic work with art media can effectively address each of the above-mentioned impediments to self-actualization, making creative activities supremely healing. First, working with art media helps individuals experience their own potential in a concrete manner; the product of their labor is evident, tangible, and meaningful. However, it must be stressed that the experience of actualization may be present even if the external product has minimal independent value, as is often the case with spontaneous or unconscious painting (Cassou & Cubley, 1995; Goldstein, 1999; Kagin & Lusebrink, 1978b). Second, fears of creativity or human potential might be expressed as resistance to creative endeavors in art therapy. This type of resistance can be effectively managed and worked through, as will be discussed in Chapter 11. Thus, individuals in art therapy need not fear their creative potential, but rather submerse themselves in it, mine it, and grow because of integrative encounters with it.

Individuals can explore the demands or stereotypical expectations placed on them by familial or societal expectations. Previously these demands may not have been consciously known. However, through the therapeutic process, they can be acknowledged and challenged such that individuals may meet their full potentials. For example, qualities such as sympathy and tenderness might have been discouraged in males by families, cultures, or societies that consider such characteristics excessively feminine. Mandala paintings and harmony drawings can be means by which both masculine and feminine traits are acknowledged and accepted (Hinz, 2006). Finally, through the artistic process, clients can be challenged to take risks and make mistakes. Therapy can include discussions of how risk and growth are related not just in art, but also in life. Courageous exploration and risk taking in one sphere demonstrate that growth is rewarding, and prompt future strivings for growth in other spheres (Hjelle & Ziegler, 1981).

Children working on the Creative level of the Expressive Therapies Continuum freely include themselves in their artwork. They show through images that they are beginning to understand themselves and their needs. In addition, through their creative productions children demonstrate their increasing ability to identify and respond to the needs of other people (Lowenfeld, 1952). Children do not necessarily have to be skillful in order to be creative, but they must be courageous in their approach to the subject matter and free to express their thoughts, feelings, and needs. The use of art media in therapy can help children discover creative potential by encouraging risk taking with media and subject matter, and through nonjudgmental acceptance of the full range of topics that can be addressed. Encouraging freedom of expression does not mean noncritically accepting all forms of behavior; as was discussed in Chapter 5, there is power in limits. All clients should adhere to a set of procedures and rules that ensure respect and safety.

Media and Experiences to Enhance Creative Functioning

Creativity has been defined as the ability to bring something new into being (May, 1975) or to produce work that is both novel and useful (Dietrich, 2004). The usefulness of creative products has been described as relevance, appropriateness, or social value (Nickerson, 1999). In art therapy, the usefulness of a product can be expressed in many ways, depending upon therapeutic goals. For example, a process or product could be useful in helping to release energy (Kinesthetic component), in expressing emotion (Affective component), or for providing insight (Symbolic component). Consequently, any media can be used in an original manner to aid in a valuable therapeutic process, and even the most mundane materials have creative potential. Individuals have used materials from dryer lint to car parts to express that which is new and relevant (Capezzuti, 2006; Kirby, Smith, & Wilkins, 2007). Further, in art expression, creativity is manifested in the ability to create order out of unstructured media, especially when the final art product contains universal emotional appeal (Lusebrink, 1990; Ulman, 1975).

Clients can be encouraged to be mindful of the effects of various media on the creative experience. Csikszentmihalyi (1998) discussed the experience of "flow" in everyday life. He wrote that when an individual's talents precisely match a specific task, she or he experiences a state of mind in which time loses meaning (it either speeds up or slows down), mental facilities are completely engaged, and a profound sense of satisfaction prevails. When using art media to promote creativity, it is important to remember that if the individual struggles too greatly to master the materials, she or he is less likely to experience the healing aspects of creativity, and more likely to experience frustration or anxiety. If the medium is so familiar as to be absolutely unchallenging, the individual will likely experience boredom and not creative flow.

Many art therapists have written about the importance of a sense of play in enhancing creativity (Betensky, 1995; Kramer, 1971; Lusebrink, 1990; Malchiodi, 1998; McNiff, 1998). Play in art therapy means becoming familiar with diverse and unfamiliar media, experimenting with various ways to use the media, and not being concerned at first with creating a product. This sort of experimentation usually has a spontaneous and carefree quality, and thus the word "play" accurately describes it. Exploration and play, especially on the Kinesthetic/Sensory level of the Expressive Therapies Continuum, allow participants to process diverse information without pressure to form premature closures (Lusebrink, 1990). By encouraging clients to have fun with the art media and to deny their wishes for finished products, many more opportunities present themselves for creative functioning.

Lusebrink (1990) describes two procedures designed to increase creative inspiration and action. Luthe (as cited in Lusebrink, 1990) coined the term *creativity mobilization* in describing an artistic process that involved producing a large number of different paint and brush exercises in a short period using inexpensive materials. The rapid and prolific paintings will bypass typical defenses to release creative tendencies (Goldstein, 1999). Lusebrink (1990) also discussed enhancing creative functioning through an exercise that involved making multiple paintings to different types of music. Music and imagery both circumvent left-brain analytical functions, again allowing for creative release. In both types of activities, clients are counseled not to decide upon a product, but rather to allow the material to surface as it will. Often disturbing material emerges in this type of unplanned work, which allows for emotional release and cognitive reflection. Making multiple images in a short period also reduces the amount of conscious planning and ego investment in the final crude images, and thus allows for more creative possibilities in the outcome. Thomas Merton (Lipsey, 2006) said of his spontaneous printmaking process, "You never quite know what is going to come out, and often it is a big surprise. These drawings may continue to awaken possibilities, consonances; they may dimly help to alter one's perceptions" (p. 39). For Merton, the process of unplanned printmaking opened numerous possibilities for creativity. Scribble drawings or blot paintings can be used in this manner.

An individual can respond creatively within the limits of his or her capabilities in a supportive environment (Lusebrink, 1990). This type of environment contains diverse art media, fosters curiosity, encourages perceptual openness, and stimulates all the senses. Interestingly, a supportive environment also includes well-defined limits. May (1975) wrote that creativity is born out of tension between spontaneity and limits, and that to a certain extent, limits are thus essential in the creative effort. As was stated above, limits can include a set of rules for the art room. Other important limits include daily or weekly session procedures, and rituals to heighten creative expression. In addition, therapists' attitudes toward client efforts can limit or promote creativity. Some clients will require unconditional acceptance of all artistic undertakings in order to feel free to create.

Others will benefit from encouragement to master both the materials and their fears and frustration in dealing with them, in order to create within a structure (Lusebrink, 1990).

An illustration of aiding client persistence happened when a woman was encouraged to use oil pastels to depict past trauma. It was hoped this medium would promote more affective functioning and the creative release of tension related to repressed pain. The art therapist wanted the client to experience the intense colors and emotional release of working with the deeply pigmented, slightly resistive oil pastels. The woman needed repeated encouragement to persevere with the unfamiliar and uncomfortable medium. However, when mastered, the rich colors of the oil pastels successfully conveyed the pain and horror of past sexual abuse. If the art therapist had not helped the young woman persist, the full extent of her emotional pain would not have been creatively expressed.

It is necessary for the art therapist to take into account the individual's developmental level and ego strength when approaching and suggesting media and activities. Creativity often involves breaking established rules and overturning previously held assumptions to arrive at something new (Lusebrink, 1990; Malchiodi, 1998). However, depending on the client age and developmental level, an unstructured and media-rich environment that encourages rule breaking can be overwhelming, and therefore not conducive to effective creative expression (Lusebrink, 1990). Clients will require various amounts of structure in order to promote creative functioning. For example, children with attention-deficit/hyperactivity disorder may require limits on the types and amounts of media available in order to benefit from creative expression (Safran, 2003). Adolescents and adults could be overcome with inner critical voices when faced with unlimited materials and choices. By providing a structured task, the art therapist can lend needed ego strength to overcome forces that previously have undermined the motivation or concentration needed for project completion.

According to McLeod (1999), more children currently are introduced to the visual arts through the computer screen than the crayon. Thus, it is necessary that art therapists be familiar with the latest advances in computer-assisted art therapy. The types of assistance available vary from location to location, but most schools are equipped with some computer technology, including drawing programs. A good starting place to familiarize oneself with available technology would be to research the computer software programs used in local school districts. Software to augment the creative process can include programs for drawing, painting, animation, photo alteration, book making, video editing, and art presentation (Malchiodi, 2000; McLeod, 1999; Peterson, Stovall, Elkins, & Parker-Bell, 2005).

Reflective Distance With the Creative Level

Reflective distance in creative interaction with media is character- ized by total involvement in the expressive act while maintaining some awareness of the interaction, or it can alternate between periods of total absorption and subsequent reflection upon that interaction (Kagin & Lusebrink, 1978b; Malchiodi, 2002). Again, we can refer to the work of Csikszentmihalyi (1998) and the concept of flow. Complete immersion in the creative process is one way people experience flow. However, in order to express an inner state or outer reality, there must be alternating periods of detached reflection, as the individual makes sure that needs, ideas, or feelings are being expressed in the desired fashion. Therefore, both low and high degrees of reflective distance are characteristic of and necessary for creative information processing.

Questions and Discussion That Promote Creative Information Processing

Creative expression usually does not need verbal reflection because it stands as a statement by itself (Lusebrink, 1990). The feelings of completion and satisfaction that accompany creative expression should be acknowledged by therapists as well as by clients. This shared knowledge is important for clients because it helps them remember and identify creative achievement and feelings in the future, and because identifying and celebrating the creative experience reinforces closure. In addition, this acknowledgment is significant because at times clients have a tendency to identify with creative excitement and accelerate their activity rather than to appreci- ate the satisfaction of concluding a creative act (Lusebrink, 1990). Slowing down to take in the satisfaction that comes from completion reinforces closure and helps clients integrate therapeutic gains.

Clients can be encouraged to be mindful of the various mood states and mind states that characterize the creative process. For example, incu- bation of creative thoughts will perhaps feel slow and deliberate, while illumination of creative insight could be defined by a sense of growing excitement. Discussion to promote functioning on the Creative level of the

Expressive Therapies Continuum also can focus on cycles of creativity and how mood states or mind states are related to creative energy and output. Clients can compare and contrast periods of relatively decreased creativity with exciting creative times, and can be encouraged to talk about what inspires them (Malchiodi, 1998). The outcome of such discussions can be that clients realize they have the ability to be creative in a number of different areas, that creativity fuels meaning and passion in life, and that they can enhance their lives by engaging in regular creative activity beyond the therapeutic sessions.

Emergent Function of the Creative Level

The discovery of new levels of expression or a new way of experiencing oneself can be seen as emerging from the creative act (Lusebrink, 1991b). The creative experience is accompanied by feelings of wholeness and satisfaction, closure and joy (Kagin & Lusebrink, 1978b; Lusebrink, 1990; Maslow, 1982). May (1975) stated that what emerges first from the creative encounter is joy, "the emotion that … accompanies the experience of actualizing one's potential" (p. 45). Secondly, and upon deliberate reflection, the creator feels a sense of gratification or satisfaction about bringing something new into being. Finally, the experience of closure helps new knowledge and emotion become integrated as part of the individual, and clients view themselves in a fresh light.

What emerges from the creative experience often is the establishment of order out of chaos, the giving of form to feelings and ideas that otherwise might not have been expressed (Lusebrink, 1990; Ulman, 1975). Again, the individual could experience himself in a new way—free of anxiety and able to express inner turmoil in a way that clarifies rather than obscures meaning. Accessing all levels of information processing on the Expressive Therapies Continuum and experiencing the final product are aspects of artistic events that help individuals liberate creativity, actualize potentials, and express uniqueness.

Overcoming Blocks to Creative Functioning

Blocks to creative functioning are many in our society (Bayles & Orland, 1993; McNiff, 1998). Barriers can be physical, emotional, or psychological. Physical barriers to creativity can include the client's actual physical disabilities or physical properties of the environment. Emotional barriers can include any problematic feeling: anxiety, fear, anger, or sadness. Psychological barriers to creativity include mental attitudes that hamper the creative process, such as perfectionism, self-criticism, and self-doubt. If the art therapist uses the word *creative*, many clients will demur, claiming not to be at all creative. This attitude toward creativity may be the most common obstacle to creative functioning faced by therapists. One approach to this potential barrier is to point out to clients the many ways that they are creative in everyday life: Choosing clothing, cooking, and child rearing are a few examples where people frequently make choices and decisions that show their original approach to problem solving (Cornell, 1990; Maslow, 1982). With some reassurance along these lines, apprehensive clients usually will take up unfamiliar artistic tasks.

Self-criticism and fear of criticism by others can stem from a powerful internal critic. This critical voice engenders doubts about one's abilities, especially when facing novel tasks (Stone & Stone, 1993). The inner critic can cause clients tremendous anxiety about their abilities to handle the media, and even more anxiety about their abilities to express themselves in original ways. Bayles and Orland (1993) wrote: "Fear about yourself prevents you from doing your best work, while fears about your reception by others prevents you from doing your own work" (p. 23). Overcoming the inner critic will take reassurance and patience on the part of the therapist. Therapists can aid clients by helping them understand that the inner critical voice usually stems from an internalized parental voice whose original intent was benign and helpful. The original purpose of the internal critic was to reduce or eliminate shame and pain. Making peace with the inner critic requires that clients appreciate the helpful—and dismiss the harmful—significance of this voice (Stone & Stone, 1993).

Children can employ certain behaviors that they learn are effective coping mechanisms or are pleasing to others. For example, overly mature and helpful behaviors can become part of an adult façade. Perfectionism can be viewed as a behavior that children take on because it is pleasing to adults, but which is not expressive of the child's true self. Perfectionism often is driven by the underlying belief that "I am not good enough." Extremely high achievement can represent repeated attempts by clients to prove that they are fundamentally good. Individuals often live with a lack of confidence in the false self and fear of discovery. This discrepancy between real self and false self can inhibit creativity as clients experience an agonizing dilemma about how to express their true identity (Rhyne, 1973). With therapeutic encouragement, creative activity can be one way to bridge the gap within the divided self and heal the shame that has developed (Johnson, 1990).

The emotional consequences of physical, sexual, or psychological trauma in childhood can greatly hinder adult creativity (Miller, 1986, 1990). When children are traumatized without anyone to witness their emotional and physical pain, they will be lastingly impaired. In abusive situations without a witness to their natural anger, and being unable to express their pain alone, children are forced to suppress their feelings and memories, and frequently idealize the persons who abused them. Without memories of the original causes for their emotional turmoil, psychic energy is interpreted destructively; children often act out their pent-up emotions on others by aggressively acting out, or on themselves through alcoholism, drug addiction, or high-risk sexual behavior. However, when someone acts as a witness to their trauma and supports them emotionally, children frequently can use their emotional upheaval for tremendous creativity (Miller, 1986, 1990; Nickerson, 1999).

Adolf Hitler and Joseph Stalin were severely abused, had no supportive adults in their lives, and were not permitted to voice their emotion or pain— both men became destroyers of multitudes. Charlie Chaplin and Chaïm Soutine also experienced devastating childhood trauma. Chaplin and Soutine's lives, however, contained caring adult companions who witnessed their pain, and the resulting emotional turmoil was expressed creatively (Miller, 1990). A therapist can become a caring witness for a traumatized child and encourage creative expression. Adult clients also benefit therapeutically from a compassionate witness to their past or current distress. In addition, the art product can contain, and creatively explain, the pain that perhaps has long gone unacknowledged and unexpressed.

Physical disabilities can lead clients to believe they have reduced expressive abilities or creative capacity. Art therapists can adapt media and mediators as well as propose alternative means of expression to demonstrate myriad abilities and possibilities for unique expression (Anderson, 1992). Computer applications also can enhance creative expression for clients with limited physical abilities (Parker-Bell, 1999). There are numerous hardware adaptations and software applications that can help physically challenged clients overcome movement and communication difficulties to achieve effective artistic expression (Malchiodi, 1998, 2000; Parker-Bell, 1999).

Beyond clients' physical limitations, there can be physical environments that deprive children, adolescents, and adults of creative opportunities. Impoverished environments have been associated with lowered achievement as well as reduced creativity (Lowenfeld, 1952; Lowenfeld &

Brittain, 1987). True expression and creativity take place when a child, adolescent, or adult can identify with the creative experience as well as with the medium. If identification does not occur, then art loses its expressive potential (Lowenfeld, 1952). An impoverished environment typically does not contain abundant art materials, and thus it can be difficult for a child raised in poverty to identify with the creative experience (Hebert & Beardsley, 2001; Nickerson, 1999). The use of art media in therapy can provide an avenue by which a world of creative possibilities opens up for impoverished children, and art instruction becomes a significant part of early endeavors (Kramer, 1971).

Understanding and Supporting Creative Functioning

Lusebrink (1990) wrote about the conditions necessary to promote the creative climate. She indicated that it was necessary to provide an atmosphere of challenging acceptance where clients felt free to express themselves, but supported at the same time to take risks and follow through on new and possibly perilous avenues. In addition, Lusebrink mentioned that the practitioner should be familiar with the psychodynamics of the creative process in order to provide effective assistance. The stages of creativity originally were proposed by Wallas (as cited in Lusebrink, 1990); they are still the focus of research in their original form, and include preparation, incubation, illumination, and verification (Bogousslavsky, 2005; Lusebrink, 1990; Nickerson, 1999).

In the phase of *preparation*, the individual is receptive to stimulation from inside (thoughts, dreams, and wishes) and outside (objects and information). An attitude of openness, an ability to see things from many points of view, and the ability to quiet the inner critic increase the likelihood of successful preparation (Goleman & Kaufman, 1992). Preparation for creative problem solving also can include instruction about effective problem finding (Nickerson, 1999). Problem finding often seems to define the first few therapy sessions, as clients claim that they do not know what to talk about or draw. With encouragement to "trust the process" (McNiff, 1998), therapeutic issues will present themselves in the first few images and discussions. For example, the collage presented in Figure 9.1 was created by a young wife and mother who was depressed and could not identify a reason for her depression. The young woman was the mother of two young children and the wife of a medical resident who worked impossibly long hours. The young wife did not believe that she had a right to feel angry at

Figure 9.1   Collage aids in creative problem finding or problem identification.

her husband for not being home or sad at his absence. After all, being away from home was not his fault; his medical training required it. Creating the collage was a successful creative problem-finding strategy. It helped the young woman identify suppressed feelings and realize that she had a "right" to feel them.

Incubation refers to a deceptively passive time where information is allowed to exist without decision making or premature closure of ideas taking place; daydreaming and actual dreaming facilitate the operation of unconscious thought processes during the incubation stage (Goleman &

Kaufman, 1992). Divergent thinking characterizes the cognitive processes during preparatory and incubation phases; thinking is nonverbal, not focused on a product; and ego boundaries are diffuse. This type of process allows the creator to think deeply and beyond the surface structure of the basic elements (Lusebrink, 1990).

The *illumination* period is characterized by convergent thinking; it is in this phase of creativity that input comes together to present a problem or propose a solution. The *verification* stage requires explicit thought and deductive reasoning. Verification can be associated with depression and the solemn acceptance of the subject matter (Lusebrink, 1990), or elation and joyous celebration. Finally, the *creative product* is the translation of thought into solution (Goleman & Kaufman, 1992). In art therapy, the final art product can represent transformation or reformulation of a problematic issue or situation: It contains and explains the solution.

Creativity does not always mean that the individual makes a completely new product with a new theme and mode with each endeavor. Sometimes creativity means repetition; repetition of an image demonstrates for its creator various aspects and moods of the same subject (McNiff, 1998). Much can be learned about the source through repetition, and by examining the image from different views and at different periods in time.

Case Example

Introduction

This case follows the 28-year-old Caucasian woman introduced in Chapter 7. The young woman was the only child of an alcoholic mother and workaholic father. Her father was an attorney who regularly worked 80-hour workweeks and spent his weekends playing golf and tennis with clients or colleagues. The young woman's mother did not work outside the home, but spent her days decorating her home, shopping, and drinking alcohol excessively. When she came home from school as a child, the young woman usually found her mother intoxicated and angry. As the afternoons and evenings progressed, the mother would rail against her husband who "abandoned" her by staying away from home for so many hours. The young woman reported that often she would make dinner for her mother and put her to bed, all the time vowing never to be like her. After college, she completed law school and became a practicing attorney. She worked approximately

60 to 90 hours per week trying to make partner and had very little social life outside of occasional drinks with colleagues after long hours at work.

Kinesthetic/Sensory Level

Upon entering the community college extension class on using art for self-expression, the young woman stated that she wanted to do something completely different from her usual law practice. She had not used art materials since elementary school. Although she voluntarily enrolled in the class, she was ambivalent about art expression. The class was structured so that there was a short introductory period followed by time for individual, free art expression. The instructor asked the woman to begin playing with various art media to see what effects they had and how she responded to them. After a period of experimentation, the young woman used paint in a Kinesthetic/Sensory fashion: swirling and mixing colors, and commenting on the sense of freedom and release that she felt during and after the process.

Perceptual/Affective Level

The young woman seemed to enjoy the fact that her first experiences were not focused on outcomes or finished products. Her focus was on movement and release of energy. A change in this process occurred during the fourth week of the eight-week course, when the young woman created the image discussed in Chapter 7 and displayed in Figure 9.2. This image began as many of the previous images had, with mixing of colors and release of energy. However, in this case, the paint stayed dryer and more contained, and the young woman was encouraged to look for and develop an image in the midst of the ambiguous mass of color. Focus on form led her to the Perceptual component of the Expressive Therapies Continuum.

Cognitive/Symbolic Level

As was mentioned in Chapter 7, the addition of the title "I of the Storm" to the image helped crystallize the young woman's thoughts about her childhood. She explained that she had kept so busy with studying and working that she did not take the time to think about her childhood or experience

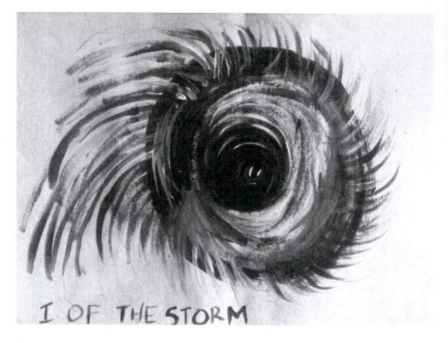

Figure 9.2   "I of the Storm": Movement to the Cognitive/Symbolic level through establishing a title for the painting.

her feelings about it. However, the hurricane and its associated meaning "I of the Storm" became symbolic of her life as a child. She was at the center of her mother's stormy rages.

In the three subsequent sessions, the young woman returned to affective expression by painting a series of images without a great deal of form, but aptly conveying her anger, sadness, and feelings of tremendous responsibility and isolation.

Creative Level

On the last week of class, the young woman brought in a paper sculpture that she had made on her own during the week. She explained that it was a three-dimensional representation of the image "I of the Storm." The paper sculpture is displayed in Figures 9.3 and 9.4. In explaining the sculpture and her impetus to make it, the young woman said that she had been thinking about being the "I" of the storm and struggling with feelings of responsibility for her mother. The young woman stated that she no

Figure 9.3 A three-dimensional representation of "I of the Storm" aids in actu-alizing creative potential.

longer wanted to be inexorably tied to her mother's well-being, and that the artistic expression during the class had helped her feel that she was ready to be free. She demonstrated how the paper sculpture was not static, but rather could move and change (as shown in Figure 9.4), reflecting the new sense of freedom that she felt. The young attorney was ready to become the best person that she could be—to actualize her potential—rather than staying trapped in an unpleasant childhood mold. The paper sculpture was symbolic of her new sense of freedom and a reminder of the promise of self-actualization. Functioning at the Creative level of the Expressive Therapies Continuum helped her match a new inner sense of herself with an outward manifestation. It pointed toward self-actualization and engen-dered a sense of freedom and joy that the young woman had previously not experienced.

Summary

The Creative level of the Expressive Therapies Continuum refers to both the synthesizing and self-actualizing tendencies of the individual. Creative experiences are integrative and expressive of the whole person. Creative

Figure 9.4   The three-dimensional representation integrates a new way of seeing the self: emotional freedom.

information processing can occur at any level and with any component process of the ETC. In addition, it can encompass functioning with all component processes, as demonstrated in the case example in this chapter. The healing dimension of the Creative level of the Expressive Therapies Continuum is creative interaction with the environment leading to self-actualization experiences. Any art media can be used in an imaginative and original manner to fashion novel and appropriate creations. The inventive use of media is facilitated if the therapist understands the creative process, beginning with incubation and continuing through verification. In addition, therapists should be familiar with media properties so they can aid clients in choosing art materials and methods that best match their therapeutic needs. If a client has to struggle too much to master the material, the therapeutic nature of the art experience is greatly diminished.

Creative functioning can be improved when therapists help clients examine and resolve mental, emotional, and physical barriers to artistic expression. Creativity also is enhanced by immersion in a creative environment: one that contains diverse art media, fosters curiosity, encourages perceptual openness, and stimulates all the senses. Further, clients are aided by a sense of play that suspends judgment and premature closure. What can emerge from such self-actualizing experiences is a profound sense of joy as one realizes talents, capabilities, and potentials. A new manner of knowing oneself can prevail when creative experiences are internalized from self-actualizing growth.

Section 3

Assessment and
Clinical Applications

10

Assessment Within the Structure of the Expressive Therapies Continuum

Introduction to Art-Based Assessment

Although most art therapists agree that assessment is a necessary element in the therapeutic process, there is some disagreement about how to carry it out appropriately (Gantt, 2004; Wadeson, 2002). Established assessment procedures are at the heart of evidenced-based treatment strategies in any health care practice, including art therapy (Gilroy, 2006). Art-based assessment grew out of psychological testing, specifically projective drawings, which originated as intuitively based—not evidenced-based—techniques. Art therapy inherited difficulties with these drawing tests, such as a lack of substantiation for sound psychometric properties, as well as problems inherent in theoretical approaches (Betts, 2006; Gantt, 2004; Kaplan, 2003). Psychologists using drawings for assessment purposes had removed drawings from their context in art. Typical projective drawing tasks such as the House-Tree-Person, Draw-A-Person, and Kinetic Family Drawing require clients to depict specific subject matter on 8½-by-11-inch paper with a pencil (Buck, 1970; Burns & Kaufman, 1972; Hammer, 1997). Scoring systems formulated by psychologists focused on precise indicators in projective drawings, trying to match specific graphic signs with psychiatric symptoms or disorders (Betts, 2006; Gantt, 2004).

Because psychiatric disorders are not homogeneous or static conditions, results from reliability and validity studies of projective drawing techniques were variable. Some studies showed high test-retest or inter-rater reliability for a rating system; others showed poor agreement. Varied results also were characteristic of studies attempting to establish the validity of drawing tests (Brooke, 2004; Feder & Feder, 1998; Handler &

Habenicht, 1994). The lack of evidence for the validity and reliability of projective drawing scoring systems caused Wadeson (2002) to suggest that art therapists abandon the use of formal assessment methods and scoring. Instead, Wadeson admonished art therapists to use their creative abilities to assess clients using informal methods that best suited their immediate and specific needs. Despite advice against doing so from such a strong voice in the field, many art therapists have continued to embrace projective drawing techniques, hopefully heeding cautions about improving scoring systems and making guarded interpretations (Neale & Rosal, 1993). Cautious interpretations based on global characteristics of drawings have demonstrated higher validity correlations than those based on specific graphic indicators (Gantt, 2004; Hammer, 1997; Hinz, Hall, & Lack, 1997; Neale & Rosal, 1993; Oster & Gould Crone, 2004).

Recent research has followed the trend of focusing on global characteristics of drawings—typically on *how* people draw, not *what* they draw. Studies with the Diagnostic Drawing Series (DDS) (Cohen, Mills, & Kijak, 1994; Mills, 2003) and the Person Picking an Apple from a Tree (PPAT) drawing scored with the Formal Elements Art Therapy Scale (FEATS) (Gantt & Tabone, 1998) have shown that the ways clients express themselves visually through formal art elements, such as form quality and color use, show promise as descriptors of clinical states. Both the DDS and the PPAT procedures are based in part on the tradition of art therapy assessment begun by Elinor Ulman, Hanna Kwiatkowska, and Edith Kramer (American Art Therapy Association [AATA], 1975; Junge & Wadeson, 2006). These three art therapy pioneers provided not just pencils, but a variety of art materials for assessments. They drew upon data from a series of artistic expressions, not merely one image. Moreover, they were interested in how their clients reacted in the context of the art therapy assessment, as much as what they created. They paid attention to verbal communication, nonverbal behavior, and attitudes. Along similar lines, Rubin (1984) proposed a diagnostic art interview in which children were given free choice of art materials and assessed over a series of images. In evaluating children, Rubin paid attention to media choices and subject matter as well as to verbal communication, working posture, and attitude toward self and therapist.

In summary, returning to the roots of art therapy assessment helps clinicians remember that the foundation of art assessment should be in the full expression of art, and that a series of images is more representative of an individual than a single image. Additionally, it is prudent to remember that it is most productive and predictive to focus art assessments on describing *how* clients draw—the visual elements included in the expression—rather than on interpreting *what* they draw. It is paramount to understand that drawings provide information about clinical states rather than personality traits, and that descriptive patterns or clusters of characteristics serve this approach (Betts, 2006; Gantt, 2004; Neale & Rosal, 1993). As proposed by Rubin (1984), art assessment can act as a structured interview in which attention is paid to the materials chosen and how they are employed, how clients describe themselves and the process, as well as their levels of commitment and frustration tolerance.

The Expressive Therapies Continuum provides a structure for art therapy assessment that takes into account the variables described above. It suggests an evaluation procedure based in the artistic experience; it provides a range of materials, and assesses a series of art expressions. Assessment within the framework of the ETC focuses on how people process information to form images, and to that end takes into account the formal elements of images, verbal communication, and behavior. It is descriptive of the current clinical state of the client, focusing both on existing positive elements and on challenges.

Assessment With the Expressive Therapies Continuum

As a framework for assessment, the Expressive Therapies Continuum centers on clients' strong points and areas of weakness in information processing. It shows how areas of basic deficit or superior skill are related to clients' experiences of life's difficulties and joys. Assessment using the structure of the ETC can provide suggestions about where to begin a course of therapy, the direction of therapeutic work, and the choice of therapeutic art media. The ETC can indicate steps toward improved functioning and help therapists determine the appropriate time to change course in therapy. The ETC does not provide a "cookbook" approach to assessment or therapy; each client is approached as an individual within this system. The ETC does provide an organized and efficient manner in which to assess client skills and abilities, devise individualized treatment goals, and conduct treatment. This chapter will explore the ways that the ETC can be used to structure art assessment. Chapter 11 will examine the ETC as a framework for formulating goals for treatment and for conducting art-based therapy.

As was mentioned above, traditional art therapy and art-based assessments require that a series of specific tasks be carried out using precisely defined media and methods. Results from assessment procedures such as the DDS and the FEATS have demonstrated correlations between graphic elements of the images produced and diagnostic categories (Gantt & Tabone, 1998; Mills, Cohen, & Meneses, 1993; Munley, 2002). Because of an emphasis on correlating formal art elements with psychiatric diagnoses, these assessment procedures must be carefully conducted, precisely following standard administration procedures.

However, prescribing tasks and media as demanded by formally structured assessments does not allow the freedom necessary to gather information about the preferred level of functioning with the Expressive Therapies Continuum. Clients need to be free to choose materials and tasks in order to demonstrate their true preferences for expression. Therefore, assessment within the framework of the ETC is nonstructured and nondirective in order to give clients choices of materials, tasks, and subject matter. Clients then reveal, through the creative process and the art expression, central facts about their preferred style of operating in the world. These preferences provide information about how clients typically approach new situations in life, and what types of attitudes and abilities can be marshaled to support change.

Assessment of Client Functional Level on the Expressive Therapies Continuum

In order to determine clients' preferred functional level(s) within the Expressive Therapies Continuum, a series of assessment tasks or sessions are carried out. In the first session at least, clients should be provided with free access to a continuum of art media from resistive to fluid, two-dimensional and three-dimensional materials, various sizes and qualities of paper, and appropriate tools for working with each medium. Therapists can introduce those media with which clients are unfamiliar and provide brief instructions for their use. In this way, clients have increased freedom of choice in terms of materials with which to demonstrate their information processing and image formation preferences.

In general, clients should be asked to carry out at least three to five tasks that will form the basis of the assessment (Kaplan, 2003). Three is a minimum number of tasks because three points potentially can reveal a trend. One piece of assessment information is not sufficient data to provide a valid assessment because one sampling could be overly influenced by the situational factors that characterize any new experience, such as nervousness at being in an unusual situation, self-consciousness at being observed, and lack of practice with art materials (Hammer, 1997). Two data points may provide contrasting or incomplete information, but three points can more reliably reveal a trend in direction or strength of preference (Levin, 2004).

Thus, the Expressive Therapies Continuum assessment begins with at least three free art tasks. Depending on time constraints, these can be carried out in one session, or in a series of three sessions. During the assessment session(s), clients are free to choose materials and content. As was mentioned in Chapter 6, free choice of subject matter has been shown to correlate with more personal and meaningful creative products (Ellenbecker, 2003). Given freedom of subject matter, the first expression often relates the most relevant and pressing therapeutic topic. This image often will reoccur near the end of therapy, reflecting resolution of the underlying issue (Lusebrink, 1990).

A free choice of art media likely will lead to the selection of materials that are at least familiar, and at best comfortable. As was discussed in Chapter 9, when materials are comfortable, their use can lead to the experience of "flow," from which a more absorbing creative experience can result (Csikszentmihalyi, 1998). The flow experience is significantly hampered if clients must struggle to master materials. Therefore, suggestions for using unfamiliar materials should be kept to a minimum in the assessment phase. Clients can be encouraged to use those media that are known to them so that time and energy do not have to be expended learning about media at this stage of the therapeutic process.

Information Gathered From Assessment Tasks

While clients are working on assessment art pieces or tasks, therapists should carefully observe their work and discourage client commentary and questions that will distract psychic energy from the creative process. The art tasks represent a sample of responses that provide clues to behaviors, emotions, and cognitions typical of the client at the time of the assessment (Kaplan, 2003). They should be completed without the interference of verbalizations that at times can serve as defenses against the creative process. Clients' descriptions of the expressive experience are gathered at the completion of each art task. Postponing verbal exchanges allows all available psychic energy to be channeled into the expressive tasks (Cohen, Hammer, & Singer, 1988). Other data come from the completed art expressions.

TABLE 10.1   Elements of Art-Based Assessment Using the Expressive Therapies Continuum Framework

Assessment Element	Component Parts
Preferred medium	Media properties
	Strength of preference
	Risk taking
Manner of interaction with medium	Responses to boundaries and limits
	Commitment and frustration tolerance
	Level of energy
	Coping skills
Stylistic or expressive elements of final art product	Developmental level
	Line quality
	Form quality
	Use of space
	Color use
	Integration
	Organic indicators
	Content and symbolism
	Organizing function
Verbal communication	Quality of verbal comments
	Rate and volume of speech
	Logic displayed

Table 10.1 summarizes the types of information gathered in the assessment sessions. In determining clients' preferred level of the Expressive Therapies Continuum, therapists will review the following information gathered over the period of the first three to five art therapy tasks:

1. Preferred medium
2. Manner of interaction with the medium to process information and form images
3. Stylistic or expressive elements of the final art product
4. Verbal communication about the creative process

Preferred Medium

Information about media preferences will provide therapists with evidence regarding clients' inclinations in information processing and structuring images. These clues help therapists decipher what is most salient for clients in decision-making processes and action tendencies. When clients choose similar media over a series of tasks, their preferences for information processing are likely to be unyielding, and may indicate that a certain type is overused, or that other types of input are ignored or repressed. If media preferences change over the series of tasks, therapists must take note of the type and direction of change. Flexibility in gaining access to and processing information from all channels is desirable. Balance in the use of these strategies is a strength and the hallmark of a well-functioning individual (Lusebrink, 1990).

Media Properties and Strength of Preference

As was mentioned in Chapter 1, the more fluid the medium chosen (watercolors, chalk pastels), the more likely a person accesses and uses emotional input when structuring images. If clients predominantly choose paint for the assessment tasks, affective input is likely of primary value in processing information, in the formation of images, and in decision making. The most psychologically healthy people are those who can accurately identify, easily access, and comfortably express their emotions (Burum & Goldfried, 2007; Ekman, 2003). Therefore, easy access to the Affective component of the ETC is an asset. On the other hand, too much emotional involvement can make it difficult for clients to think clearly and will interfere with sound decision making and effective problem solving (Linehan, Bohus, & Lynch, 2007).

The more resistive the choices of medium, the more likely clients are to depend on cognition as the preferred manner of information processing. After evaluation of all data gathered during the assessment phase, it could be concluded that emotion is suppressed or avoided when clients demonstrate a firm preference for resistive media and the Cognitive component. A preference for cognitive functioning can be a positive feature when balanced with other methods. Valued cognitive behaviors include confident memory, effective planning, and efficient problem solving.

If clients consistently select media from the middle of the media properties continuum, their choices can suggest flexibility. As was mentioned above, flexibility in information gathering and processing is a desirable attribute. Generally, more and varied data means a greater number of options for responding. On the other hand, a choice of medium midway between fluid and resistive qualities, such as familiar watercolor markers, could represent a common drawing material not requiring movement from a familiar working zone. If markers were the preferred medium over all assessment sessions, it could be hypothesized that the client did not want to stray from what was well known and comfortable.

Risk Taking

Given free choice of a variety of different media, the choice to work with the same medium over a series of assessment tasks also could expose clients' unwillingness to take risks. Risk avoidance is related to a relatively high level of discomfort with the unknown and unfamiliar. Client discomfort with risk taking also can be related to (1) highlighting potential negative outcomes; (2) perceived low level of competence and control; (3) unwillingness to play, experiment, or reach out; or (4) a high level of self-discipline and not knowing how to play (Maner & Schmidt, 2006). Careful questioning about media choices and preferences can help provide clues to motivation for persisting with the familiar or experimenting with the untried and unknown.

Those who avoid risk due to high levels of anxiety or fear must be gently guided into using unfamiliar ETC processes. The issues of risk taking and risk avoidance in decision-making processes can be addressed as part of the therapeutic process. One goal of therapy is to help clients actively experience risk taking in this safe environment, so that they begin to gather and process information through all channels. Using various media types is one way to help ensure that all components are available for use. Risk taking later can be generalized to other areas of life. Clients who spontaneously experiment with various and unknown media demonstrate an adventurous attitude; for these clients, risk taking is a strength that can be built upon to enhance therapeutic gains.

Manner of Interaction With Media to Process Information and Form Images

Assessment within the context of the ETC requires as much attention to the behaviors of clients interacting with media as it does to the images themselves. The ways in which clients use art materials to form images will demonstrate their predominant organizing processes in operation during information processing, in response to boundaries and limits, and in their level of commitment to the task. In addition, the manner of interaction with art materials gives a window for viewing clients' levels of energy applied to tasks, as well as coping skills employed in unfamiliar situations. All of the above factors help to flesh out a picture of the individual client and his or her action tendencies in life. Clients express their preferred component functioning almost regardless of the type of media used. As an example, paint can be used in a perceptual manner with emphasis on the precise outlines of forms, or it can be used in a fluid manner with emphasis on the expression of emotion. Other media also can be used in various ways demonstrative of component processing preferences.

Responses to Boundaries and Limits
Clients' knowledge of when to stop the creative process is one kind of boundary or limit that therapists attend to in the assessment phase. Other types of limits are determined by the size of paper used and the amount of medium applied. In general, larger papers contain greater amounts of thoughts, ideas, and emotions. Clients who are more expansive use larger pieces of paper and more supplies. Expansiveness can be related to a preference for the Affective dimension of the Expressive Therapies Continuum. Alternatively, some clients will choose smaller paper and use lesser amounts of materials to convey meaning. Constricted interaction with boundaries usually points to avoidance of affective input and expression. Clients ordinarily respect the physical boundaries of the paper; they create within the confines imposed by the edges. If they do not, and their drawings extend over the edges of the paper, it may be hypothesized that cognitive information processing strategies are impaired (Lusebrink, 1990).

Commitment and Frustration Tolerance
Much can be learned about clients' level of commitment to themselves and the learning process of therapy through observing their commitment to the art tasks and their level of frustration tolerance. Clients who quickly quit a task when frustrated reveal, through their low level of frustration tolerance, a tendency to act out in an emotional manner, indicating an emphasis on the Affective component. On the other hand, clients can persist too long in a task, agonizing about how to determine when work is complete. Often images are spoiled or even obscured by overthinking and overworking as clients continue to add "finishing touches." Overthinking and overworking can demonstrate overuse of cognitive information processing and a lack of faith in perceptual (trusting how the image looks) or affective (trusting how it feels) processing.

A well-balanced person integrates information from several ETC components to inform decisions about commitment to a project. Information from the kinesthetic channel provides physical feedback and the answer to the question "Has adequate tension been released?" Perceptual feedback helps determine the question "Does the image look the way I wanted it to look?" Feedback from the Symbolic component answers the question "Is it meaningfully symbolic to me?" The Affective component informs the question "How do I feel about the expression and the process?" The more processes actively recruited into the therapeutic session, the more likely the experience will be rewarding on some level, and not frustrating. This reward will activate commitment to the current session as well as to subsequent therapeutic sessions.

Level of Energy
Clients put forth effort and energy on a continuum from very low to very high, and energy expended correlates with the level of commitment clients demonstrate in attempting to work through difficulties. One would expect a well-functioning individual to demonstrate high levels of energy and commitment in order to see a task through to completion. A high level of energy would be viewed as a client asset associated with interest and internal motivation. Extremes of these variables suggest inappropriate use of the Affective and Kinesthetic components of the Expressive Therapies Continuum. A high level of energy coupled with a low level of commitment could indicate expression with the Kinesthetic component of the ETC, and perhaps point to a diagnosis of attention-deficit/hyperactivity disorder (AD/HD). Low levels of energy and commitment would indicate a blocked Affective component or a diagnosis of depression.

Gantt and Tabone (1998) have shown that the level of implied energy in PPAT drawings of adult psychiatric patients is significantly correlated with depression and bipolar illness. Decreased implied energy has been correlated with major depressive disorder; high levels of implied energy have been correlated with bipolar disorder, hypomanic phase. These examples support the proposal that details from interaction with the media can provide important clues to information processing styles.

Coping Skills
From their manner of interaction with the materials during the creative process, clients offer evidence about how they approach unfamiliar tasks in life. Often clients have not used art media for many years, and thus the materials are novel and the assessment tasks foreign to them (Kaplan, 2003). Therapists can gauge clients' types of coping skills and their flexibility from the amount of energy and commitment they bring to bear in the unfamiliar situation, the level of frustration tolerance demonstrated,

and the manner in which they make decisions and respect the boundaries and limitations of the materials and tasks (Matto, Corcoran, & Fassler, 2003). A woman in an art therapy group explained that she made a mistake while creating an image and she wanted to throw it away. After some thought, she did not dispose of the paper, but chose to rework the image. She explained that giving in to frustration would represent her "old way" of approaching problems. She wanted to respond differently, so she chose to revise the picture until the image was pleasing to her. Her success in modifying her old way of responding demonstrated flexibility of coping skills.

Stylistic or Expressive Elements of the Final Art Product

Expressive elements, or formal elements of visual expression, include components such as developmental level, line and form quality, use of space, color use, organic indicators, and content and symbolism. Relationships have been demonstrated between elements of artistic expression and various personality characteristics or diagnostic categories (Cohen, Mills, & Kijak, 1994; Gantt & Tabone, 1998; Ulman & Levy, 1973). Within the framework of the Expressive Therapies Continuum, these elements offer indications about dominant organizing functions. Each feature just listed will be examined individually in the following sections, and the information will be integrated and summarized.

Developmental Level

Chapter 1 introduced the concept that the Expressive Therapies Continuum represents a developmental hierarchy. Information processing and image formation develop from simple Kinesthetic/Sensory dealings to the complex workings of the Cognitive/Symbolic level. Stylistic features from final art products can indicate clients' developmental level and the preferred ETC component. These details are especially salient if they differ from that which would be expected given client age and level of education (Malchiodi, Kim, & Choi, 2003; Oster & Gould Crone, 2004; Simon, 1992).

Expressions on the Kinesthetic/Sensory level are indicative of the scribble stage of graphic development. In the scribble stage, art materials often are used for their sensory qualities or as passive facilitators of action. Children incorporate sensorimotor feedback as a significant source of learning. The art product itself is frequently not as important as the action involved in creation. Clients who are capable of fully formed visual images may engage in Kinesthetic/Sensory activities in a regression to an earlier stage of development as a way of conveying primary material. When clients are at an age where a higher level of graphic development is expected but not achieved, hypotheses are generated about the interfering presence of conditions such as mental retardation, dysgraphia, AD/HD, or resistance to the art process. Images created on the Perceptual/Affective level of the ETC are characteristic of the schematic stage of graphic development, where the emphasis is on the formal elements of visual expression or form deviations due to affective influences. At the Cognitive/Symbolic level, one can expect graphic representations from the schematic through the naturalistic and adolescent stages. Drawings can be used to visually communicate complex thoughts and ideas, humor, irony, and significant symbolism.

Line and Form Quality

Fine details and carefully shaped forms—those requiring thought, precision, and planning—generally are indicative of a preference for the Cognitive component. An emphasis on the formal elements, such as form, line, space, and color in the visual expression, would suggest that perceptual functioning was the dominant mode of information processing (Lusebrink, 1990). Distorted forms, overemphasis on some parts of forms, or disappearance of details indicate functioning with the Affective component of the ETC (Gantt & Talbone, 1998; Kramer, 1975b). In addition, affective influence in the form of anxiety is suggested by heavy shading (Hammer, 1997; Koppitz, 1968). Poor line quality can be associated with overinvolvement with the Kinesthetic component (Gantt & Tabone, 1998; Munley, 2002).

Use of Space

The use of space in the final image also can suggest preferred information processing and image formation strategies. Most people use two-thirds of the page in order to create a picture (Oster & Gould Crone, 2004; Ulman & Levy, 1975). Greater use of space is indicative of the overuse of the Affective component, as would be seen in mania. Using very little space and creating tiny figures would be indicative of greater perceptual information processing and lower affective expression, as in major depressive disorder (Gantt & Tabone, 1998; Hammer, 1997). Space use also can correlate with kinesthetic dominance, if the paper were covered with markings due to increased movement and level of energy. Where Perceptual or Cognitive component processes are central, space usage is likely strategically planned and well executed. The use of space where sensory or symbolic processes are dominant is likely to be unremarkable, as sensuousness or symbolism are primary in the experience.

Color Use

As was demonstrated in Chapter 6, color use is correlated with the evocation of emotion. In art assessment, color use is associated with emotional involvement in several ways. Depression has been correlated both with the use of dark colors and with the absence of color (Gantt & Tabone, 1998; Hammer, 1997; Wadeson, 1980). Hammer has noted that when presented with crayons for use, the most "emotionally avoidant" persons tended to use them like pencils, with no coloring in, and to opt for dark colors, such as black, brown, or blue. Persons in the hypomanic phase of bipolar disorder typically use a great deal of color in their drawings; many and varied colors are used and color fills the page (Gantt & Tabone, 1998).

Color changes and color fit are two other variables to be examined when considering color use in assessment. Important emotional shifts in therapy can be indicated by changes in the colors used in children's drawings (Gregorian, Azarian, DeMaria, & McDonald, 1996). In general, cool colors such as blue are associated with internalizing tendencies, and warm colors such as red with externalizing qualities and behavior (Elliot, Maier, Moller, Friedman, & Meinhardt, 2007; Hauschka, 1985). Gantt and Tabone (1998) have shown that reduced cognitive processes are associated with idiosyncratic uses of color. Bizarre color combinations are seen in schizophrenia, probably related to psychotic thought processes. Visual expressions of persons suffering from organic mental disorders such as delirium and dementia show lack of color fit, which is defined as colors not related to the items depicted.

Organic Indicators

Cognitive impairment characterized by memory loss and reduced executive functioning occurs in many elderly clients (Stewart, 2006; Wald, 2003). Formal drawing tests such as the Bender Gestalt Test, various projective drawings, and informal assessments have been used to determine the presence of organic mental disorders (Hammer, 1997; Koppitz, 1969, 1975; Stewart, 2006; Wald, 2003). In general, drawings by patients with dementia and delirium demonstrate deficits in graphic abilities to integrate information and depict realism. Other organic indicators include inappropriate rotations, simplification, fragmentation, and perseveration (Gantt & Tabone, 1998; Hammer, 1997, Koppitz, 1975; Wald, 1984, 2003).

Content and Symbolism

The above factors, including developmental level, line and form quality, use of space and color, and organic indicators, are concerned with *how* people draw, and can perhaps be considered objective signs obtained from stylistic or expressive elements. The last type of information available from art products concerns *what* people draw. This type of information is more subjective because it derives from the content and symbolism of the subject matter. The subjective nature of art content stems from the fact that viewers project their own understanding onto images that, of course, may differ from the conscious intentions of the creator.

Art therapists can be equally liable to project their own thoughts and feelings onto drawings, and are trained to recognize and alter this tendency. Clients are the foremost authorities on their own images and should be the first to provide information about the content and symbolism included in them. On the other hand, therapists should not become so conservative in their approach to client imagery that they forget their education has provided them with knowledge of symbolism that can be used to reveal subject matter to reluctant clients. The evaluation of content and symbolism necessitates a careful balance of client-provided information and therapist input as needed to clarify and crystallize meaning (Hinz, 2008; McConeghey, 2003).

Organizing Functions

An organizing function represents the way a person typically gathers and processes information to form images, and these correspond to the six components of the Expressive Therapies Continuum. Stylistic features of the art expressions have been discussed separately above; this section attempts to integrate the data and to provide a more complete picture of strengths and weaknesses with each preferred component, as well as to describe the area of creative transition. Lusebrink (V. B. Lusebrink, personal communication, March 3, 2008) created Table 10.2 to describe the cardinal characteristics and strengths of visual expression on different levels of the ETC, as well as pathological variations, such as overuse or underuse of each component. In addition, the table describes the qualities of expression to be expected at the area where the two bipolar components meet: the creative transition area. As can be seen from the information in Table 10.2, in well-functioning individuals, the integration of information from each component is seen as a strength. For example, the integration of affect into an image is an asset in that it helps produce emotionally expressive forms.

TABLE 10.2   Predominant Characteristics of Visual Expressions of Expressive Therapies Continuum Levels

K = Kinesthetic level: Emphasis on kinesthetic expressions and action	CRk-s = Creative transition area	S = Sensory level: Emphasis on sensations and sensory exploration
Kx = Psychopathological variations		Sx = Psychopathological variations
Kx ⇦	CRk-s	⇨ Sx
	K ⇦ CRk-s ⇨ S	
Rhythm as integration	Dynamic kinesthetic expression with concurrent sensory feedback	*Sensory integration*
Agitated scribbles		Overabsorption in sensory experience
Agitated throwing	Scribbling	Stillness or very slow movements
Disregard of limits	Stabbing	
Destruction of materials	Daubing	Avoidance of sensory experience
	Sensory exploration of materials and textures	Lack of sensory integration
Poor line quality	Rolling	
Disregard of line	Sensory exploration of surfaces	Extreme sensory sensitivity
Increased space use		

continued

TABLE 10.2 (continued)   Predominant Characteristics of Visual Expressions on Different Levels of the Expressive Therapies Continuum

| P = Perceptual level: Emphasis on form expression | | CRp-a = Creative transition area | | A = Affective level: Emphasis on affective and individual images |
| Px = Psychopathological variations | | | | Ax = Psychopathological variations |
Px ⇔	P ⇔	CRp-a	⇔ A	⇔ Ax
	Perceptual integration	Good or complex gestalts	*Affective integration*	Disintegration of color
Geometrization of forms	Form predominance	Color-enlivened forms	Open forms	Disintegration of form
Stereotypical images		Abstract or reality oriented	Aesthetic ordering of forms	Dynamic outlines
Incomplete forms				Agitated forms
Poorly integrated forms	Line/shape mixture	Dynamic/forms	Incomplete outlines	Affective images as hallucinations
Perseveration of forms	Shape variations	Involvement in expression	Schema variations	Large forms
Predominance of outlines	Gestalt variations		Overlapping forms	Overtly clashing colors
Overemphasis on details	Differentiation of details		Color use predominant	More space used
Very small forms		Descriptive use of color		
Minimal use of color	Adequate use of space		Affectively expressive forms	
Decreased use of space				

C = Cognitive level: Emphasis on symbolic expression Cx = Psychopathological variations		CRc-sy = Creative transition area		Sy = Symbolic level: Emphasis on cognitive operations Syx = Psychopathological variations
Cx ⇔	**C** ⇔	**CRc-sy**	⇔ **Sy**	⇔ **Syx**
	Cognitive integration		*Integrative symbolism*	
Loss of conceptual meaning	Concept formation	Intuitive problem solving	Symbolic meaning	Overidentification with symbols
Surface structure disintegration	Objective meaning	Self-discovery	Symbolic relationships between forms	Idiosyncratic symbolism
Illogical or incomplete relations between forms	Spatial integration	Spiritual search	Intuitive concept formation	Obscure symbolism
Spatial disintegration	Abstractions	Self-acceptance	Subjective meaning	Symbolic perceptions of reality
Obscure abstractions	Problem solving		Self-searching	Symbols as defenses
Rigid structures	Word inclusion			
Overuse of words	Stepwise planning			
Extreme poverty of images	Cognitive maps			
	Pictographs			

Note: The examples provided in this table are only descriptive of the particular components of the ETC and are not meant to be all-inclusive or exclusive.

Kinesthetically dominant people are movement oriented, prone to using media as facilitators of action. A free choice assessment session likely will be dominated by acting or doing: daubing paint, scribbling, and drawing with dynamic lines. The actions involved in the process typically are more therapeutically meaningful than the final art expressions. Kinesthetic dominance can be a strength when it provides a tension-relieving vent for stress or an aid in the integration of a healing rhythm. When kinesthetic action is overused, art products show poor line quality (Munley, 2002) or a disregard for limits (Gantt & Talbone, 1998). Kinesthetic functioning can be a challenge when unfocused action blocks image formation, inhibits project completion, or contributes to the destruction of images.

When the Sensory component is dominant, clients will embrace sensuous responding to art materials. Clients can become caught up in textures, aromas, or sights. An interesting sound made by the incidental use of a material may be repeated for the sheer pleasure of listening. Similar to the kinesthetic dominant experience, the final art product usually is secondary to the process of experiencing the materials themselves. The ability to integrate sensory information into decision-making and problem-solving activities is a benefit. The sensory-dominant person can be highly sensitive to internal and external stimuli, capable of experiencing tremendous beauty and uniquely rich and creative synesthesia experiences (Ackerman, 1991). Alternatively, the sensory-dominant person risks being overwhelmed by unfamiliar, multiple, or noxious stimuli (Aron, 1996; Zeff, 2004). Extreme overinvolvement in sensory experiences or difficulties with sensory integration can lead to difficulties with behavior regulation, self-absorption, and poor interpersonal relationships (Miller, 2006).

The person for whom the Affective component is dominant has open access to emotions. Emotions serve as appropriate signals to action; they are acknowledged, understood, and expressed. In a free choice assessment session, the affectively dominant person would be drawn to colorful and fluid media. Colorful paint or pastels facilitate emotional expression. In addition to the predominant use of color, characteristics of the image would include schema variations, as well as open and overlapping forms. Forms are used for affective communication: they are dynamic and expressive. With excessive affective functioning one notices greater space use, the agitated use of form, and large or looming forms (Gantt & Talbone, 1998; Lusebrink, 1990; Simon, 1992). When Affect is the central organizing factor in expression, colors may clash and forms disintegrate, at times compromising meaningful expression.

When Perceptual is the influential component, one notices emphasis on the formal elements of visual expression. As can be seen in Table 10.2, form would dominate images, and if color were used, it would describe or delineate form. Images could be either abstract or reality oriented, and they would be characterized by shape variations and differentiation of details. Perceptual integration would be noted with adequate use of space. In extreme underuse of the Perceptual dimension, perceptual integration diminishes. In addition, one would see incomplete forms, decreased use of space, and lack of details. These features are characteristic of organic mental disorders such as dementia (Gantt & Tabone, 1998; Koppitz, 1975; Wald, 1984, 2003). In the pathological extreme, overuse of the Perceptual component, geometric forms predominate. Drawings exhibit small forms, overemphasis on details, and perseveration (Gantt & Talbone, 1998).

Images created in the creative transition area of the Perceptual/Affective level are dynamic and expressive. They demonstrate good or complex gestalts and are both aesthetically ordered and emotionally impactful. This area of expression acts as a bridge between the two components; it is where the most effective artistic expression on this level of the ETC transpires.

The creation of images by a cognitive-dominant person would reveal spatial integration, stepwise planning, and problem solving. These characteristics reflect the involvement of the frontal cortex and the brain's executive functions, as discussed in Chapter 7. Cognitive dominance can be a weakness when overuse promotes adherence to rigid structures, or when excessive word use interferes with image formation. Illogical or incomplete spatial relationships, loss of conceptual meaning, and extreme poverty of image would be characteristic of underuse of cognitive processes. These manifestations of reduced cognitive functioning are seen in organic disorders and schizophrenia (Gantt & Talbone, 1998; Lusebrink, 1990).

The person for whom the Symbolic component is the primary organizing principle often thinks and communicates in metaphoric images and language. Symbolic processing can be a strength when it promotes self-searching, realization and appreciation of connections between diverse cultures, as well as connections between common elements of the past, present, and future. Deep connectedness to symbols is confirmed in assessment through the selection of collage materials that allow the demonstration of associations with archetypal figures, the symbolic use of color, and implied meaning. In its extreme manifestation, the symbolically involved client remains preoccupied with idiosyncratic or obscure symbols or uses symbols as defenses.

The search for meaning and purpose supported by solid symbolic processing, when combined with superior problem-solving skills from the Cognitive component, leads to intuitive problem solving. Individuals produce images of self-discovery and spiritual searching at the creative transition area between the two poles of the Cognitive/Symbolic level. Often words cannot describe the sort of experiences that occur; the ultimate in creative expression at this level would be acceptance of new information about the self.

It is not always the case that a single organizing process is strongly dominant. The well-functioning person demonstrates facile and integrated use of all or a majority of the ETC components. In addition, intellectual level or artistic training can distort information garnered from a free art assessment (Ulman & Levy, 1975). Persons with artistic training will show mastery of materials and subject matter that alter common interpretations. A trained artist will likely show preferences for a variety of media, for a newly mastered material, or a rediscovered old favorite. This flexibility of expression can be related to exposure and experience, or equally to information processing preferences. When discerning the primary organizing function, it must be kept in mind that the organizing principle is the form of information processing that the client finds most comfortable and familiar. *Discovering the primary organizing function does not correspond to assigning a diagnosis.* Information about the dominant organizing process can inform a psychiatric diagnosis, but it is not equivalent to it.

Verbal Communication

The fact that verbal communication is a determining factor in assessment means that drawings should be collected only when the administrator is present, and drawings should not be interpreted "blindly" (Hammer, 1997; Kaplan, 2003; Oster & Gould Crone, 2004). When the administrator is present with the client during the assessment phase, a whole host of information is available from verbal communication. Discussion following creation, or postdrawing inquiry, will include query regarding feelings experienced during the creative activity, associations to the images, and meanings of the expression. Further, the preferred manner of expression may be revealed verbally, indicative of the various components of the Expressive Therapies Continuum. As was mentioned previously, discussion during the expressive experience should not be encouraged; available psychic energy should be concentrated on the task rather than on talking. Nevertheless, all comments made during assessment should be noted and clarified in the postdrawing inquiry. Features of verbalizations to be observed include quality of speech, including self-talk and comments addressed to the examiner, rate and volume of speech, and logic displayed in communications with the self and examiner (Rubin, 1984; Matto, Corcoran, & Fassler, 2003).

During inquiry, clients have the least difficulty discussing those processes that are associated with left-hemisphere abilities: cognitive, perceptual, and kinesthetic. As noted in Table 10.2, cognitive processes frequently include words that are readily expanded upon in verbal description. Talking about elements of visual expression facilitates the discussion of perceptual experiences. Clients normally find it effortless to discuss the action-oriented nature of kinesthetic functioning. In contrast, clients seldom find words adequate to describe the right-hemisphere-dominated processes: sensory, affective, and symbolic. The counselor using art in therapy must be confident that words are not always necessary when creative activity is involved. A creative experience can be therapeutic even when clients do not find words to describe it (Lusebrink, 1990; McNiff, 1998).

Quality of Verbal Comments
The types of remarks that clients make to themselves and to the administrator provide clues to their preferred level of information processing and image formation on the Expressive Therapies Continuum. What clients say about themselves, the assessment process, and their final expression can, for example, demonstrate an inclination for sensory processing if they focus on how the materials feel in their hands. Clients also might concentrate on how the materials smell or the striking visual impact that they make (Evans & Dubowski, 2001). Alternatively, a kinesthetic predilection would be demonstrated by concentrated attention to and pleasure in the movement aspects of the experience. Kinesthetically involved clients sometimes prefer to stand and move about freely rather than sit down to work. These clients would center the experience on the release of energy through movement.

An affective focus would be demonstrated by attention to the emotional aspects of the self, the process, or the product. Comments would underscore the feelings experienced by clients during the creative process or evoked by the final product. Clients at times deride themselves for their lack of abilities, or disparage the final product, for it not being what they imagined it would be. Further, the affectively dominated person would express emotions clearly without words during the assessment session. A preference for perceptual functioning would be shown through an emphasis on the formal elements of visual expression.

A cognitive penchant could be demonstrated in a number of ways. Clients can show their consideration of planning and envisioning a task by talking to themselves or the therapist about the steps required to execute the image. Those for whom cognitive processing is overused frequently focus more on talking than on making images. The quality of this speech could include rationalizing about their artistic abilities, intellectualizing about the process of art making, or denying the importance of carrying through with the project. The use of these types of verbal defense mechanisms by clients reveals that cognitive processes are more comfortable than the action-oriented tasks required in the art assessment. Conversely, impaired cognitive processing is seen through deficits in executive functions, such as planning, organizing, and sequencing, as is seen in various forms of dementia (Stewart, 2006).

Clients who prefer working with the Symbolic component of the Expressive Therapies Continuum would demonstrate this inclination by showing their interest in and affinity for symbolic implications and meanings of the images. Additionally, persons who speak in metaphorical language certainly are processing information comfortably with the Symbolic component. A depressed client referred to herself as a "conduit" and easily drew the pipe-like structure that allowed good things, such as advice and spiritual direction, to pass through her to other people, but did not allow positive elements to remain and nourish her sense of self-esteem. Metaphorical language and self-symbols continuously appeared in the assessment sessions; this was a person for whom rich imagery and symbolism were essential for successful art therapy.

Rate and Volume of Speech

Quality of verbal comments also includes information about the rate and volume of speech, which can give clues to information processing strategies. Slow, deliberate speech can be indicative of dominant thought processes characteristic of the Cognitive component of the Expressive Therapies Continuum. Qualities of speech also can be indicative of involvement with the Affective component. Rapid and loud speech or excessive talkativeness would likely be indicative of bipolar disorder, hypomanic or manic phase (American Psychiatric Association [APA], 2000). Another indicator would be pressured speech accompanied by flight of ideas, demonstrated through rapid changes in unrelated subject matter. Depression would be demonstrated by quiet, tearful speech, and lack of spontaneous speech, as was illustrated in the case example discussed in Chapter 6.

Logic Displayed

Certain types of communication difficulties are characterized by lack of logic in verbalizations. Impaired logic can be a sign of deteriorating brain function, as seen in dementia or psychotic disorders (APA, 2000; Wald, 2003). The quality of logic as displayed through speech in most psychotic disorders is characterized as incoherence or disorganization. Poverty of speech and an inability to explain oneself logically have also been identified as characteristics of psychotic disorders (APA, 2000; Gantt & Talbone, 1998). Logic and language deficits, as well as other signs of impaired cognitive functioning, also are demonstrated in the case of delirium (APA, 2000). The FEATS contains a scoring category for logic displayed in the execution of the PPAT drawing (Gantt & Talbone, 1998). Although this quality refers to the visual elements of the drawing, in discussing the drawing the logic usually is evident, and thus can be assessed through verbal communication.

Preferences for processing information will not always be demonstrated fully and completely through verbal communication. This is just one method of obtaining information during the assessment phase. In addition, there likely will be overlap between components of the Expressive Therapies Continuum, as expression occurs on different levels and with various components. However, the presence of strong preferences will offer ideas about therapeutic directions.

Case Example

A 15-year-old Hispanic girl suffering from anorexia nervosa demonstrated an initial preference for cognitive information processing through her choice of materials, the strength of that preference, and a low level of risk taking. She chose to work with collage materials over the course of 8 to 10 biweekly art therapy sessions without deviation from this preference. Collage materials are conceptualized as engaging cognitive information processing because of the complex thought processes involved in identifying, selecting, and arranging words and images.

Her manner of interaction with the materials showed a great deal of persistence and commitment, a high level of frustration tolerance, and an interesting interaction with boundaries. This young girl carefully cut images to fit the entire page without leaving any of the background paper exposed.

Hammer (1997) mentioned that when clients consistently create images that test the boundaries of the page, they are experiencing constraints from external limitations and feel a need to overcompensate for this restriction. This confrontation of boundaries was one indication that emotions, which needed expression, were occurring beneath the obvious cognitive control. In addition, the girl used tape instead of glue to affix the images to her background paper, demonstrating an avoidance of the sensory input that would be evoked by the sticky substance. It was hypothesized that sensory input would have called forth the emotions that she was trying to avoid with her intense focus on cognitive information processing.

Stylistic elements from the collages themselves also indicated a preference for cognitive information processing. The number of words outweighed the number of pictures used in the final images. However, the messages of the collages and the words that the girl spoke to herself and the therapist as she created again showed a great deal of emotion under the surface. The collages spoke of a Eurocentric beauty ideal and the supermodel-thin body, perhaps what this large-framed Hispanic girl knew was for her an unobtainable goal. The words that she spoke to the art therapist emphasized her disappointment that she was not what she saw in the myriad fashion magazines she surrounded herself with and out of which she created her collages. Elements of the assessment are summarized in Table 10.3. Results of the assessment revealed that the young girl was almost exclusively using, and definitely overemphasizing, cognitive information processing to avoid affective stimulation.

Summary

Assessment within the structure of the Expressive Therapies Continuum begins with a series of tasks or sessions to determine clients' functional level, or most comfortable approach to processing information. This point frequently becomes the targeted starting point for expressive therapy experiences. The types of information attended to in the assessment phase include preferred media, manner of interaction with media to process information and form images, stylistic or expressive elements in the final art product, and verbal communication during the creative process. All of these elements are surveyed and information compiled in order to formulate hypotheses about typical approaches to information processing, decision making, and action tendencies. Knowledge of these factors aids in the formulation of treatment goals and treatment planning.

TABLE 10.3   Assessment of Preferred Component of Expressive Therapies Continuum by 15-Year-Old Hispanic Female Client

Assessment Element	Component Parts
Preferred medium	Collage
	Strong preference over 8–10 sessions
	Low risk taking
Manner of interaction with medium	Precision with scissors
	Precise interaction with boundaries of paper
	High level of commitment
	High level of frustration tolerance
	Avoids sensory stimulation by using tape
Stylistic or expressive elements of final art product	Adolescent collage topic
	Precise alignment
	More words than images
	Negative content
	All available space used
Verbal communication	Negative comments about self
	Disappointment expressed about not meeting Eurocentric beauty standard

11

Individual Interventions

Introduction to Therapeutic Intervention With the Expressive Therapies Continuum

Therapists conceptualize the beneficial actions and effects of creative expression in many different ways. The use of art in therapy has been characterized as helping challenge and change problematic thoughts and behaviors (Rosal, 2001; Steele, 2003). Art can illuminate difficulties and help children learn skills (Safran, 2003). Viewed from a psychoanalytic perspective, art can quickly and effectively bring unconscious conflicts to the surface and aid in their working through (Naumburg, 1966; Wilson, 1987). Jungian approaches to therapy employ artistic expression to help integrate feared or rejected archetypal contents and to eliminate complexes (Edwards, 1987; Wallace, 1987). Regardless of their theoretical orientation, all therapists have to choose the most appropriate art materials and expressive methods to use with each client. Art therapy students often ask for techniques with which to help their clients, but what is more important is a theoretical framework from which to choose appropriate materials and methods (Wadeson, 1980). The Expressive Therapies Continuum can guide these critical healing decisions.

Art-based therapies have been used with the majority of psychiatric disorders (Malchiodi, 2003a). Children and adolescents, adults, and elders have been treated successfully with art therapy in schools, hospitals, nursing homes, and prisons, among other locations (Malchiodi, 1998). Image making can be a way to approach immigrant and minority clients for whom language and culture can make verbal psychotherapy intimidating or impossible (Berkowitz, 2007; Henderson & Gladding,

1998). Regardless of client age, ethnicity, or venue, therapists using art expression must find a way to initiate and maintain a nonthreatening and productive visual dialogue with their clients. This dialogue can be structured within the Expressive Therapies Continuum to enhance understanding and communication about treatment goals, to formulate interventions, to promote therapeutic progress, and to facilitate the termination of therapy.

An art therapy graduate student recently told me about her experience listening to a presentation at the American Art Therapy Association conference. She attended a presentation in which the speaker, a registered art therapist, lamented the fact that she had spent five months working with a client in a trial-and-error fashion before hitting upon an effective therapeutic strategy. The student commented that she asked the presenter if she knew about the Expressive Therapies Continuum, and the presenter said she had heard of it. The student went on to tell me that she thought if the therapist had employed knowledge of the ETC in her work, the presenter would not have spent such a long time working in a hit-or-miss manner before finding a helpful intervention. I believe the student was correct, and that this occurrence is not an isolated one. Without a theoretical framework to guide them, therapists often struggle to find an effective therapeutic strategy.

After assessment guided by the Expressive Therapies Continuum, therapists will have a good idea as to clients' preferred method of information processing and image formation. Assessment findings can point toward client strengths and challenges, potentially blocked components, and overused functions. Knowledge gained through assessment guides treatment planning. As has been previously mentioned, well-functioning individuals have balanced access to all ETC component functions (Lusebrink, 1990). Information can be gathered, processed, and executed through all channels. The ETC can help clinicians conceptualize treatment strategies that include making connections between previously blocked component processes to increase options for resourceful action, opening the client to underused functions to improve flexibility in thought, emotion, and action, and reducing overdependence on any one kind of component function that restricts emotional, behavioral, or cognitive options. The ETC provides a method of formulating therapeutic objectives that includes where to begin in therapy, how to create individualized interventions, and possible directions for treatment.

Formulating Treatment Goals Within the Framework of the Expressive Therapies Continuum

Determining a Starting Place for Therapy

Following assessment, therapists will understand with which Expressive Therapies Continuum component(s) clients are most comfortable. This knowledge provides a starting place for psychotherapeutic intervention. Clients should begin working in therapy with the most comfortable component and gradually be introduced to other information processing and image formation strategies. Starting therapy where clients are familiar will reduce anxiety, raise clients' comfort level, and increase clients' trust and confidence in both the therapist and the process of therapy. Art therapists, like the one in the earlier example, often begin therapy in the manner they *think* would be most beneficial, or in a manner with which they are very comfortable, rather than where the *client* is most comfortable. Time and energy are wasted waiting to stumble upon a productive intervention. When therapists assess clients using the structure of the ETC, they appreciate their clients' preferences, and achieve an accurate idea of an initially helpful component process.

Therapy is a practice requiring a balance between experiencing what is known and comfortable, and venturing into the feared unknown (Cozolino, 2002). Clients must feel some degree of control over the material divulged in therapy, alternating with uncertainty about the direction and nature of the therapeutic work. The interplay between familiarity and the unidentified, between control and uncertainty creates tension that prompts therapeutic progress. Using art materials usually is stressful due to its unfamiliarity. Therefore, clients' feelings of control in an already stressful situation can be enhanced by beginning therapy with the most comfortable ETC component process. For example, an individual who, during assessment, created images with pencil would work best with pencil in the initial therapy sessions. If first asked to use paint, distress caused by the fluidity, color, and emotionally evocative properties of the medium would possibly outweigh any therapeutic benefits for the client. When provided with familiar materials and processes with which to begin work, clients are more likely to feel in control and relax into the therapeutic process. After some experience in therapy, movement to a different medium or component process can be undertaken.

Establishing a Client-Therapist Partnership

The Expressive Therapies Continuum offers a framework for including clients as active partners in deciding upon objectives for treatment. A partnership between client and therapist helps increase rapport with the therapist and trust in the therapeutic process (Knapp & VandeCreek, 2006). Client involvement is especially vital when using art materials and expressive processes in therapy. In order to increase trust and promote client wholehearted investment in the use of art, clients should be involved in decision making about the therapeutic process and should understand enough about the Expressive Therapies Continuum to participate meaningfully in the formulation of treatment goals. Explaining the ways in which people process information not only to form images, but also to make decisions and solve problems, can be a way to engage clients in thinking about and carrying through their desired goals for treatment. In addition, when clients fully understand why and how they are engaging in therapeutic creativity, they are more likely to continue to use the creative process after the termination of therapy (Curtis, 2006; Hinz, 2006).

Clients with similar diagnoses will not always benefit from similar treatment strategies because different underlying Expressive Therapies Continuum functions can be dominant even within a similar diagnostic category. Therefore, treatment goals clearly articulated within the context of the ETC will be specific to the individual. For example, a client diagnosed with major depressive disorder can operate predominantly with the Cognitive component of the Expressive Therapies Continuum, as was true for the client described in the case example in Chapter 10. This client required many sessions of cognitively oriented therapy before she was able to work in a more emotionally expressive fashion with the Affective component. The client, named Carla, introduced in Chapter 5, also was diagnosed with major depressive disorder, but demonstrated a preference for the Affective component. Therapy with Carla required moving away from emotionally evocative expression toward containment with perceptual processes.

Involving clients in creating goals for therapy increases the transparency of the process; therapists perhaps are better able to explain, and clients better able to understand, the healing properties of the art process and product when they must actively work together to define therapeutic goals. Transparency is especially important when using art in therapy, as clients often voice the fear that their drawings will be "analyzed" in a way that is mysterious to them, and that places the therapist in a position of untenable power. Partnership equalizes power in the therapeutic relationship; it increases levels of trust in the therapist and the therapeutic process. Involving clients in the formulation of treatment goals also reduces the likelihood of withdrawal from treatment prior to successful completion (Knapp & VandeCreek, 2006).

Conceptualizing Treatment Guided by the Expressive Therapies Continuum

Initiating Art-Based Treatment

The Expressive Therapies Continuum provides an outline of basic information processing strategies that must be connected, augmented, or reduced in frequency of use. Therapy begins with the most comfortable component process, and treatment proceeds by making connections between blocked functions, increasing underused functions, and controlling overused processes. Additionally, therapy highlights the importance of component process strengths. These goals can be reached by increasing emphasis on the underused pole of a bipolar ETC level, or by focusing on an emergent function that prompts expression on a higher ETC level.

Chapters 3 to 10 include case examples that demonstrate how therapy can be conducted within the context of the Expressive Therapies Continuum. The goals in each case were to teach and reinforce functioning where it previously was not strong, to impart appreciation for well-learned skills, and to reduce overuse of any particular component process. Often, a reduction in the overuse of a component process occurs without direct intervention. This change happens with the introduction of other avenues for information processing and is strengthened when clients become more adept at using alternative strategies. For example, Chapter 3 contains a case example in which the child client named Adam overemphasized kinesthetic expression, almost to the exclusion of other components. The goal of treatment was to increase the child's ability to profit from other modes of information processing, and specifically to emphasize cognitive control over his behavior. There was no direct attention to reducing kinesthetic functioning; Adam's overreliance on it naturally abated when other information processing strategies were practiced.

Therapy began with the Kinesthetic component and evolved from pure kinesthetic release of energy when the client demonstrated the ability to perceive form. The perceptual focus allowed him to give form to feelings and provided some structure for the discharge of energy. Work with the Affective component proceeded after Adam had obtained a structure for his emotions. Therapeutic intervention with the Affective component allowed the boy to express emotions appropriately, to understand the importance of emotions for motivating behavior, and to begin exerting conscious control over his emotions. After demonstrating some mastery of the affective material, Adam proved himself ready to move to the Cognitive/Symbolic level by producing a free drawing of stoplights. Symbolic work with the traffic light, as well as the tortoise and the hare metaphor, helped reinforce the desired cognitive regulation of behavior that did not exist prior to therapy. This cognitive control was demonstrated by the ability to think through and carry out complex projects. Although no intervention directly targeted reducing kinesthetic activity, a natural reduction in this behavior occurred as a result of opening up other component functions.

Chapters 4 to 8 also contain examples of art activities that would elicit functioning with a particular component process. These examples, summarized in tables at the ends of Chapters 3 to 9, represent a mere fraction of the art interventions that are therapeutically useful, and that can operate as springboards for other ideas. Knowledge of the Expressive Therapies Continuum can give a definite healing structure to the formulation of interventions. Without knowledge of the ETC, a therapist could have all clients use markers to draw the same subject. While this process could be enlightening for some, it also could be limiting for others. It has been shown throughout the discussion of the ETC that one medium and one technique will never be adequate to address all client needs. Fortunately, the ETC can aid in deciding the most suitable materials and methods for each client. Further, therapists must remember that the use of art in therapy, or as homework outside of therapy, is not always benign and must be undertaken with thoughtful preparation (Farrelly-Hansen, 2001; Kramer, 1971; Robbins & Sibley, 1976; Vick & Sexton-Radek, 2005). Using the framework of the ETC to guide planning and implementation of treatments can reduce the likelihood that art intervention could cause undue harm. The ETC will provide information about how to proceed in the most beneficial direction.

Through therapy, clients can become more discriminating about the circumstances under which a preferred function works best. The treatment goal would not necessarily be to reduce reliance on an overused function, but to decide when a component is employed to its best advantage. In addition, clients can be shown through the creative process that the bipolar nature of the ETC levels can be used to their benefit. For example, clients can learn that if they are caught up emotionally, perceptual processing can help contain emotion. As was mentioned in Chapter 5, Curry and Kasser (2005) demonstrated that people could achieve relief from feelings of anxiety by increasing their focus on the Perceptual component of the ETC, through coloring predrawn mandala shapes.

Making Planned Therapeutic Changes

Altering components or levels of the Expressive Therapies Continuum ideally should occur with forethought and planning. Changing ETC levels allows new expression to emerge, and these novel experiences often are accompanied by the greatest therapeutic change, creativity, and joy (Lusebrink, 1990). Changing component processes in therapy can come about when therapists suggest that clients work with a new medium. A new level also can be accessed when the therapist directs clients' attention to a new component through the types of questions asked. In addition, specific tasks can be assigned that allow clients to attain functioning at the desired level.

There are several indications that modifying a component process may be the necessary next step in therapy. These occur when clients become restless with the current mode of expression, or when change has the potential to allow deeper expression than the current experience affords (McNiff, 1981). Therapeutic work can reach the limits allowed by a current component process. Transitioning to a new component process also can be prompted by mutual feelings between client and therapist that progress is at a standstill. When work has proceeded for several sessions with the Cognitive component, for example, client and therapist could decide that moving to the Affective level would allow deeper exploration of topics under consideration. A young woman exploring body image issues worked on the Cognitive level to explore and understand the influences of media, ethnicity, and family on the development of her body image. Movement to the Affective level helped her begin to work through her feelings of body image dissatisfaction.

Media Properties
Changing component processes of the Expressive Therapies Continuum can occur when therapists encourage the use of a new medium because the physical properties or emotional, schematic, or symbolic potential is

believed have the ability to guide clients in the desired therapeutic direction. As has been mentioned previously, fluid media are likely to evoke emotion, and expression with the Affective component. The same is true with brightly colored media. Color and fluidity allow the release of feelings in art therapy. Alternatively, resistive media are likely to promote cognitive functioning. Media that allow for the production of ambiguous forms can nurture expression with the Symbolic component.

Switching to a new medium while working on a piece might show a client how she or he can continue to work through a problem by changing tactics rather than starting over. A client working with watercolor paint could decide that darker pigment was needed to express the desired sentiment. Adding water-soluble oil pastels can highlight the validity of the expression and infuse it with greater intensity. Giving up on an image typically brings about feelings of failure, whereas amending a piece engenders feelings of accomplishment.

When transitioning to a new medium, the change does not have to be abrupt. Elements of the new medium can be added gradually in order to facilitate incremental movement toward the desired component. If a client were working with wood, for instance, the therapist could suggest the addition of yarn or soft wood chips to move the experience in a more fluid direction. Further, a gradual progression from pencil to colored pencils, then to pastels might be an easier transition to the Affective component than an abrupt change from pencil to pastel.

Task Complexity

New task instructions, due to their level of complexity or structure, can change the type of information processing involved in an activity (Lusebrink, 1990). Task instructions, which are low in complexity and structure, enhance the free flow of emotional expression. As was demonstrated in Chapter 2, in Table 2.1, the thought necessarily involved with highly structured or complex directions is likely to contain emotional flow and evoke cognitive information processing. Alternatively, poorly defined or overly complicated directions can disrupt or confuse the thought necessary for successful task completion.

Therapists can assign particular media or tasks in order to prompt functioning with the desired component. A six-year-old boy suffering from unresolved anxiety following the terrorist attacks on September 11, 2001, repeatedly expressed his emotions in drawings similar to the one shown in Figure 11.1. Creating this type of image allowed for release of tension and emotion, but did not promote overall resolution of the trauma.

Figure 11.1   Kinesthetic expression of trauma by a 6-year-old boy following September 11, 2001, terrorist attacks.

The kinesthetic aspects of the experience amplified the anxiety the boy felt about the possibility of future attacks. The therapist wanted to move the boy toward greater cognitive mastery of his fears, so she asked him to make the hero collage shown in Figure 11.2. The hero theme required that the boy think about the definition of hero and identify and select examples in magazine images. Making the collage required that the images be integrated into a coherent assembly. The change in media, as well as the specific task instructions, assisted the young client in identifying figures representing help and safety, which was a first step in resolving his unremitting anxiety.

Questions and Discussion

The transition to a new component process also is facilitated by therapists asking questions about topics supporting new strategies. When therapists wish to move toward Kinesthetic/Sensory processing, questions focus on how the medium feels in the hands or appeals to the eyes; what the client is doing at the moment. Therapists can encourage movement and emphasize the rhythmic aspects of the experience. When Perceptual/Affective

Figure 11.2   Movement to the Cognitive component with a change of media and assignment of hero collage task.

functioning is the goal, questions naturally center around feelings experienced (Affective) and formal elements of visual expression perceived (Perceptual). Discussion can help clients focus on internal organization or emotional expression, depending on the desired therapeutic direction. Finally, if movement to the Cognitive/Symbolic level is desired, discussion would highlight the thinking through of experiences or the complex symbols produced. Chapters 3 to 8 each contain a section dealing with questions and discussions. These further explain the use of verbal dialogue to stimulate information processing with particular components.

In summary, goals for therapy guided by the Expressive Therapies Continuum include increasing connections between component functions, removing obstacles to blocked functions, reducing emphasis on overused functions, and increasing appreciation of strengths as they are reflected in component processes. Therapy is initiated using the client's preferred information processing mode, with planned therapeutic shifts between levels or components to be made when therapeutic progress becomes limited, when clients become restless with the current process, or when delving deeper into a therapeutic topic might be achieved with another mode of information processing. Transitions to new levels are facilitated through questions and discussions directed at the desired component process, through changing media, or through changing task instructions.

Becoming open to and connecting on the Kinesthetic/Sensory level can have the effect of allowing for more sensuous enjoyment of life experiences, and promoting the release of tension. Therapeutic work to unblock or enhance the Perceptual/Affective level can encourage clients to organize their perceptions differently and support the appropriate expression of emotion. Connections to enhance Cognitive/Symbolic functioning can reframe thoughts about experiences, strengthen cognitive processes, and encourage integration of previously feared or rejected symbolic material. Creativity can optimize the use of all personal potential and encourage self-actualization.

Negotiating Unplanned Changes

Changes in Expressive Therapy Continuum components or levels can occur without therapist planning. Clients may spontaneously choose to work with a different medium or change their manner of interacting with a frequently used medium. Further, changes can occur when, through their therapeutic work, clients begin to perceive things differently, conceive of things in a new way, or experience their emotions for the first time. New forms of information processing can provoke further exploration and modification. A change in ETC components does not have to be planned by the therapist in order to be beneficial. Therapists should respect the fact that clients themselves may shift media choices or expressive processes to best meet their needs (Hinz, 2006).

Gene was a 75-year-old client suffering from major depressive disorder. During the first few sessions, he preferred to process information cognitively and had done considerable work with the Cognitive component of the Expressive Therapies Continuum. After some weeks in therapy, therapist and client agreed that movement toward greater emotional expression would be beneficial. Rather than move abruptly from the Cognitive to the Affective component, the therapist thought it prudent to start with a perceptual representation of *four primary emotions*. The therapist hoped that in this way, form would predominate, yet there would be a moderate degree of emotional involvement in the expression. Gene overlooked the therapist's instructions and painted the picture shown in Figure 11.3, which he titled "Storm in the Night." The image is dominated by a large form, muddied colors, and dynamic outlines. It is a much more purely affective, if not pathologically affective (see Table 10.2), expression than was intended by the therapist. However, when discussing the experience of painting, Gene stated that he "let go" of previously held

Figure 11.3　"Storm in the Night": Affective functioning allows the discharge of emotion.

emotions. He explained that during and after the completion of the painting he cried tears of relief, and that he experienced several days of "feeling good" during the week, which had not previously occurred during the course of therapy. In this case, Gene sensed that a free and pure emotional expression was the proper therapeutic direction, and the expression was healing. However, client choice and therapist prescription must be carefully balanced, as unmonitored art making can have harmful effects (Graham-Pole, 2002; Farrelly-Hansen, 2001; Vick & Sexton-Radek, 2005).

Avoiding Nontherapeutic Movement

Change to a different level or component of the Expressive Therapies Continuum is not always beneficial. Clients might stay with a certain subject matter or medium because it is known and feels safe. A new medium or subject can be too great a hazard to self-esteem by threatening to uncover feelings or issues that clients do not yet feel capable of facing. Therefore, shifts to different component functions or levels of the ETC typically must be planned, and always carried out with sensitivity. Movement to new components or levels should be avoided if the therapist does not have sufficient time to dedicate to a new process, if a significant process could possibly be overlooked or disregarded, or if changing to a new component process has the potential to adulterate important therapeutic moments.

It would be counterproductive to move to another component of the Expressive Therapies Continuum if therapists did not take ample time to introduce and explain an unfamiliar process. As was mentioned earlier, using art in therapy increases anxiety due to the relative unfamiliarity of the materials. Changing therapeutic tactics without adequate explanation likely will be perceived by the client as anxiety provoking and disrespectful. Movement to a new component process or level of the ETC can be facilitated by therapists introducing the medium and its properties, explaining the desired effects of its use, and obtaining client agreement to try it. Further assistance can be given to clients trying a new medium by therapists demonstrating for clients how a new medium can function, and even working side by side with clients the first time to ease anxiety. Another way to introduce a new medium or material can be to incorporate it gradually into a project that already uses a familiar one.

If a change happens too quickly, clients can feel incapable of performing with new materials or in a new way in a new situation. Therapists must try their best to ensure that clients have the mental, emotional, and physical capacities to function on a new level, or the change can be frustrating rather than rewarding. If a client were not ready to engage in a particular therapeutic process, that process could be devalued due to client discomfort. This is especially true of work on the Kinesthetic/Sensory level: If clients were not well prepared for the experience, the tension-releasing effects of work with the Kinesthetic component would be lost. The clients themselves could be lost, as they might not return to therapy following such an uncomfortable experience.

Shifting to a new component process would be disruptive if the change took the focus away from a primary experience. When processing grief, for example, each component of the complex emotional state must be acknowledged and worked through (Rogers, 2007). When the primary experience is centered on the expression of anger about death, changing from affective expression to a perceptual or cognitive process would disruptively change the necessary therapeutic focus. Typically, individual therapists have flexibility in choice of subject matter, task instructions, and media to focus the experience on any expression as long as it is therapeutically necessary. This can be a challenge in a structured and time-limited therapeutic group, as will be discussed in the next chapter.

Too many changes in one session can be counterproductive because the sheer amount of activity can weaken the import of key therapeutic moments. Clients need time to appreciate and internalize newly experienced emotions, thoughts, and behaviors. It is important to remember that sometimes less is more. There are times when words are not necessary for the client to truly grasp the healing qualities of an expressive experience. A client processing information satisfactorily with the Affective component, if abruptly asked to use materials and methods consistent with cognitive functioning, would likely feel that the primary experience of affective processing was diminished. As has been stated before, no one level or component process is inherently superior or inferior to another. The idea is not to be disconnected from any process, or trapped using only a fraction of one's resources. One goal of therapeutic endeavors using the Expressive Therapies Continuum is to ensure that all components are accessible.

Finally, movement to a different level would be considered nontherapeutic if it led to unstructured emotional expression or excessive anxiety due to the unfamiliar or regressive nature of the media involved (Kramer, 1971). Clay can facilitate regressive experiences because, due to its tactile properties, it can evoke memories with textural and kinesthetic properties that are potentially very upsetting (Sholt & Gavron, 2006). Regression of this sort can be carefully managed in art therapy, but must be thoughtfully planned and monitored so that the effect remains positive and therapeutic.

Facilitating Termination

The framework of the Expressive Therapies Continuum can offer various ways to approach the termination of therapy. Goals that were formulated within the components and levels at the start of therapy can be reviewed.

Progress toward goals can be examined against the backdrop of the hier-archical structure of the ETC. When establishing a therapeutic alliance with clients, therapists can discuss one view of optimal health as an ability to use all component functions in an integrative manner. The person who can integrate information from all levels of the ETC experiences life fully and lives joyfully. Mary, the woman discussed in the case study at the end of Chapter 9, provided an ideal example of such integrated functioning.

After participating in art therapy for approximately eight months and nearing the end of her treatment, Mary made a visit to Paris. She had been to Paris on many previous occasions, but stated that this trip was remark-able because she experienced it with her whole person. She took it in with all of her senses and felt her heart brimming with joyous emotion as she shared the events with her husband. Mary gave one example of eating a delicious sorbet while walking through the city. She and her husband stopped to admire the architecture of a particularly beautiful bridge, when across the water came lovely voices floating out of a cathedral. As they walked across the bridge, she thought of the symbolism of begin-ning a new life with all of her senses keen and her heart full. When Mary returned from Paris, she knew that she had gained everything that she needed from therapy: She was living fully and completely, harmoniously processing sensations, emotions, thoughts, and behaviors.

Of course, not all indications for termination are as dramatic as a trip to Paris, but the structure of the Expressive Therapies Continuum helps therapists comprehend whether clients are open to information pro-cessing on all levels, and the possibility for living in an integrated and self-actualized fashion. Congruence of thoughts, emotions, and action is especially important. Clients can be educated about the importance of continuing to experience life through a variety of means and having their decisions informed by many sources. In this way, integrated processing is likely to continue following the termination of therapy.

At termination, therapists should arrange a review of client artwork so that clients can see for themselves the progress they have made in therapy. This final evaluation acts as a summary of progress, and reinforces the inte-gration of knowledge gained in therapy; it should not be omitted. Therapists can reinforce the value of flexibility in processing information through all channels by reviewing the art therapy experiences through the structure of the Expressive Therapies Continuum. Clients will see and remember the challenges and advantages of each component process as they review a portfolio of their completed work. Examples of Kinesthetic/Sensory experiences support the connection to important bodily information.

Perceptual/Affective work emphasizes the interplay between expression and containment of emotion. The appraisal of previous Cognitive/Symbolic work reinforces life meaning. This retrospective journey also will reinforce the importance of continuing to use art for healing after therapy.

Managing Resistance to the Use of Art in Therapy

It is not unusual for therapists to encounter resistance to the use of art media and artistic processes during the early phases of therapy. According to Lusebrink (1990), resistance to art therapy can take many forms. Clients can show opposition by using excessive verbalization, or by silence, by producing stereotypical images, by copying another person's artwork, or by presenting unmanageable emotions. Resistance also is seen through engaging in excessive motor behavior, and by clients destroying their own artwork. Resistances often are based on clients' fears of revealing themselves, internally or externally, in ways they do not know how to control. Any sort of reluctance to engage in the art process should be queried and explored to determine its power to disrupt therapeutic rapport or future goals. Client resistance can occur on any level of the Expressive Therapies Continuum, and identifying the underlying ETC component aids therapists in devising an appropriate therapeutic approach.

Resistance can occur on the Cognitive/Symbolic level, when overinvolvement with cognitive processing leads to excessive and unnecessary verbalization. Resistance to the formation or use of images in therapy can take the form of clients defensively engaging in so much preparatory discussion that there is too little time for the creative process (Jacobse, 1995). Therapists' responses to excessive verbalization in the early stages of treatment set the stage for later client behavior. *Therapists must not be seduced into believing that words have more value than images.* Creative action must consistently be promoted because change takes place through active engagement in the therapeutic process, not through talking about it (Jacobse, 1995; Wiener & Oxford, 2003).

Lack of verbalization can be another kind of resistance experienced, especially with reluctant adolescent clients (Linesch, 1988; Riley, 1999). This sort of resistance can be worked through successfully with art, because words are not essential for successful therapy. Adolescents can be assured that they are not required to discuss the meanings of their images; therapist and client can trust that the creative process is healing even without the addition of verbal interpretation (McNiff, 1998; Riley, 2003;

Williams, 2002). Working together on an image in an alternating fashion to establish a pictorial dialogue is an effective way to engage nonverbal clients (Stone, 1968). Therapists' comfort with silence demonstrates their trust in the process of art therapy.

Resistance involving the Perceptual/Affective level is demonstrated through the use of stereotypical images, or in the form of unmanageable emotions that interfere with the creative process. For most individuals, being asked to use art media, perhaps for the first time in many years, brings up overwhelming feelings of uncertainly and insecurity. Claiming lack of artistic ability may be the only way clients think they can control these uncomfortable emotions. This sort of resistance to beginning, as well as reluctance to completing the art task, usually is dealt with by providing reassurances that artistic ability is not required in order to create in a meaningful manner. Providing a period of experimentation with the materials in order for clients to refamiliarize themselves with media also can help counter resistance to beginning art therapy (Betensky, 1995; McNiff, 1998; Rubin, 1999). Rozum and Malchiodi (2003) advise avoiding the word *art* altogether in describing the products of art therapy. Instead, the authors counsel using the word *image* because it is less value laden. Therapists can explain that images represent a unique and meaningful therapeutic language, or a different way of gathering information. Resistance to completing art tasks can be dealt with by providing predrawn images (Henley, 1989, 1991), changing modes of expression or media (Lusebrink, 1990), or working together side by side with participants to complete images (Killick, 1997).

Stereotypical images do not reveal personal information about the creator and can indicate resistance through overuse of the Perceptual component processes (Kramer, 1971). Clichéd images, such as rainbows and roses, give the impression of imparting information, but usually do not reveal the clients' genuine thoughts or emotions. However, Kramer points out

> Conventional, stereotypical production does not always mean lost opportunity for creative expression. It can also be the first step toward any kind of organization in a chaotic person or it may be a defense against the threat of chaos and confusion. (p. 130)

Chapter 5 detailed therapeutic approaches to stereotypical images, including helping the client perceive and elaborate on any deviation from the conventional form.

Copying another's artwork is related to the client's lack of faith in his or her own abilities, a fear of being judged, or frustrated competitive strivings. In general, copying can be seen as a form of resistance to revealing personal information. The person who copies another's artwork usually feels awkward and ashamed, sometimes belligerent, but does not have access to these emotions. He or she should not be admonished for attempting to use another person's ideas or images. Rather, both the copier and the one whose work was reproduced can be assured that although the images look similar, stylistic elements make each one personal to the creator. The person unwilling to reveal personal information might be encouraged to talk about the visual elements that make his or her image unique, such as variations in color or form. In this manner, the client can be gently led into more personal disclosures by first using the language of formal elements of visual expression.

Clients often link their desire to destroy artwork to being disappointed by their expressive efforts. However, destruction of artwork also can be related to confrontation of emotions, memories, or meanings emerging from the images created (Levens, 1990; Lusebrink, 1990). Therapists should explore destructive urges carefully in order to determine if disturbing underlying significance or emotion exists, and should become a focus of therapy. Clients will learn through the process of therapy that the negative or shadow parts of themselves cannot be destroyed, but rather must be accepted to reinforce wholeness of personality and build strength of character (Hinz, 2006; Jung, 1972). Planned destruction of artwork can be carried out as an activity using Kinesthetic component processing, with the goal of releasing energy leading to the expression of emotion.

Excessive motor behavior is another type of resistance seen during the early stages of therapy. While functioning predominantly with the Kinesthetic component of the Expressive Therapies Continuum, internal images are not readily formed. Excessive motor activity might represent a defense against the formation of threatening images (Lusebrink, 1990). This type of resistant client must be met in therapy where he or she is, first using the Kinesthetic component. Later, the client can be gently guided to a nonthreatening process where the formation of images is no longer intimidating. One example of this sort of work was presented in Chapter 3. The young boy described in the case example displayed resistance to image formation until he was met where he was comfortable—releasing energy through dropping markers—at the Kinesthetic component. Eventually the young client could connect the dots to form an image, and he was able to process information with the Perceptual component.

In summary, various types of resistances to the use of media and images are encountered when using art in therapy. Most forms of resistance can be viewed as expressions of clients' lack of faith in their artistic abilities, communication skills, or personal uniqueness. Resistances can occur on every level of the Expressive Therapies Continuum. Discovering the principal component involved helps therapists plan appropriate therapeutic approaches. With understanding and preparation by the therapist, the majority of resistances will be discovered and worked through early in therapy. However, a change in medium or a change to a new level of the ETC can provoke further resistance that will need to be worked through in turn.

Working Through Therapeutic Obstacles

Understanding the Expressive Therapies Continuum can help therapists accurately identify and effectively work through obstacles to optimal functioning. As is presented in Table 11.1, obstacles to optimal functioning can arise from the lack of an essential skill. The presence of a difficult emotion such as anxiety or fear also can hinder effective functioning, and problematic beliefs about self or negative perceptions of situations can be the obstacles blocking a component process. Results of assessment sessions usually will provide clues as to the nature of obstacles blocking effective functioning; other obstacles will become obvious during the course of treatment.

When the lack of an essential skill proves to be a block to effective functioning, that skill often can be taught and reinforced using the Cognitive component. For example, if a lack of assertive communication is a block

TABLE 11.1   Using the Framework of the ETC to Identify Therapeutic Obstacles and Strategies to Overcome Them

Obstacle to Component Functioning	Strategy to Overcome Obstacle
Deficient skill	Skill can be taught with the Cognitive component through cartooning, cause-and-effect collage, drawing images of role play, or imaginary situations
Difficult emotion	Emotion can be identified and worked through with the Perceptual, Cognitive, or Affective components
Problematic belief or attitude	Belief can be identified and worked through with the Perceptual or Cognitive components, for example, through the changing point of view exercise

to successful functioning, assertiveness skills can be learned through cognitively oriented experiences. Such experiences must take into account client age, intellectual ability, and developmental level. Cognitive activities could include cartooning of the process, cause-and-effect collage work, or drawings indicating role-play responses. As was mentioned in Chapter 7, a fairly advanced developmental level must be reached before higher-level cognitive processes can be demonstrated. Certain cognitive processes might always remain too abstract or too advanced for clients with mental retardation, for children and young adolescents, or for the elderly. Color-coded stickers or precut collage pictures representing aspects of problem solving or pro and con decision-making exercises can significantly increase function for these populations. These aids ground the desired cognitive skill in a concrete process.

When fear or another emotion is the obstacle to component processing, work with the Affective component may be necessary to clear the way to effective use. Alternatively, work with another component function, such as a perceptual or cognitive process, might be a necessary first step prior to commencing affectively charged work. A client with a history of child abuse unconsciously may have blocked access to sensory information processing. Because of its association with trauma, opening the sensory channel would cause a flood of uncontrollable emotion. In all likelihood, the client would not understand the fear of sensory involvement and would not be able to articulate it at the outset of therapy. However, working with the client with perceptual experiences that give shape to the fear and organize its contents around formal elements of visual expression would help the client first identify and then work through the obstacle.

Anger is another common emotional block to effective processing with all components of the Expressive Therapies Continuum. Unexpressed anger can cause somatic symptoms and depression, substance abuse, and relationship difficulties (Koh, Kim, Kim, & Park, 2005; Wilson, 2003). Helping clients identify anger through pictorial representations safely organizes the information around color, line, and form. Drawing an emotion, such as the sadness depicted in Figure 11.4, is a type of perceptual manifestation of feeling often acceptable as an initial therapeutic intervention (Malchiodi, 2002; Rhyne, 1973). Drawing emotional topics can provide richer subsequent narrative descriptions of those events (Lev-Wiesel & Liraz, 2007).

Client attitudes can prove to be obstacles to information processing strategies. Changing attitudes and revising perceptions of situations can be addressed through the Perceptual or Cognitive components. As was described in Chapter 5, the *changing point of view* exercise can help clients

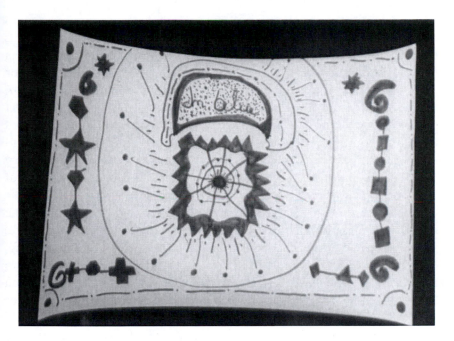

Figure 11.4 "I'm Blue": Emotions represented in a perceptual fashion, such as this depiction of sadness, often are an acceptable starting place in therapy.

understand how their current view of a situation or themselves influences how they feel and act. An adolescent wishing to interact in a more mature manner with her parents might be able to perceive, through the changing point of view exercise, how she sees herself as a child in negotiations with her parents. This attitude can be approached on the Perceptual dimension by teaching a new vision of the self, or it can be approached with the Cognitive component by reinforcing effective adult negotiation skills.

Transference and Countertransference Issues Unique to the Expressive Therapies Continuum

Clients' transference feelings about therapists can be negatively enacted through expressive means in art therapy (Ball, 2002; Betensky, 1973; McMurray & Schwartz-Mirman, 1998). Detrimental transference issues often are experienced as recurrent behaviors or images that inhibit therapeutic progress (McMurray & Schwartz-Mirman, 1998). Changing modes of expression can produce beneficial shifts in ETC component processes that decrease the focus on transference, and allow the creative process to proceed. Ball (2002) described a young girl who was predominantly acting out negative transference feelings kinesthetically by cutting and tearing paper. Transference was successfully addressed, and the client's behavior dramatically changed, when she engaged on the Symbolic level—she began creating works imbued with personal meaning.

Similarly to the clients they work with, therapists have natural or learned affinities and aversions to media and Expressive Therapies Continuum component processes. If therapists are not aware of these tendencies, they potentially can cause countertransference reactions and unduly influence clients in ways that are obstructive or harmful (Hinz, 2006; 2008). Therapists working with art media must be familiar with all types of materials and methods so that through their knowledge and experience, they can provide their clients with a full range of creative therapeutic experiences. Therapists must carefully assess and understand their own most preferred and least preferred information processing strategies, and be aware of how these preferences and aversions potentially can influence work with clients.

If therapists prefer working with Cognitive/Symbolic processes, they must be careful not to project their own meaning and symbolism onto client artwork. When this preference is strong, work with the Kinesthetic/Sensory level sometimes is not fully appreciated. A therapist with a cognitive penchant, or viewing the world symbolically, may avoid work with the Kinesthetic/Sensory level, believing it to be unmanageable and overly simplistic. Clients who would benefit from movement or sensation will not progress in treatment at the same rate when they only work on the Cognitive dimension. Alternatively, when therapists are uncomfortable working on the Cognitive/Symbolic level, they will not be able to help a client derive symbolic or abstract meaning from an image.

Therapists who prefer work with the Affective component could potentially misread or disregard their clients' needs for more organization and structure for their emotions and experiences. Alexithymic clients, unable to access their emotions and creativity due to excessive intellectualizing, potentially could be judged as overly defensive by therapists who value affective processing. If therapists work too quickly to expose these clients to a wide range of emotional experiences, the resulting fear of the unfamiliar could cause clients to leave therapy. Often therapists rush too quickly to do what they believe is right and clients do not return to therapy.

When the Kinesthetic/Sensory mode is overemphasized, clients might not attain adequate understanding of their therapeutic work. A modicum of cognitive processing aids clients in generalizing change to other areas of their lives. As was mentioned in Chapter 9, consistent rules and firm boundaries are necessary to foster constructive creative experiences. This is especially true with work on the Kinesthetic/Sensory level because unchecked energy release potentially can increase Kinesthetic/Sensory processing to a destructive point. Overabsorption in sensory processing can detract from the application of learning to other realms. Respect for the boundaries of the person, materials, and space is a key element when working with a preference for the Kinesthetic/Sensory level.

Another potentially harmful countertransference reaction can occur if therapists try to predict and force responding with a particular Expressive Therapies Continuum component process before a client is ready to make the change. Because an experience *can* occur does not mean that it *will* occur in the manner that we predict. Therapists must conduct an ongoing assessment of clients' progress through the components and levels of the ETC to understand what steps their clients are ready to make in therapy. An interesting and harmless example of this phenomenon occurred to an art therapy student working on a class assignment. The student began an art experience on the Kinesthetic/Sensory level by vigorously swirling finger paint. She related that she wanted to perceive a figure and change the experience to the Perceptual component. She really wanted to see a particular shape from a previous art experience, and move to the Symbolic component, but no form emerged. The experience remained one of tension release with the Kinesthetic component. She could not force a form to appear, and even if she had, forcing the appearance of a form would not have led to a genuine healing experience.

Summary

Art therapy has been used with all age groups in a vast array of therapeutic situations. Although the historic roots of art therapy are psychoanalytic, art therapists practice from numerous theoretical perspectives. Art materials and processes are universal activities that are common to all counselors using art in therapy. The Expressive Therapies Continuum is a theory that unites art therapists regardless of their beliefs about the healing nature of art in therapy. The Expressive Therapies Continuum cuts across various theoretical orientations to provide a framework from which to choose appropriate materials and methods in therapy. In addition, the ETC provides guidance about where to begin treatment, how to structure and make therapeutic changes, and when to do so. Therapeutic shifts involve movement to new levels or components, and these changes should be made with foresight and planning to reduce the likelihood of regression or anxiety. Nontherapeutic movement occurs when changes are made without preparing clients, and those changes take the focus away from significant therapeutic topics or actions.

Resistances to art therapy likely will be demonstrated during the early stages of treatment and can give information about comfort levels with components of the Expressive Therapies Continuum. The majority of resistances encountered during assessment can be understood as manifestations of clients' lack of faith in their abilities or self-worth. With therapist knowledge, patience, and support, most client resistances can be effectively managed so that they do not impede long-term therapeutic progress. Both resistances and obstacles to therapeutic progress can be understood through the organization of the ETC components and levels. From this structure, obstacles can be systematically analyzed and worked through.

Transference issues can be conceptualized and successfully handled with knowledge of the Expressive Therapies Continuum. Movement to a new component process can aid in reestablishing progress after disruption through problematic behaviors or expressions. The structure of the ETC helps therapists become aware of their own media preferences and information processing biases, so that they do not become countertransference obstacles to successful treatment.

12

Couples, Families, and Groups

Introduction

Clients are referred to couples, family, and group therapy to explore and change their ways of relating with others (Yalom, 1995; Riley, 2001, 2003). The therapy group is a microcosm where patterns of interaction and communication can be noted and transformed, with new patterns practiced and reinforced (Yalom, 1995). Group therapy is used to impart information, to teach skills, and to provide therapy in an economical fashion (Pollock & Kymissis, 2001). The use of art in groups adds a visual dimension to the work of therapy that can significantly enrich learning as the group process is made visible (Riley, 2001). It can aid couples and families in saying what previously has not been put into words, and can say more than a family is capable of expressing in speech. Art helps group participants discover universal themes; it helps couples and family members externalize their problems and rework them (Carlson, 1997).

Art therapists have discussed the mechanics of conducting group art therapy (Liebmann, 2003; Riley, 2001; Wadeson, 1980, 2000) and family art therapy (Riley & Malchiodi, 1994, 2003; Landgarten, 1981; Wadeson, 1980, 2000). They have discussed the various forms that groups can take (Riley, 2001), and special topics and techniques useful in group and family art therapy (Hoshino, 2003; Kerr & Hoshino, 2007; Klorer, 2003; Landgarten, 1981; Malchiodi, 2003d; Wadeson, 2000). But beyond these practical approaches, art therapists have not often discussed a theoretical orientation that unites art therapists in orchestrating the complicated interactions that comprise couple, family, or group art therapy. Group and family art therapy typically have been integrated into other theories rather than being developed as distinct entities (Arrington, 2001; Kerr & Hoshino, 2007; Riley & Malchiodi, 2003; Sobol & Williams, 2001). The Expressive Therapies Continuum can provide a theoretical framework to emphasize the unique contributions of art to group and family therapy. Application of this framework in group and family therapy can aid both therapists and clients in appreciating that clients can demonstrate the quality of their inner experience through action, form, and symbol. It can help therapists determine the purposes and goals of the therapeutic work in each of these various areas.

Multiple client interactions are notably more complicated than those with a single client. Art has been described as a way of helping organize and focus these complex exchanges involving more than one client (Landgarten, 1981; Riley & Malchiodi, 1994; Riley, 2003). According to Sobol and Williams (2001), in order to best manage the interactions of group and family therapy,

> The art therapist must subject every aspect of the design of the group, her behavior in group, and her understanding of what occurs within the group, to the same intense scrutiny with which she would critique a piece of artwork. (p. 278)

This chapter will demonstrate how knowledge of the ETC can aid therapists in conceptualizing family and group treatment interventions, as well as in individualizing activities for participants. Knowledge of the ETC also can assist therapists in deciding upon materials and methods that most fully meet the individual and combined therapeutic goals of the group, family, or couple.

Conducting Group Therapy in the Expressive Therapies Continuum Framework

The structure of the Expressive Therapies Continuum can be used to devise group activities that highlight individual group member goals or that emphasize group dynamics. In general, optimal group therapy work is not entirely preplanned, but based upon immediately expressed concerns and needs (Yalom, 1995). Ideally, group psychotherapy begins with participants sitting in a circle and checking in with the group leader(s) about their current feelings and topics of interest (Riley, 2001). The circular arrangement provides visual balance and organization, which through the process of isomorphism engenders feelings of protection and order within group participants (McNiff, 1981). After listening to group members' concerns at check in, therapists formulate an art therapy directive that best addresses current needs, themes, and emotions using the ETC as a framework for organization.

Kaplan (1995) attributed her successful group experience with chronic schizophrenic patients in a day treatment facility in part to the use of the Expressive Therapies Continuum. Kaplan assessed the level of the ETC where the group process was taking place and planned activities accordingly. She used the structure of the ETC to choose activities to meet the group goals, as well as to tailor activities to the individual needs of each group member. The author explained that understanding the ETC helped her realize that starting on the Cognitive/Symbolic level with the creation of a self-collage was inappropriate due to the group members' lack of essential skills needed to benefit from the higher-order cognitive processes involved in the creation of self-symbols.

After the first group session, Kaplan changed activities to the Kinesthetic/Sensory level because "the sensory quality of bodily experience provides the primary foundation for later development of object relationships and eventual symbolization" (p. 19). Later, the group moved from the Kinesthetic/Sensory level to the Perceptual/Affective level when the appropriate expression of affect was associated with a mask-making activity. Participants experienced group cohesion, cooperation, and use of combined strengths in the completion of their project. In addition, they were able to express authentic sentiment toward one another upon group termination.

As demonstrated in the above example, the structure of the Expressive Therapies Continuum can be used to conceptualize activities that emphasize general therapeutic factors of group psychotherapy, such as increasing cohesiveness, establishing trust, allowing catharsis, and providing vicarious learning experiences (Malchiodi, 2003d; Riley, 2001; Yalom, 1995). In addition, the ETC can afford group therapists with a structure from which to build interventions that accentuate significant and ever-changing group dynamics. These rich therapeutic experiences can occur on all levels of the ETC, as will be discussed below.

Kinesthetic/Sensory Level

Initial group therapy goals often include reducing discomfort or tension among new members, and building group cohesion (Liebmann, 2003; Riley, 2001). These goals can be assisted by work on the Kinesthetic/Sensory level of the ETC. Art materials can function as catalysts to amplify action and to release energy. Group members can be encouraged to create sound, rhythm, or music to accompany their illustrations as a way to release tension and connect with universal rhythms. These art activities can facilitate feelings of cohesion. Participants can improvise with tempo and cadence to create a healing release within the group and build unity (Winkelman, 2003; McNiff, 2004). Recall from Chapter 3 that a feeling can emerge from a Kinesthetic/Sensory experience. Establishing a common group rhythm is one way to engender feelings of empathy among participants.

Destruction of artwork is another kinesthetic activity that can underscore release of energy and tension reduction. The planned destruction of artwork can be worked through as a group ceremony, leading to an integrative creative experience. Old artwork, or images created specifically for the ritual, can be destroyed through cutting, tearing, or burning. Participants focus on the release of tension as the artwork is destroyed. The experience can continue on the Perceptual dimension as participants are asked to concentrate on the changed shape (smoke or shreds of paper) of the formerly problematic material or use it to create a new image (Luzzatto & Gabriel, 2000). Frequently the visual language involved in creating the new image allows a new freedom of expression. The experience can move to the Symbolic component as participants talk about the significance of what they have destroyed or released, and what they have created or added to their lives in the process.

Sensory experiences in group settings can heighten awareness of sensations, the information gained from them, and their importance in decision making. Sharing feelings accessed by using sensuous materials such as feathers, beads, and glitter can open up previously closed group members (Jensen, 1997; Kahn-Denis, 1997). Group sensory experiences can help instruct clients about distinguishing positive and negative touch, establishing trust, and setting appropriate boundaries. Kaplan (as cited in Moore, 1983) discussed a group sensory art experience in which participants created paint from cornstarch, cold cream, and food coloring. Adolescent group members experimented with increased openness, establishing trust, and boundary setting as they painted one another's faces.

The sensory-rich experience of group art therapy can sometimes break through the isolation and depression that characterizes elderly clients with Alzheimer's disease (Wald, 2003). Group sensory experiences have been used to improve memory functioning and develop personal meaning in aging clients (Jensen, 1997). Using sensuous materials, including rich fabrics, potpourri and spices, and nostalgic music, can evoke individual memories. Sharing memories in a group therapy setting can boost long-term memory retrieval in fellow participants. Other benefits of group sensory experiences are that they promote primary motor and sensory functions, increase sociability and social skills, reinforce procedural memory and habitual skills, and heighten humorous experiences (Jensen, 1997; Riley, 2001).

Perceptual/Affective Level

Group work with a focus on the formal elements of visual expression can help members better attend to and understand the organization of social relationships. Group members can explore how they fit together in a cohesive whole. Perceptual work can help members understand their influences on one another, as well as appreciate that the group as a whole has a character that is more than the sum of its individual members (Sobol & Williams, 2001). These kinds of experiences teach valuable lessons about the impact and importance of community. Riley (2001) discussed how projects such as group murals can shed light on the complex group character. Group mosaics or paper quilting experiences also can show participants that the nature of the group is more than just the addition of separate parts. When group members can participate in a project more than one time, with some new and some old group members, it is especially instructive of how relationships between group members influence not just the composition, but also the character of the group. In addition, the change in character of a time-limited group can be seen from first session to last by comparing group murals from the beginning and end of the group (Riley, 2001). Typically, murals created at the end of group demonstrate increased richness of visual expression and more complex and pleasing gestalts than at the beginning of group. Participants frequently comment that the more satisfactory pictures made at the end of group therapy reflect the growth in trust and deepening of relationships that occurred during treatment.

Riley (2001) discussed how art experiences can become ritualized as part of the process of conducting group therapy. The author used a "marking in" mural for clients to check in at the beginning of each group. Riley stated that this mural could be a visual reminder of the permanence of the group as well as the individuality of group participants. As the author explained it, members entered the group session and "marked in" on a mural with an image that demonstrated their feelings and concerns of the day. This growing graffiti wall also functioned as a visual testament to the growth and healing of the group members as it changed over time. Riley also discussed a ritual of confidentiality in which group members pledged to keep group information private by tracing their overlapping hand patterns. This image of the group pact was displayed as a concrete reminder to participants of the sanctity of information shared.

Although universality and discovering universal themes has been found to be a hallmark element of group psychotherapy (Yalom, 1995), it is also through successful group therapy that participants realize that people perceive things in different ways. Group work on the Perceptual level can help promote what has been called "representational diversity" (Siegel & Hartzell, 2003), or the ability to understand that different people may view one image or belief in different ways. As was mentioned in Chapter 1, a classic example of representational diversity is that of Rubin's vase, which is viewed by some as a vase, and by others as two faces. Concentrating on the foreground or background can lead to an equally valid perception of one or other view. Focusing on the perceptual qualities of an image can emphasize that certain group members see an image one way, and others see it entirely differently. All views are recognized as valid, and this acceptance of diversity can promote tolerance among group members that is generalized to families, friends, and communities.

Group work greatly enhances affective information processing, especially for participants with previous difficulties identifying and expressing their feelings. A group warm-up exercise can require group members to paint to music (Lusebrink, 1990). Later, when sharing their various portrayals, participants learn that perception and expression are extremely diverse. Group members who demonstrate less facility depicting emotions can gain ideas and confidence by viewing the affective images of others. In addition, having group members participate in an experience where all depict the same feeling and share their final products helps those less practiced learn that emotion can take on various forms and expressions. It is significant to learn that emotional expression is not right or wrong, but can change depending on situational or personal factors.

Participants also can experience feelings firsthand with one another through art experiences and be encouraged to discuss them in the safe group environment. The *pass-around drawing* is one such group activity designed to encourage active and immediate affective expression (Liebmann, 2003; Riley, 2001). In this exercise, group members choose one colored marker and begin a drawing. After a short time, participants are instructed to pass their drawings to the person on one side of them, who uses his or her "own" color to add to the drawing. The image is passed around the group until it reaches the originator, a completely different drawing. Participants are then encouraged to talk about the feelings they experienced as they drew on someone else's image, and how it felt to have their image altered by others. Group members who previously may not have been capable of sharing their emotions with others often find this activity an effective springboard for discussions of interpersonal affective content.

Cognitive/Symbolic Level

Work with the Cognitive dimension of the Expressive Therapies Continuum can occur when group members plan activities, negotiate issues, or solve problems together. In an eating disorders group, for example, the Cognitive component is engaged when members are asked to create a group collage depicting the three most detrimental effects of the media on body image. Group members must negotiate what they believe are the three significant issues. They must discuss and choose images that represent the options, and finally, they must work together to create the collage in a way that is satisfactory to all. The active negotiating, compromising, and problem solving contributing to the successful completion of the collage are cognitive processes. The creation of a group picture can be used as a way to engage participants in conflict resolution (Liebmann, 2003). Power struggles between group members can be actively worked through in the present.

Group members can examine their interactions and influences upon one another on the Cognitive/Symbolic level by building a structure to represent the group. Various materials can be provided, such as cardboard boxes, paper towel rolls, and construction paper. Group processes such as negotiation and problem solving reveal and emphasize functioning with the Cognitive component. Symbolic processes are revealed through the structure itself, and the personal meanings that participants ascribe to it.

Groups can gain more experience with the Symbolic component of the Expressive Therapies Continuum when they use metaphor and symbol to represent themselves, their families, and their worlds. Sharing a self-symbol, as discussed in Chapter 8, is one way to engage the Symbolic component. A former participant wrote about her experiences in group psychotherapy, saying she felt validated by other group members' reactions to her images. She added that the imagery and symbolism that seemed obvious to her, but new and exciting to others, helped increase her appreciation of her own artwork (Warriner, 1995). As in this example, acknowledgment by the group can have significant effects on a participant's sense of self-esteem.

Work with the Symbolic component also can assist participants in understanding their impact upon one another. Group members can individually depict their defenses, which typically do not operate on a fully conscious level. These images of defense mechanisms can subsequently be joined to make a group picture. In combining their images, participants can examine what might be revealed about their previously unconscious influence on each other.

In summary, the Expressive Therapies Continuum provides a framework for conceptualizing and constructing group goals that emphasize universal healing factors involved in group participation. In addition, knowledge of the ETC can help leaders formulate treatment goals that meet the immediate needs of group members, and that provide for long-term gains. Group work can be conducted within any component of the ETC, each having different merits for illuminating group dynamics.

Individualizing Group Art Therapy Using the Expressive Therapies Continuum

Although it is ideal for group therapy to be based on members' immediate concerns, feelings, and needs, at times group sessions are structured and carried out based on a predetermined treatment plan. The content of these structured groups often is dictated by the clinical or administrative staff of treatment centers and cannot take into account individual needs (Klorer, 2003). However, art therapists can vary art therapy directives or media assigned in structured group treatment to help individual participants achieve a desired therapeutic effect (Hinz, in press). The customizing of task instructions or media use to meet individual needs can be explained at the outset, to enlist clients as partners in formulating and implementing treatment goals. Participants will understand that various activities and media have the ability to evoke different desired responses, and their thoughtful implementation will be part of individualized treatment planning.

Media can be displayed in therapy groups arranged along a continuum. At one end of the continuum would be fluid media, those most likely to promote affective processing, such as paint. Resistive media, those most likely to promote cognitive responding, such as a pencil, would be located at the other end of the continuum. This kind of media presentation can be discussed to facilitate participants' choices of media that best meet existing needs. The media continuum can be elaborated upon as a component of the art therapy group that will be considered in the prescription of individualized art experiences (Hinz, in press). This arrangement allows group members to appreciate the different qualities of the various media options, and helps therapists devise the most effective art interventions for each individual. As was stated in Chapter 1, in an activity designed to explore the first of the 12 steps in Alcoholics Anonymous, Cox and Price (1990) discussed the use of incident drawings with chemically dependent adolescent clients. The authors used paint in order to heighten group participants' feelings of unmanageability. It can be imagined that there could be a group member for whom the use of paint would be too emotionally evocative, and for whom the therapists could provide a more controlled medium. When media properties have been explained and their variation anticipated, group members need not feel negatively judged when prescribed a different medium (Hinz, in press).

Art therapy directives can be altered to fit individual group member goals and needs. Group members sometimes alter their experience themselves, as was discussed in Chapter 11. This modification of task instructions need not be looked upon as resistance, but can be understood as clients intuitively knowing what type of experience would be most therapeutic (Hinz, 2006). When asked to make an abstract family collage, a group member might instead use the torn paper to create an image of how she or he is feeling. The client should be given an opportunity to explain how alteration of the activity met his or her needs. With an understanding of media properties and the components of the Expressive Therapies Continuum, the group member who altered task instructions should be able to articulate that a pressing feeling needed an outlet, or an idea required expression; the feeling or thought did not fit the parameters of the original directive.

The structure of the Expressive Therapies Continuum can help therapists more sensitively apply group art experiences in structured situations. As has been stated in preceding chapters, one medium and method cannot meet all group members' needs. Understanding the potentials of the various ETC components can help therapists determine if some variation of task instructions might be necessary for particular group participants. At times, clients come to inpatient groups greatly distressed by individual therapy sessions, previous appointments with other staff, or family therapy sessions. After listening to client concerns, therapists will understand if emotion needs expression, thoughts require working through, or if the client would benefit from gaining a different perspective about an experience. An individual art expression could take precedence over the structured group directive, or could be incorporated into it.

Termination of Group Art Therapy

The structure of the Expressive Therapies Continuum can be used to help therapists make certain that group participants fully process the important event of termination. From the background of the ETC, therapists can ensure that members are aided in consolidating the learning that took place in group, and in expressing their ideas about how the group changed their lives. In addition, therapists will want to help participants express their feelings toward their fellow group members and about the end of their therapy experience. Experiences on the Cognitive/Symbolic level of the ETC can help group members consolidate and integrate the learning that took place in group. Group members can be instructed to make a collage detailing the concepts that they will take away from treatment. They can be encouraged to create a self-symbol that demonstrates skills learned or abilities strengthened by their group participation. Group members can make and exchange "gifts" that help each other remember important lessons. For example, one participant in a group for sexually abused women made a small model of an aerosol can out of construction paper and labeled it "shame away spray." She presented the gift to another group member whom she wanted to remind not to succumb to feelings of shame after therapy was over.

The Perceptual/Affective pass-around drawing discussed above, where group members add symbols to and alter each other's drawings, can be performed at termination. In this way, group members possess an image that demonstrates through the formal elements of visual expression how they have influenced each other over the course of the therapy experience. In addition, each participant can be reminded that they are keeping with them a meaningful part of the group experience (Hinz, 2006). The affective qualities of these images can be amplified by the addition of a group-created poem that expresses their sentiments toward each other and about group termination.

Finally, the conclusion of a group experience can be marked by a ceremony that includes Kinesthetic/Sensory aspects in which old ways of being are left behind and new ways embraced. Images can be created that commemorate the ceremony and its importance for changing beliefs and feelings. Rituals are healing in and of themselves, but creating images of them can help clients concretely retain their healing effects.

It has been demonstrated that the framework of the Expressive Therapies Continuum can aid in the planning and organization of group art therapy. Knowledge of the ETC can help group therapists plan group interventions that accentuate the healing elements of group therapy or that underscore immediate group dynamics. Working from the structure of the ETC also can help therapists individualize group therapy goals to meet particular client needs. Finally, the ETC provides a way for therapists to plan and organize termination from group treatment, ensuring that feelings are appropriately expressed and learning is reinforced.

The Expressive Therapies Continuum in Couples and Family Therapy

Art therapy is a relatively young field, and there are only a modest number of textbooks and articles about family art therapy. Most of these authors agree, however, that the introduction of art into family therapy is challenging (Arrington, 2001; Kwiatkowska, 1978; Riley & Malchiodi, 1994, 2003). Using art in therapy can upset the usual manner of communication and interaction among family members (Riley & Malchiodi, 1994, 2003; Wadeson, 2000). Adults typically have an advantage over children in family therapy because they are more masterful at verbal communication. This puts family members on unequal footing right from the start of family therapy, and often mimics the distribution of power in the household. Yet, the opposite may be true when using art in therapy. Because children have more familiarity with art materials through their more frequent use, they could feel an advantage over adults in art-assisted family therapy (Wadeson, 1980; Riley & Malchiodi, 1994).

Explanation of the Expressive Therapies Continuum can provide a way to balance power at the beginning of therapy, by helping family members understand that different persons take in and process information in various ways. Assessments exist that can help determine different learning styles (Gardner, 1999). Family members can be assured that all types of information processing will be used and honored in art therapy. Families can be introduced to the various ETC component processes, and to the concept that preferences for one or another can be affected by temperament or training (Armstrong, 1987; Gardner, 1999). They can be reminded that although the ETC is arranged in a hierarchical fashion, higher-order processing is not valued over lower. All components are necessary for effective problem solving and living. Family members may be taught that preferences can be deeply ingrained, but that they can be modified through therapy. One goal of couples or family therapy can be explained as helping family members appreciate each other's preferred ways of processing information. Understanding and appreciating information processing strategies can reduce conflict and increase communication among family members.

The structure of the Expressive Therapies Continuum can guide therapists in choosing methods and activities for use in family intervention. Art therapy experiences on the Kinesthetic/Sensory level of the ETC can help increase enjoyment and expansion through the senses, as well as discovery of the energy-releasing properties of movement. Family members can experience an enhanced sense of well-being from integrating creative endeavors involving the body and the senses. Experiences on the Perceptual/Affective level can allow family members the opportunity to see each other in ways that they previously have not, and to increase their appreciation for their similarities and differences. Art therapy can be used on the Cognitive/Symbolic level to examine and change patterns of communication, problem solving, and conflict resolution among couples and families. In addition, visual images can aid in the synthesis and transcendence of opposites, allowing new elements of the relationship to emerge, and helping couples and family members overcome obstacles from the past that may find expression in symbolic form.

Kinesthetic/Sensory Level

Optimally functioning families are characterized by good communication, cohesiveness, and playfulness (Dermer, Olund, & Sori, 2006). Kinesthetic/Sensory activities usually are not result oriented; they require action, but not necessarily achievement. Their use can reduce competitive feelings among family members and help them have fun together (Dermer & Foraker-Koons, 2007). Kinesthetic/Sensory activities can include finger painting, clay work, puppetry, and papier-mâché, all of which aid in the release of tension, and thus can enhance a sense of fun. Bubble painting, in which colored soap bubbles are used to create images, and face painting, to emphasize personality characteristics, also can help family members remember that play is an essential element in the functional family.

Engaging in art activities on the Kinesthetic/Sensory level of the Expressive Therapies Continuum can emphasize essential connections with healing rhythms, build trust, and be used to emphasize cohesiveness while at the same time enforcing appropriate boundaries among family members and family subsystems (Landgarten, 1981). Work on the Kinesthetic/Sensory level can help newly married couples and blended families establish their own rhythms and define their new roles.

Perceptual/Affective Level

According to Riley and Malchiodi (1994), family members yearn to be accurately seen by one another. Typically, people have only words with which to explain themselves; words are often inadequate to explain the depths of feelings needing to be discussed, and sometimes words are incendiary. Language can be especially ineffectual at portraying people when family members come from different cultures or are significantly different ages (Hoshino & Cameron, 2007; Riley, 2003; Riley & Malchiodi, 1994). Work on the Perceptual/Affective level of the Expressive Therapies Continuum can help couples and families see their problems objectively rather than continuing to argue or complain about them. Riley and Malchiodi (1994) gave an example of a couple with marital difficulties that was asked to "draw how it was (in their youth) when one opened the door and entered into their family home" (p. 26). In sharing their separate depictions with one another, it seemed as if the husband and wife were seeing each other for the first time. Disparities in the artistic elements of their drawings helped the couple see their personal differences objectively. This neutral view was a first step in their developing new feelings of empathy for one another.

A couple can use perceptual processes to represent their perceptions and expectations of their relationship, as well as hope for relationship improvement. Dattilio (2000) discussed a technique that he called *graphic perceptions* in which couples use line, shape, and color to represent various aspects of their lives, such as physical, social, emotional, and spiritual. The graphic representations can give couples a visual means of understanding the similarities and differences in their perceptions that can profoundly affect their relationships. The author reported that this activity could be carried out several times throughout the course of therapy to assess progress toward shared goals.

Examples of the graphic perceptions exercise that husband and wife completed at the outset of marital therapy are shown in Figures 12.1

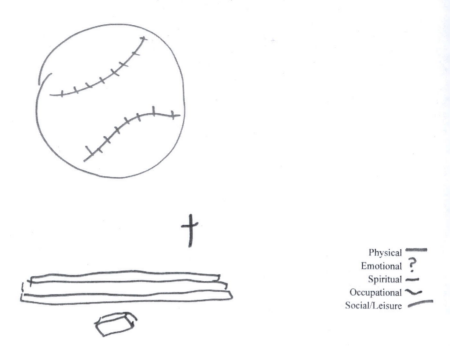

Figure 12.1 Husband's graphic representation of his life.

and 12.2. They were asked to each make a picture using lines, shapes, and color to show five aspects of their lives: physical, emotional, spiritual, occupational, and social/leisure. When the couple presented for therapy, the husband stated that they "argued about everything." The images helped the couple more clearly define the vague dissatisfaction that they were experiencing in their marriage. The husband was able to see that his interest in a city softball team was the largest aspect of his life, and that there was no representation of his wife or marriage in the drawing. The wife used the drawing to illustrate her depression, which she drew as clouds "overshadowing everything." The other important aspect of the image was her spirituality, which she believed was helping her overcome the depression. This depiction helped the wife understand how both the depression and her spiritual focus were not allowing time for social and leisure activities (in which she depicted herself and her husband as two ants on two separate blades of grass). These graphic representations of their lives allowed the couple to see their difficulties more objectively, and to shift their energies so that the marriage began to have a more prominent place in their thinking and their lives.

Physical
Emotional
Spiritual
Occupational
Social/Leisure

Figure 12.2   Wife's graphic representation of her life.

Work with the Perceptual/Affective level also can help couples in cross-cultural relationships depict differences in role expectations, child-rearing practices, and spiritual beliefs (Hoshino & Cameron, 2007). These images can be used to help husbands and wives acknowledge complementary abilities and roles, and validate contrasting beliefs and desires stemming from different cultures. Images of diversity can be deconstructed, and a third reality created that incorporates elements of both previous views, but includes the tolerance and flexibility to make the new couple unique (Perel, 2000). This third view can celebrate strengths taken from both cultures, religions, and ethnic backgrounds. The integrative construction can be used in subsequent therapy sessions to aid the couple in defining role expectations, discussing child-rearing strategies, and deciding spiritual practices.

When each family member constructs an abstract family collage, work on the Perceptual/Affective level can help family members clearly see typical relationship dynamics, and interactions among subsystems in the family. Figure 12.3 is an example of an *abstract family collage* created by one member of a family that helped demonstrate enmeshed family relationships. The anorexic patient who created this picture was considered

Figure 12.3   Work on the Perceptual level of the Expressive Therapies Continuum demonstrates family enmeshment.

the "problem" in the family. However, when other siblings made similar images depicting enmeshment, the combined impact of their visual depictions greatly emphasized the need for increased separation of behaviors, thoughts, and emotions among *all* family members.

Research has demonstrated that alexithymia is characteristic of certain psychiatric disorders, and that the difficulties with identifying, discriminating, and expressing feelings seen in alexithymic parents are associated with similar difficulties in their offspring (Espina, 2003; Guttman & Laporte, 2002). Some difficulties with this type of expression seem to be learned and passed down from one generation to the next (Fukunishi & Paris, 2001). Art therapy with the Affective component of the Expressive Therapies Continuum can intervene to teach emotional identification, discrimination, and expression in families where expression of feelings was previously unknown or avoided. Family members can create images of *four primary emotions*, as described in Chapter 6, as an introduction to this new language. From this perceptually oriented expression, family members can graduate to *cause-and-effect collages* in which basic feelings are identified and depicted along with their potential antecedents and consequences.

These structured approaches to emotion can transition into free art expression, allowing family members to describe and express their feelings.

The images produced by family members will vary widely, which can mimic varieties of affective experiences. Exposure to the framework of the Expressive Therapies Continuum and acceptance of various styles of information processing can lay the groundwork for tolerance of emotional expression. Movement of the family to the Cognitive/Symbolic level of the ETC can teach the signaling function of emotions and reinforce appropriate behavioral responses.

Cognitive/Symbolic Level

Families can use the *problem-solving or decision-making collages* discussed in Chapter 7 to help them define, implement, and reinforce appropriate behavioral choices in response to various feeling states. Cognitive/Symbolic activities render concrete and observable cycles of violent or abusive behavior that have been passed down through generations (Arrington, 2001). These art experiences can become the first steps toward productive change.

Work with the Symbolic component of the Expressive Therapies Continuum can help new couples and blended families, or couples and families in conflict, increase cohesiveness and form a new identity. Symbolic work allows the integration of opposites, the intuitive rendering of new definitions of relationships, and the recognition of unconscious obstacles to effective functioning. Part of the work that new couples and families must do is to separate from their families of origin and define themselves in terms of values, beliefs, and behaviors with their new partner or relatives. The creation of a *family coat of arms* is an example of one way that a newly married couple or blended family could define the combined unit. This symbolic definition can separate it from the past and establish a new path for the future. In addition, therapists can suggest that the creation of art become part of a family tradition to commemorate the New Year or to express gratitude at Thanksgiving.

Frequently, discrepancies in role expectations between husbands and wives cause the first marital discord experienced by married couples (Dattilio, 2000; Riley & Malchiodi, 1994). Couples and family members can use symbols to explore role expectations. These images might contain more information than the couples understand on a conscious level. However, symbolic representation can be a nonthreatening opportunity to make role expectations conscious and work toward compromise or resolution. Skilled art therapists understand and trust that not every interaction requires words. This confidence translates into helping members of couples and families acknowledge and respect that which is revealed in the art process as providing the foundation for positive change.

When families operate predominantly with the Cognitive component, verbal processes can become overemphasized, and family members can become fixed in defensive rationalizations and arguments. Work with the Cognitive component of the Expressive Therapies Continuum can help identify constructive and destructive patterns of communication, interaction, and problem solving. One way to explore these interactions is through an activity called the *family construction project* (Staton & Lucey, 2004). In this exercise, families are asked to build a bridge or similar structure while therapists observe communication patterns and problem-solving strategies. During construction, therapists can deflect typical negative interactions or reinforce positive strategies (Staton & Lucey, 2004). The construction experience requires that the family actively experience and alter their communication patterns and problem-solving strategies (Wiener & Oxford, 2003).

This same kind of learning also can be carried out through *nonverbal communication experiences*. In a nonverbal communication, family members are asked to "converse" with one another on paper using signs and symbols, without the benefit of spoken language (Riley & Malchiodi, 1994; Wadeson, 1980). This exercise visually emphasizes typical patterns of constructive and destructive communication among couples or family members that can be changed or reinforced to aid growth and healing.

Creative Level

It has been my experience that family members remember and embrace what they have creatively experienced, especially activities involving expression on all levels of the Expressive Therapies Continuum. One such experience, called *family sculpting*, can be carried out in family therapy, group therapy, or multifamily group therapy (Root, 1989). In this art experience, family members first use plasticene modeling clay to make and arrange a model of their family. Each family member works on his or her own representation of the whole family. Working with the modeling clay allows activity on the Kinesthetic/Sensory level of the ETC.

These small sculptures can be sketched or photographed so that they may be referred to in the future. Family members can talk about what they see when they look at each sculpture. A discussion of the formal elements of visual expression—color, shape, and size—involves the Perceptual component. The activity can be moved to the Cognitive/Symbolic level, as family members talk about the significance of the relative positions of the sculpture components, and the underlying communication and relationship patterns demonstrated. In the next part of this experience, family members are asked to pose as the sculpted family groups. This reinfuses the activity with kinesthetic energy and can ignite emotions. After the members are posed, they are asked to talk about what feelings emerge from being in their respective positions. The final element of the activity asks family members together to create a new sculpture that expresses the energy, emotion, and interaction that they would like to feel in their family in the future.

When conducting multifamily group therapy I have seen that when participants talk about their experiences in family therapy, they often refer to the family sculpting activity as one that influenced them greatly. Creative activity involving all components of the Expressive Therapies Continuum encourages family members to integrate the learning they experienced into new ways of thinking, feeling, and behaving.

McNamee (2005) introduced the use of bilateral art in family therapy as a creative experience using both the left and right hand to process information about therapeutic conflicts. Using bilateral art, information is processed sequentially through the Kinesthetic/Sensory mode, Perceptual/Affective channels, and Cognitive/Symbolic level. Changes in thoughts and feelings, ultimately influencing behavioral change, are the desired outcomes of bilateral art.

Termination of Couples and Family Therapy

Couples and families can look upon termination from therapy as a graduation. Through their successful participation in therapy, participants have gained a level of knowledge and experience that will support a new family structure in the future. The same process of reviewing artwork discussed in the termination of individual art therapy can mark the end of couple or family therapy. Members of couples and families can appreciate their progress by viewing the various works of art created over the course of therapy. They can review what they learned from the creation of each image in terms of the various component processes of the Expressive Therapies Continuum.

After reinforcing the learning and changes that have taken place through therapy, the family or couple can be asked to create an image of what they would like the household to look like in six months, in one year, or at any time interval (Riley & Malchiodi, 1994). This future projection can help family members express their hopes and expectations on the Perceptual/Affective level. The family can display this concrete representation of their wishes to help maintain the desired focus after the termination of therapy.

If couples and families repeatedly created similar images in therapy, they can be reviewed for evidence of progress toward desired goals (Dattilio, 2000). The same image or graphic representation can be repeated at termination to reinforce the message of change on the Perceptual/Affective level. Stories can be created in the form of family myths that project the lives of family members into the future. Symbols can be reviewed for their ability to integrate opposites and allow new meaning to emerge. These creations on the Cognitive/Symbolic level celebrate change and help maintain therapeutic gains. Couples and families can be encouraged to keep scrapbooks that visually chronicle individual family member's growth and change, as well as the evolution of the family identity.

Summary

Clients are referred to group, family, and couples therapy to understand and change their problematic ways of communicating and relating. These multiple client interactions are complicated and intense; art activities have been used to organize and focus these complex interactions. Knowledge of the Expressive Therapies Continuum can help therapists decide upon materials and methods that best meet the individual and combined goals of the group, couple, or family. Each component of the ETC has distinct properties that can be used to reinforce universal healing themes or highlight group dynamics. Activities on the Kinesthetic/Sensory level of the ETC can be used to reduce initial tension, promote bonding, and enhance cohesiveness. Perceptual/Affective processes are suited for exposing diversity and teaching tolerance, as well as for helping clients identify, discriminate, and express emotions. Work on the Cognitive/Symbolic level can strengthen negotiating, problem-solving, and conflict resolution skills. It can help illuminate synthesis and transcendence of opposites, allowing new aspects of relationships be defined. Couples and family members can realize and overcome obstacles from the past that may have found expression in symbolic form.

Families and couples are small groups that benefit from the same learning experiences brought about by Expressive Therapies Continuum component processes. The ETC provides an ideal framework for helping couples and families understand and appreciate their similarities as well as their differences in thinking, feeling, and behaving. Discrepancies in views of role expectations, beliefs about child rearing, and religious practices often are the basis for the first disagreements experienced by couples and families. Difficulties with communication and conflict resolution can continue and exacerbate disagreements into escalating negative patterns of interaction. The structure of the ETC can aid family art therapists in providing therapeutic interventions for couples and families in conflict.

Perceptual/Affective activities can help family members view each other more objectively and learn to express feelings appropriately with one another. Cognitive/Symbolic activities provide a foundation for examining communication patterns, and improving negotiation and conflict resolution skills. Kinesthetic/Sensory activities can help couples and families explore boundary issues, enhance bonding, and reinforce the importance of having fun together. Creative activities do not always require words, but are often the most treasured events that families experience together in therapy.

Termination from couples, family, or group psychotherapy can be facilitated by knowledge of the Expressive Therapies Continuum. This theoretical framework provides a way to structure and reinforce the learning that has taken place in therapy, and it can uniquely promote the view that individual differences in information processing should be respected and appreciated. A review of the artwork created during treatment aids in the integration of therapeutic gains by providing a means of conceptualizing the information in terms of the component processes and their associated healing elements.

The addition of art making to the ongoing life of a couple or family is important. Art can maintain a sense of playfulness, good communication, and cohesiveness that characterize an optimally functioning family.

Epilogue

Art touches body, mind, and spirit; it involves the creative process, the maker and viewer, and the product itself. Constructing a theory that takes into account all of the complexities of art therapy is a formidable task; however, in conceptualizing the Expressive Therapies Continuum, Dr. Lusebrink did a remarkable job of encompassing the myriad bodily, mental, and spiritual processes tapped by the conceptualization, creation, and appreciation of art.

My own admiration of the Expressive Therapies Continuum initially was sparked by the fact that it was a theoretical structure that was unique to the expressive therapies. It is not an attempt to fit art therapy into a psychological theory, but it has room to understand and explain the therapeutic uses of art applied in the majority of psychological disciplines. My appreciation of the Expressive Therapies Continuum deepened during the years of reading, researching, and teaching this remarkable theoretical framework. In writing this book, I worked to simplify and clearly relate the concepts of this comprehensive structure.

In the last couple of years, my focus in writing the chapters on the separate Expressive Therapies Continuum component functions has been to conceptualize and write about them as distinctly as possible. When I began writing about assessment and treatment, I understood more fully how the previous chapters reinforced the artificiality of the separation of component processes into discrete functions. I wrote that separating the influences of one type of information processing from another was necessary for the purposes of clarifying the unique component processes, but difficult, if not undesirable, in practice. I think that this information bears repeating.

Expressive Therapies Continuum components represent predominant, not exclusive, modes of information processing and visual expression. Especially within the context of an art therapy session, the influence of one type of component processing remains and influences the next. This power is discussed in the elicitation of the emergent function of each component. A new level of functioning often emerges from an art experience that leads a client to a new mode of feeling, action, or experience.

My appreciation of the Perceptual/Affective level as a bridge exemplifying this process between the Kinesthetic/Sensory and Cognitive/Symbolic levels was greatly enhanced during the writing of this book. As was mentioned in Chapter 1, the Perceptual/Affective level is pivotal in many therapeutic undertakings. It helps translate into concrete visual images mental

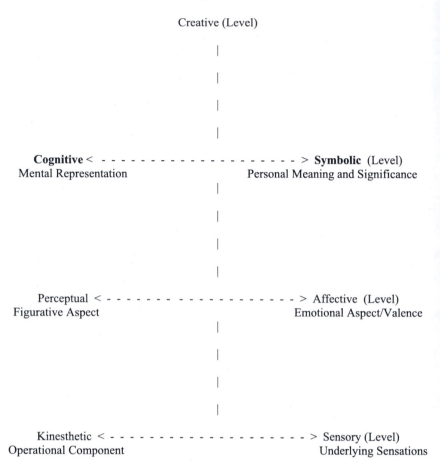

Figure E.1 The complex influences of each ETC level and component on the others as demonstrated in the process of symbol formation.

sensation, energy, and bodily movement brought about by participation in art experiences. These images with their representation in formal visual qualities such as shape, size, color, and implied movement allow differentiation and description of complex feeling states to which more cognitive processes can be applied and meaning attributed.

The Perceptual component is what allows many experiences to be differentiated, described, and contained for future use. The transitional nature of the Perceptual/Affective level between the Kinesthetic/Sensory level on the one hand, and the Cognitive/Symbolic level on the other is exemplified in the process of symbol formation and is demonstrated in Figure E.1.

According to Piaget, symbols have both a figurative component and an operational component (Lusebrink, 1990). The figurative aspect is manifested through the Perceptual component, and the operational aspect involves the Kinesthetic component. Symbol formation in this context means a mental representation instead of a personal symbol in the Jungian or Freudian sense, and in this context, it utilizes the Cognitive component. The creation of a symbolic representation allows an action to be contemplated. Similarly, the Affective component provides a transition between the Sensory level and the Symbolic level since affect, based on internal sensations, gives personal meaning and significance to images as symbols. This is exemplified by the Jungian concept of the feeling function of symbols (V. Lusebrink, personal communication, May 1, 2008).

In summary, the Expressive Therapies Continuum is a complex theoretical structure capable of encompassing the numerous ways in which art functions therapeutically. The component processes work together, influencing one another to promote therapeutic progress and enhance growth. It is hoped that this book stimulates a new generation of scholars who take up the challenge of providing an even stronger foundation for the field of art therapy based on this theoretical and practical framework.

References

Ackerman, D. (1991). *A natural history of the senses*. New York: Vintage.

Ahmed, T., & Miller, B. L. (2003). Art and brain evolution. In A. Toomela (Ed.), *Cultural guidance in the development of the human mind* (pp. 87–93). Westport, CT: Ablex Publishing.

Allen, P. B. (1992). Artist-in-residence: An alternative to "clinification" for art therapists. *Art Therapy, 9*, 22–29.

American Art Therapy Association (Producer). (1975). *Art therapy: Beginnings* [Film]. Alexandria, VA: Producer.

American Psychiatric Association. (2000). *Diagnostic and statistical manual of mental disorders* (4th ed., text rev.). Washington DC: Author.

Anderson, F. E. (1992). *Art for all the children: Approaches to art therapy for children with disabilities* (2nd ed.). Springfield, IL: Charles C. Thomas Publisher.

Armstrong, T. (1987). *In their own way: Discovering and encouraging your child's personal learning style*. Los Angeles: Jeremy P. Tarcher.

Arnett, J. J. (2006). *Adolescence and emerging adulthood: A cultural approach* (3rd ed.). New York: Prentice Hall.

Arnheim, R. (1966). *Toward a psychology of art: Collected essays*. Berkley: University of California Press.

Arnheim, R. (1969). *Visual thinking*. Berkley: University of California Press.

Arnheim, R. (1992). *To the rescue of art: Twenty-six essays*. Berkley: University of California Press.

Aron, E. N. (1996). *The highly sensitive person*. Secaucus, NJ: Berol Publishing.

Arrien, A. (1993). *The four-fold way: Walking the paths of the warrior, teacher, healer and visionary*. San Francisco: Harper.

Arrington, D. B. (2001). *Home is where the art is: An art therapy approach to family therapy*. Springfield, IL: Charles C. Thomas Publisher.

Azara, N. (2002). *Spirit taking form: Making a spiritual practice of making art*. Boston: Red Wheel/Weiser.

Ball, B. (2002). Moments of change in the art therapy process. *The Arts in Psychotherapy, 29*, 79–92.

Bayles, D., & Orland, T. (1993). *Art and fear: Observations on the perils (and rewards) of artmaking*. Santa Barbara, CA: Capra Press.

Beck, J. (1995). *Cognitive therapy: Beyond the basics*. New York: Guilford Press.

Berkowitz, S. (2007). Art therapy for this multicultural world. In F. Kaplan (Ed.), *Art therapy and social action* (pp. 244–262). London: Jessica Kingsley Publishers.

Betensky, M. (1973). *Self-discovery through self-expression: Use of art psychotherapy with children and adolescents*. Springfield, IL: Charles C. Thomas Publisher.

Betensky, M. G. (1995). *What do you see: Phenomenology of therapeutic art expression*. London: Jessica Kingsley Publishers.

Betts, D. J. (2006). Art therapy assessments and rating instruments: Do they measure up? *The Arts in Psychotherapy, 33*, 422–434.

Birren, F. (1988). *The symbolism of color.* New York: Citadel Press.

Blackett, P., & Payne, H. L. (2005). Health rhythms: A preliminary inquiry into group-drumming as experienced by participants on a structured day services programme for substance-misusers. *Drugs: Education, Prevention and Policy, 12*, 477–491.

Bogousslavsky, J. (2005). Artistic creativity, style and brain disorders. *European Neurology, 54*, 103–111.

Bradt, J. (2002). The effects of music entrainment on postoperative pain perception in pediatric patients. *Dissertation Abstracts International, 62*, 5073.

Brooke, S. L. (2004). *Tools of the trade: A therapist's guide to art therapy assessments* (rev. ed.). Springfield, IL: Charles C. Thomas Publisher.

Bruch, H. (1973). *Eating disorders: Obesity, anorexia nervosa, and the person within.* New York: Basic Books.

Buck, J. N. (1970). *House-tree-person technique: Manual.* Los Angeles: Western Psychological Services.

Burns, R. C., & Kaufman, S. H. (1972). *Actions, styles and symbols in kinetic family drawings (K-F-D): An interpretive manual.* New York: Brunner/Mazel.

Burum, B. A., & Goldfried, M. R. (2007). The centrality of emotion to psychological change. *Clinical Psychology: Science and Practice, 14*, 407–413.

Callejas, A., Acosta, A., & Lupianez, J. (2007). Green love is ugly: Emotions elicited by synesthetic grapheme-color perceptions. *Brain Research, 1127*, 99–107.

Cane, F. (1951). *The artist in each of us.* New York: Pantheon Books.

Capacchione, L. (2001). *Living with feeling: The art of emotional expression.* New York: Tarcher/Putnam.

Capezzuti, C. (2006). The national lint project: Artist's statement. *Studio Capezzuti* [Online]. Retrieved January 19, 2008 from http://www.studiocapezzuti.com/lint/artist_statement.htm.

Carlson, T. D. (1997). Using art in narrative therapy: Enhancing therapeutic possibilities. *American Journal of Family Therapy, 25*, 271–283.

Carolan, R. (2007). Adolescents, identity, addiction, and imagery. In D. B. Arrington (Ed.), *Art, angst, and trauma: Right brain interventions with developmental issues* (pp. 99–115). Springfield, IL: Charles C. Thomas Publisher.

Carter, R. (1998). *Mapping the mind.* Berkeley: University of California Press.

Cary, J. (1958). *Art and reality: Ways of the creative process.* Freeport, NY: Books for Libraries Press.

Cassou, M., & Cubley, S. (1995). *Life, paint and passion: Reclaiming the magic of spontaneous expression.* New York: Jeremy Tarcher/Putnam.

Cohen, B. M. (1983). Combined art and movement therapy group: Isomorphic responses. *The Arts in Psychotherapy, 10*, 229–232.

Cohen, B. M., Hammer, J. S., & Singer, S. (1988). The diagnostic drawing series: A systematic approach to art therapy evaluation and research. *The Arts in Psychotherapy, 15*, 11–22.

Cohen, B. M., Mills, A., & Kijak, A. K. (1994). An introduction to the diagnostic drawing series: A standardized tool for diagnostic and clinical use. *Art Therapy*, *11*, 105–110.

Collie, K., Backos, A., Malchiodi, C. A., & Spiegle, D. (2006). Art therapy for combat-related PTSD: Recommendations for research and practice. *Art Therapy*, *23*, 157–164.

Cooper, B. F., & Milton, I. B. (2003). Group art therapy with self-destructive young women. In D. J. Wiener & L. K. Oxford (Eds.), *Action therapy with families and groups using creative arts improvisation in clinical practice* (pp. 163–196). Washington, DC: American Psychological Association Press.

Cooper, C. L., & Dewe, P. (2004). *Stress: A brief history*. Malden, MA: Blackwell Publishing.

Cornell, J. (1990). *Drawing the light from within*. New York: Prentice Hall.

Cottrell, R. P., & Gallant, K. A. (2003). The elders drum project: Enhancing quality of life for long-term care residents. *Physical and Occupational Therapy in Geriatrics*, *22*, 57–79.

Cox, K. L., & Price, K. (1990). Breaking through: Incident drawings with adolescent substance abusers. *The Arts in Psychotherapy*, *17*, 333–337.

Cozolino, L. (2002). *The neuroscience of psychotherapy: Building and rebuilding the human brain*. New York: Norton.

Curry, N. A., & Kasser, T. (2005). Can coloring mandalas reduce anxiety? *Art Therapy*, *22*, 81–85.

Curtis, A. S. (2006). Expressing trauma: Comparing the client's art-making to the artist's work. *Canadian Art Therapy Association Journal*, *19*, 2–10.

Csikszentmihalyi, M. (1998). *Finding flow: The psychology of engagement with everyday life*. New York: Basic Books.

Damasio, A. R. (1994). *Descartes' error*. New York: Putnam & Sons.

Dattilio, F. M. (2000). Graphic perceptions. In R. E. Watts (Ed.), *Techniques in marriage and family counseling* (Vol. 1, pp. 49–51). Alexandria, VA: American Counseling Association.

De Petrillo, L., & Winner, E. (2005). Does art improve mood? A test of a key assumption underlying art therapy. *Art Therapy*, *22*, 205–212.

Detre, K. C., Frank, T., Kniazzeh, C. R., Robinson, M. C., Rubin, J. A., & Ulman, E. (1983). Roots of art therapy: Margaret Naumburg (1890–1983) and Florence Cane (1882–1952): A family portrait. *Art Therapy*, *22*, 111–123.

Dermer, S. B., & Foraker-Koons, K. (2007). Couples drawing together. In L. Hecker & C. F. Sori (Eds.), *The therapist's notebook: More homework, handouts, and activities for use in psychotherapy* (Vol. 2, pp. 3–9). New York: Haworth Press.

Dermer, S. B., Olund, D., & Sori, C. F. (2006). Integrating play therapy in family therapy theories. In C. F. Sori (Ed.), *Engaging children in family therapy: Creative approaches to integrating theory and research in clinical practice* (pp. 37–65). New York: Routledge/Taylor & Francis Group.

Dickman, S. B., Dunn, J. E., & Wolf, A. W. (1996). The use of art therapy as a predictor of relapse in chemical dependency treatment. *Art Therapy*, *13*, 232–237.

Dietrich, A. (2004). The cognitive neuroscience of creativity. *Psychonomic Bulletin and Review, 11*, 1011–1026.

DK. (2003). *DK illustrated Oxford dictionary*. New York: Dorling Kindersley and Oxford University.

Doczi, G. (1981). *The power of limits: Proportional harmonies in nature, art and architecture*. Boston: Shambhala.

Donders, J. (2002). The behavior rating inventory of executive function: Introduction. *Child Neuropsychiatry, 8*, 229–230.

Edinger, E. F. (1973). *Ego and archetype*. New York: Penguin Books.

Edwards, B. (1989). *Drawing on the right side of the brain*. Los Angeles: Jeremy P. Tarcher.

Edwards, M. (1987). Jungian analytic art therapy. In J. Rubin (Ed.), *Approaches to art therapy: Theory and technique* (pp. 92–113). New York: Brunner/Mazel.

Ekman, P. (2003). *Emotions revealed*. New York: Henry Hold Publishers.

Ellenbecker, T. K. (2003). Effect of content choice freedom on drawer's creative engagement. *Art Therapy, 20*, 22–27.

Elliot, A. J., & Maier, M. A. (2007). Color and psychological functioning. *Current Directions in Psychological Science, 16*, 250–254.

Elliot, A. J., Maier, M. A., Moller, A. D., Friedman R., & Meinhardt, J. (2007). Color and psychological functioning: The effect of red on performance attainment. *Journal of Experimental Psychology: General, 136*, 154–168.

Eriksen, H. R., & Ursin, H. (2004). Subjective health complaints, sensitization, and sustained cognitive activation (stress). *Journal of Psychosomatic Research, 56*, 445–448.

Espina, A. (2003). Alexithymia in parents of daughters with eating disorders: Its relationship with psychopathology and personality variables. *Journal of Psychosomatic Research, 55*, 553–560.

Etzel, J. A., Johnsen, E. L., Dickerson, J., Tranel, D., & Adolphs, R. (2006). Cardiovascular and respiratory responses during musical mood induction. *International Journal of Psychophysiology, 61*, 57–69.

Evans, K., & Dubowski, J. (2001). *Art therapy with children on the autism spectrum*. London: Jessica Kingsley Publishers.

Exkorn, K. S. (2005). *The autism sourcebook*. New York: Regan Books.

Exner, J. E. (1993). *The Rorschach: A comprehensive system: Basic foundations* (Vol. 1). New York: John Wiley & Sons.

Eysenck, H. (1995). *Genius: The natural history of creativity*. Cambridge, England: Cambridge University Press.

Farrelly-Hansen, M. (2001). Nature: Art therapy in partnership with the earth. In M. Farrelly-Hansen, (Ed.), *Spiritual art therapy: Living the connection* (pp. 137–158). London: Jessica Kingsley Publishers.

Feder, B., & Feder, E. (1998). *The art and science of evaluation in the arts therapies: How do you know what's working?* Springfield, IL: Charles C. Thomas Publisher.

Feen-Calligan, H. (1995). The use of art therapy in treatment programs to promote spiritual recovery from addiction. *Art Therapy, 12*, 46–50.

Feldman, E. B. (1972). *Varieties of visual expression: Art as image and idea.* Englewood Cliffs, NJ: Prentice-Hall.

Fox, M. (2002). *Creativity: Where the divine and the human meet.* New York: Tarcher/Putnam.

Freud, S. (1938). The interpretation of dreams. In A. A. Brill (Ed.), *The basic writings of Sigmund Freud* (pp. 181–549). New York: The Modern Library.

Friedman, D. (2007). *The writer's brush: Paintings, drawings, and sculpture by writers.* Minneapolis, MN: Mid-List Press.

Froehlich, J., Doepfner, M., & Lehmkuhl, G. (2002). Effects of combined cognitive behavioural treatment with parent management training in ADHD. *Behavioural and Cognitive Psychotherapy, 30,* 111–115.

Fukunishi, I., & Paris, W. (2001). Intergenerational associations of alexithymic characteristics for college students and their mothers. *Psychological Reports, 89,* 77–84.

Furth, G. (1988). *The secret world of drawings: Healing through art.* Boston: Sigo Press.

Gabriels, R. L. (2003). Art therapy with children who have autism and their families. In C. A. Machiodi (Ed.), *Handbook of art therapy* (pp. 193–206). New York: Guilford Press.

Gantt, L. (2004). The case for formal art therapy assessments. *Art Therapy, 21,* 18–29.

Gantt, L., & Tabone, C. (1998). *The formal elements art therapy scale: The rating manual.* Morgantown, WV: Gargoyle Press.

Gardner, H. (1999). *Intelligence reframed: Multiple intelligences for the 21st century.* New York: Basic Books.

Germer, C. K., Siegel, R. D., & Fulton, P. R. (2005). *Mindfulness and psychotherapy.* New York: Guilford Press.

Gilroy, A. (2006). *Art therapy, research and evidence-based practice.* Thousand Oaks, CA: Sage Publications.

Gladwell, M. (2005). *Blink: The power of thinking without thinking.* New York: Little, Brown, and Company.

Goldberg, N. (1997). *Living color: A writer paints her world.* New York: Bantam.

Goldstein, V. B. (1999). *The magic of mess painting: The creativity mobilization technique.* Sausalito, CA: Trans-Hyperborean Institute of Science.

Goleman, D., & Kaufman, P. (1992). The art of creativity. *Psychology Today* [Online]. Retrieved December 14, 2007 from www.psychologytoday.com/articles/pto-19920301-000031.html

Gonick-Barris, S. E. (1976). Art and nonverbal experiences with college students. In A. Robbins & L. B. Sibley (Eds.), *Creative art therapy* (pp. 188–197). New York: Brunner/Mazel.

Grady, D. (2006). Self-portraits chronicle a descent into Alzheimer's. *New York Times* [Online]. Retrieved January 21, 2007 from www.nytimes.com/2006/10/24/health/24alzh.html

Graham-Pole, J. (2002). The creative arts: What role do they play? In S. Scott (Ed.), *Handbook of comlementary and alternative therapies in mental health* (pp. 475–495). San Diego, CA: Academic Press.

Gregorian, V. S., Azarian, A., DeMaria, M. B., & McDonald, L. D. (1996). Colors of disaster: The psychology of the "black sun." *The Arts in Psychotherapy, 23*, 1–14.

Greenspan, M. (2004). *Healing through the dark emotions: The wisdom of grief, fear and despair.* Boston: Shambhala.

Greenspan, S. I., & Shanker, S. G. (2004). *The first idea: How symbols, language, and intelligence evolved from our primate ancestors to modern humans.* Cambridge, MA: De Capo Press.

Guttman, H., & Laporte, L. (2002). Alexithymia, empathy, and psychological symptoms in a family context. *Comprehensive Psychiatry, 43*, 448–455.

Hammer, E. F. (1997). *Advances in projective drawing interpretation.* Springfield, IL: Charles C. Thomas Publisher.

Handler, L., & Habenicht, D. (1994). The kinetic family drawing: A review of the literature. *Journal of Personality Assessment, 62*, 440–464.

Hanes, M. J. (2007). "Face-to-face" with addiction: The spontaneous production of self-portraits in art therapy. *Art Therapy, 24*, 33–36.

Hanh, T. N. (1999). *The miracle of mindfulness.* Boston: Beacon Press.

Harmon, K. (2004). *You are here: Personal geographies and other maps of the imagination.* New York: Princeton Architectural Press.

Hauschka, M. (1985). *Fundamentals of artistic therapy: The nature and task of painting therapy.* London: Rudolf Steiner Press.

Haynes, D. J. (2003). *Art lessons: Meditations on the creative life.* Boulder, CO: Westview Press.

Hebert, T. P., & Beardsley, T. M. (2001). Jermaine: A critical case study of a gifted black child living in rural poverty. *Gifted Child Quarterly, 45*, 85–103.

Heilman, K. M. (2005). *Creativity and the brain.* New York: Psychology Press.

Henderson, D. A., & Gladding, S. T. (1998). The creative arts in counseling: A multicultural perspective. *The Arts in Psychotherapy, 25*, 148–154.

Henderson, P., Rosen, D., & Mascaro, N. (2007). Empirical study on the healing nature of mandalas. *Psychology of Aesthetics, Creativity and the Arts, 1*, 148–154.

Henley, D. R. (1989). Stereotypes in children's art. *The American Journal of Art Therapy, 27*, 116–125.

Henley, D. R. (1991). Facilitating the development of object relations through the use of clay in art therapy. *The American Journal of Art Therapy, 29*, 69–76.

Hill, A. (1945). *Art versus illness: The story of art therapy.* Liverpool, England: Tinling & Co., Ltd.

Hinz, L. D. (In press). Order out of chaos: The Expressive Therapies Continuum as a framework for art therapy interventions in substance abuse treatment. In S. Brooke (Ed.), *Creative art therapies in substance abuse treatment.* Springfield, IL: Charles C. Thomas Publisher.

Hinz, L. D. (2006). *Drawing from within: Using art to treat eating disorders*. London: Jessica Kingsley Publishers.

Hinz, L. D. (2008). Walking a thin line: Passion and caution in art therapy. *Art Therapy, 25*, 38–40.

Hinz, L. D., Hall, E., & Lack, H. S. (1997, August). *The person-in-the-rain drawing: A normative study*. Paper presented at the American Psychological Association, Chicago.

Hinz, L. D., & Ragsdell, V. (1991, August). *Art therapy exercises with adult incest survivors*. Paper presented at the American Psychological Association, San Francisco.

Hjelle, L. A., & Ziegler, D. J. (1981). *Personality theories: Basic assumptions, research, and applications*. New York: McGraw Hill.

Horay, B. J. (2006). Moving towards gray: Art therapy and ambivalence in substance abuse treatment. *Art Therapy, 23*, 66–72.

Horowitz, M. J. (1970). *Image formation and cognition*. New York: Appleton-Century-Crofts.

Horowitz, M. J. (1983). *Image formation and psychotherapy*. New York: Jason Aronson.

Hoshino, J. (2003). Multicultural art therapy with families. In C. A. Malchiodi (Ed.), *Handbook of art therapy* (pp. 375–386). New York: Guilford Press.

Hoshino, J., & Cameron, D. (2007). Narrative art therapy within a multicultural framework. In C. Kerr & J. Hoshino (Eds.), *Family art therapy: Foundations of theory and practice* (pp. 193–220). New York: Routledge.

Hoss, R. J. (2005). *Dream language: Self-understanding through imagery and color*. Ashland, OR: Innersource Books.

Iarocci, G., & McDonald, J. (2006). Sensory integration and the perceptual experience of persons with autism. *Journal of Autism and Developmental Disorders, 36*, 77–90.

Jacobse, A. (1995). The use of dramatherapy in the treatment of eating disorders. In D. Doktor (Ed.), *Arts therapies and clients with eating disorders* (pp. 124–143). London: Jessica Kingsley Publishers.

Jensen, E. (2001). *Arts with the brain in mind*. Alexandria, VA: Association for Supervision and Curriculum Development.

Jensen, S. M. (1997). Multiple pathways to self: A multisensory art experience. *Art Therapy, 14*, 178–186.

Johnson, D. R. (2000). Creative therapies. In E. B. Foa, T. M. Keane, & M. J. Friedman (Eds.), *Effective treatments for PTSD: Practice guidelines from the International Society for Traumatic Stress Studies* (pp. 302–316). New York: Guilford Press.

Johnson, L. (1990). Creative therapies in the treatment of addictions: The art of transforming shame. *The Arts in Psychotherapy, 17*, 299–308.

Jung, C. G. (1964). *Man and his symbols*. Garden City, NY: Doubleday.

Jung, C. G. (1969). *Archetypes and the collective unconscious: The collected works of C. G. Jung* (Vol. 9, Pt. 1, 2nd ed.). Princeton, NJ: Princeton University Press.

Jung, C. G. (1972). *Mandala symbolism*. Princeton, NJ: Bollingen/Princeton.

Junge, M. B., with Asawa, P. (1994). *A history of art therapy in the United States.* Mundelein, IL: American Art Therapy Association.

Junge, M. B., & Wadeson, H. (2006). *Architects of art therapy: Memoirs and life stories.* Springfield, IL: Charles C. Thomas Publisher.

Kabat-Zinn, J. (2005). *Wherever you go, there you are: Mindfulness meditation in everyday life.* New York: Hyperion.

Kagin, S. L., & Lusebrink, V. B. (1978a). The expressive therapies continuum. In L. Gantt, G. Forest, D. Silverman, & R. J. Shoemaker (Eds.), *Proceedings of the Ninth Annual Conference of the American Art Therapy Association, 9,* 4.

Kagin, S. L., & Lusebrink, V. B. (1978b). The expressive therapies continuum. *Art Psychotherapy, 5,* 171–180.

Kahn-Denis, K. B. (1997). Art therapy with geriatric dementia clients. *Art Therapy, 14,* 194–199.

Kaplan, D. E. (1995). Creating a frame: Object relations theory and the Expressive Therapies Continuum. *Pratt Institute Creative Arts Therapies Review, 16,* 17–22.

Kaplan, F. F. (2003). Art-based assessments. In C. A. Malchiodi (Ed.), *Handbook of art therapy* (pp. 25–35). New York: Guilford Press.

Karges, C. (1999). *Ignite your intuition.* Deerfield Beach, FL: Health Communications.

Keane, T. M., Weathers, F. W., & Foa, E. B. (2000). Diagnosis and assessment of PTSD. In E. B. Foa, T. M. Keane, & M. J. Friedman (Eds.), *Effective treatments for PTSD: Practice guidelines from the International Society for Traumatic Stress Studies* (pp. 18–36). New York: Guilford Press.

Kearns, D. (2004). Art therapy with a child experiencing sensory integration difficulty. *Art Therapy, 21,* 95–101.

Kellogg, R. (1970). *Analyzing children's art.* Mountain View, CA: Mayfield Publishing.

Kerr, C., & Hoshino, J. (Eds.). (2007). *Family art therapy: Foundations of theory and practice.* New York: Routledge.

Killick, K. (1997). *Art, psychotherapy and psychosis.* New York: Routledge.

Kirby, D., Smith, K., & Wilkins, M. (2007). *Muffler men* [Online]. Retrieved January 19, 2007 from http://www.roadsideamerica.com/muffler/index.html

Klorer, P. G. (2003). Sexually abused children: Group approaches. In C. A. Malchiodi (Ed.), *Handbook of art therapy* (pp. 330–350). New York: Guilford Press.

Knapp, S. J., & VandeCreek, L. D. (2006). *Practical ethics for psychologists: A positive ethical approach.* Washington, DC: American Psychological Association.

Koh, K. B., Kim, D. K., Kim, S. Y., & Park, J. K. (2005). The relation between anger expression, depression and somatic symptoms in depressive disorders and somatoform disorders. *Journal of Clinical Psychiatry, 66,* 485–491.

Koppitz, E. M. (1968). *Psychological evaluation of children's human figure drawings.* Needham Heights, MA: Allyn and Bacon.

Koppitz, E. M. (1975). *The Bender Gestalt Test for young children: Research and application, 1963–1973* (Vol. II). New York: Grune & Stratton.

Kramer, E. (1971). *Art as therapy with children.* New York: Schocken Press.

Kramer, E. (1975a). Art and emptiness. In E. Ulman & P. Dachinger (Eds.), *Art therapy in theory and practice* (pp. 33–42). New York: Schocken.

Kramer, E. (1975b). The problem of quality in art. In E. Ulman & P. Dachinger (Eds.), *Art therapy in theory and practice* (pp. 43–59). New York: Schocken.

Kramer, J. H., Mungas, D., Reed, B. R., Wetzel, M. E., Burnett, M. M., Miller, B. L., Weiner, M. W., & Chui, H. C. (2007). Longitudinal MRI and cognitive change in healthy elderly. *Neuropsychology, 21,* 412–418.

Kurihara, H., Chiba, H., Shimizu, Y., Yanaihara, T, Takeda, M., Kawakami, K., & Takai-Kawakami, K. (1996). Behavioral and adrenocortical responses to stress in neonates and the stabilizing effects of maternal heartbeat on them. *Early Human Development, 46,* 117–127.

Kwiatkowska, H. (1978). *Family therapy and evaluation through art.* Springfield, IL: Charles C. Thomas Publisher.

Lacroix, L., Peterson, L., & Verrier, P. (2001). Art therapy, somatization, and narcissistic identification. *Art Therapy, 18,* 20–26.

Lambert, D. (1995). *The life and art of Elizabeth "Grandma" Layton.* Waco, TX: WRS Publishing.

Landgarten, H. B. (1981). *Clinical art therapy: A comprehensive guide.* New York: Brunner/Mazel Publishers.

Landgarten, H. B. (1993). *Magazine photo collage.* New York: Brunner/Mazel.

Langer, S. K. (1967). *Philosophy in a new key: A study in the symbolism of reason, rite, and art.* Cambridge, MA: Harvard University Press.

Large, E. W., & Jones, M. R. (1999). The dynamics of attending: How people track time-varying events. *Psychological Review, 106,* 119–159.

Lee, Y.-J., & Lee, J. (2006). The development of an emotion model based on color combinations. *International Journal of Consumer Studies, 30,* 122–136.

Levant, R. F. (2003). Treating male alexithymia. In L. B. Silverstein & T. G. Goodrich (Eds.), *Feminist family therapy: Empowerment in social context* (pp. 177–188). Washington, DC: American Psychological Association Press.

Levens, M. (1990). Borderline aspects in eating disorders: Art therapy's contribution. *Group Analysis, 23,* 277–284.

Levens, M. (1995). *Eating disorders and magical control of the body: Treatment through art therapy.* London: Routledge.

Levick, M. F. (1983). *They could not talk so they drew: Children's styles of coping and thinking.* Springfield, IL: Charles C. Thomas Publisher.

Levin, I. P. (2004). *Relating statistics and experimental design: An introduction.* Thousand Oaks, CA: Sage Publications.

Leviton, C. D., & Leviton, P. (2004). What is guided imagery? The cutting-edge process in mind/body medical procedures. *Annals of the American Psychotherapy Association, 7,* 22–29.

Lev-Wiesel, R., & Liraz, R. (2007). Drawings vs. narratives: Drawing as a tool to encourage verbalization in children whose fathers are drug abusers. *Clinical Child Psychology and Psychiatry, 12,* 65–75.

Liebmann, M. (2003). Developing games, activities, and themes for art therapy groups. In C. A. Malchiodi (Ed.), *Handbook of art therapy* (pp. 325–338). New York: Guilford Press.

Lin, H., Chan, R. C. K., Zheng, L., Yang, T., & Wang, Y. (2007). Executive functioning in healthy Chinese people. *Archives of Clinical Neuropsychiatry, 22,* 501–511.

Linehan, M. M. (1993). *Cognitive-behavioral treatment of borderline personality disorder.* New York: Guilford Press.

Linehan, M. M., Bohus, M., & Lynch, T. R. (2007). Dialectical behavior therapy for pervasive emotion dysregulation: Theoretical and practical underpinnings. In J. J. Gross (Ed.), *Handbook of emotion regulation* (pp. 581–605). New York: Guilford Press.

Linesch, D. S. (1988). *Adolescent art therapy.* New York: Brunner/Mazel.

Lipsey, R. (2006). *Angelic mistakes: The art of Thomas Merton.* Boston: New Seeds.

Lowell, S., & Harris, J. (1994). *The tortoise and the jackrabbit.* Flagstaff, AZ: Rising Moon Books/Northland Publishing.

Lowenfeld, V. (1952). *Creative and mental growth* (2nd ed.). New York: Macmillan.

Lowenfeld, V., & Brittain, W. L. (1987). *Creative and mental growth.* (8th ed.). New York: Macmillan.

Lubbers, D. (1991). Treatment of women with eating disorders. In H. B. Landgarten & D. Lubbers (Eds.), *Adult art psychotherapy: Issues and applications* (pp. 49–82). New York: Brunner/Mazel.

Luscher, M. (1969). *The Luscher color test.* New York: Random House.

Luscher, M. (2006). *Luscher color diagnostic.* Retrieved October 1, 2007 from http://www.luscher-color.com

Lusebrink, V. B. (1990). *Imagery and visual expression in therapy.* New York: Plenum Press.

Lusebrink, V. B. (1991a). Levels of imagery and visual expression. In R. G. Kunzendorf (Ed.), *Mental imagery: Proceedings of the 11th and 12th annual conferences of the American Association for the Study of Mental Images* (pp. 35–43). New York: Plenum Press.

Lusebrink, V. B. (1991b). A systems oriented approach to the expressive therapies: The expressive therapies continuum. *The Arts in Psychotherapy, 18,* 395–403.

Lusebrink, V. B. (2004). Art therapy and the brain: An attempt to understand the underlying processes of art expression in therapy. *Art Therapy, 21,* 125–135.

Lusk, J. T. (1993). *Thirty scripts for relaxation, imagery and inner healing.* Duluth, MN: Pfeifer-Hamilton Publications.

Luzzatto, P., & Gabriel, B. (2000). The creative journey: A model for short-term group art therapy with post-treatment cancer patients. *Art Therapy, 17,* 265–269.

Makin, S. (2000). *More than just a meal: The art of eating disorders.* London: Jessica Kingsley Publishers.

Malchiodi, C. A. (1998). *The art therapy sourcebook.* Los Angeles: Lowell House.

Malchiodi, C. A. (2000). *Art therapy and computer technology: A virtual studio of possibilities.* London: Jessica Kingsley Publishers.

Malchiodi, C. A. (2002). *The soul's palette: Drawing on art's transformative powers for health and well-being*. Boston: Shambhala.

Malchiodi, C. A. (2003a). Art therapy and the brain. In C. A. Malchiodi (Ed.), *Handbook of art therapy* (pp. 16–24). New York: Guilford Press.

Malchiodi, C. A. (2003b). Expressive arts therapy and multimodal approaches. In C. A. Malchiodi (Ed.), *Handbook of art therapy* (pp. 106–117). New York: Guilford Press.

Malchiodi, C. A. (2003c). Psychoanalytic, analytic, and object relations approaches. In C. A. Malchiodi (Ed.), *Handbook of art therapy* (pp. 41–57). New York: Guilford Press.

Malchiodi, C. A. (2003d). Using art with medical support groups. In C. A. Malchiodi (Ed.), *Handbook of art therapy* (pp. 351–361). New York: Guilford Press.

Malchiodi, C. A., Kim, D.-Y., & Choi, W. S. (2003). Developmental art therapy. In C. A. Malchiodi (Ed.), *Handbook of art therapy* (pp. 93–105). New York: Guilford Press.

Maner, J. K., & Schmidt, N. B. (2006). The role of risk avoidance in anxiety. *Behavior Therapy, 37,* 181–189.

Manheim, A. R. (1998). The relationship between the artistic process and self-actualization. *Art Therapy, 15,* 99–106.

Marshall, L. H., & Magoun, H. W. (1998). *Discoveries in the human brain*. Totowa, NJ: Humana Press.

Martin, E. (2003). The symbolic graphic lifeline: A connection of line quality and feeling expression. *Art Therapy, 20,* 100–105.

Maslow, A. H. (1970). *Motivation and personality* (2nd ed.). New York: Harper and Row.

Maslow, A. H. (1982). *Toward a psychology of being* (2nd ed.). New York: Van Nostrand Reinhold.

Matto, H., Corcoran, J., & Fassler, A. (2003). Integrating solution-focused and art therapies for substance abuse treatment: Guidelines for practice. *The Arts in Psychotherapy, 30,* 265–272.

May, R. (1960). The significance of symbols. In R. May (Ed.), *Symbolism in religion and literature* (pp. 12–49). New York: George Braziller.

May, R. (1975). *The courage to create*. New York: Norton.

McConeghey, H. (2003). *Art and soul*. Putnam, CT: Spring Publications.

McGriffin, M. (2002). *Reflections in clay*. Bloomington, IN: Author.

McLeod, C. (1999). Empowering creativity with computer-assisted art therapy: An introduction to available programs and techniques. *Art Therapy, 16,* 201–205.

McMurray, M., & Schwartz-Mirman, O. (1998). Transference in art therapy: A new look. *The Arts in Psychotherapy, 25,* 31–36.

McNamee, C. M. (2004). Using both sides of the brain: Experiences that integrate art and talk therapy through scribble drawings. *Art Therapy, 21,* 136–142.

McNamee, C. M. (2005). Bilateral art: Integrating art therapy, family therapy, and neuroscience. *Contemporary Family Therapy, 27,* 545–557.

McNiff, S. (1977). Motivation in art. *Art Psychotherapy, 4*, 125–136.

McNiff, S. (1981). *The arts and psychotherapy.* Springfield, IL: Charles C. Thomas Publisher.

McNiff, S. (1998). *Trust the process: An artist's guide to letting go.* Boston: Shambhala.

McNiff, S. (2004). *Art heals: How creativity cures the soul.* Boston: Shambhala.

Meerlood, J. A. M. (1985). The universal language of rhythm. In J. J. Leedy (Ed.), *Poetry as healer: Minding the troubled mind* (pp. 3–16). New York: Vanguard Press.

Meijer-Degen, F., & Lansen, J. (2006). Alexithymia—A challenge to art therapy: The story of Rita. *The Arts in Psychotherapy, 33*, 167–179.

Miller, A. (1986). *Pictures of a childhood: Sixty-six pictures and an essay.* New York: Farrar, Straus & Giroux.

Miller, A. (1990). *The untouched key: Tracing childhood trauma in creativity and destructiveness.* New York: Anchor/Doubleday.

Miller, L. J. (2006). *Sensational kids: Hope and help for children with sensory processing disorder.* New York: G.P. Putnam's Sons.

Mills, A. (2003). The diagnostic drawing series. In C. A. Malchiodi (Ed.), *Handbook of art therapy* (pp. 401–409). New York: Guilford Press.

Mills, A., Cohen, B. M., & Meneses, J. Z. (1993). Reliability and validity tests of the diagnostic drawing series. *The Arts in Psychotherapy, 20*, 83–88.

Moon, B. (1992). *Essentials of art therapy training and practice.* Springfield, IL: Charles C. Thomas.

Moore, R. W. (1983). Art therapy with substance abusers: A review of the literature. *The Arts in Psychotherapy, 10*, 251–260.

Munley, M. (2002). Comparing the PPAT drawings of boys with AD/HD and age-matched controls using the formal elements art therapy scale. *Art Therapy, 19*, 69–76.

Muri, S. A. (2007). Beyond the face: Art therapy and self-portraiture. *The Arts in Psychotherapy, 34*, 331–339.

Naumburg, M. (1966). *Dynamically oriented art therapy: Its principles and practice.* New York: Grune & Stratton.

Neale, E., & Rosal, M. E. (1993). What can art therapists learn from the research on projective drawing techniques for children: A review of the literature. *The Arts in Psychotherapy, 20*, 37–49.

Nickerson, R. S. (1999). Enhancing creativity. In R. J. Sternberg (Ed.), *Handbook of creativity* (pp. 392–430). Cambridge, England: Cambridge University Press.

Orr, T. J., Myles, B. S., & Carlson, J. K. (1998). The impact of rhythmic entrainment on a person with autism. *Focus on Autism and Other Developmental Disabilities, 13*, 163–166.

Osborne, J. (2003). Art and the child with autism: Therapy or education? *Early Child Development and Care, 173*, 411–423.

Oster, G. D., & Gould Crone, P. (2004). *Using drawings in assessment and therapy* (2nd ed.). New York: Brunner-Routledge.

Parker-Bell, B. (1999). Embracing a future with computers and art therapy. *Art Therapy, 16*, 180–185.

Panter, B. M., Panter, M. L., Virshup, E., & Virshup, B. (1995). *Creativity and madness: Psychological studies of art and artists*. Burbank, CA: AIMED Press.

Perel, E. 2000. A tourist's view of marriage: Cross-cultural couples—Challenges, choices, and implications for therapy. In P. Papp (Ed.), *Couples on the fault line: New directions for therapists* (pp. 178–204). New York: Guilford Press.

Peterson, B. C., Stovall, K., Elkins, D. E., & Parker-Bell, B. (2005). Art therapies and computer technology. *Art Therapy, 22,* 139–149.

Piaget, J. (1962). *Play, dreams, and imitation in childhood*. New York: Norton.

Piaget, J. (1969). *The psychology of the child*. New York: Basic Books.

Plutchik, R. (2003). *Emotions and life: Perspectives from psychology, biology, and evolution*. Washington, DC: American Psychological Association Press.

Pollock, K. M., & Kymissis, P. (2001). The future of adolescent group therapy. *Journal of Child and Adolescent Group Therapy, 11,* 3–11.

Ray, O. (2004). How the mind hurts and heals the body. *American Psychologist, 59,* 29–40.

Redish, A. D. (1999). *Beyond the cognitive map: From place cells to episodic memory*. Cambridge, MA: MIT Press.

Rhyne, J. (1973). *The gestalt art therapy experience*. Monterrey, CA: Brooks/Cole Publishing Company.

Rhyne, J. (1987). Gestalt art therapy. In J. A. Rubin (Ed.), *Approaches to art therapy* (pp. 167–187). New York: Brunner/Mazel.

Rich, J. M., & Devitis, J. L. (1996). *Theories of moral development* (2nd ed.). Springfield, IL: Charles C. Thomas Publisher.

Rider, M. S. (1987). Treating chronic disease and pain with music-mediated imagery. *The Arts in Psychotherapy, 14,* 113–120.

Riley, S. (1999). *Contemporary art therapy with adolescents*. London: Jessica Kingsley Publishers.

Riley, S. (2001). *Group process made visible: Group art therapy*. Philadelphia: Taylor & Francis Publishing Group.

Riley, S. (2003). Art therapy with couples. In C. A. Malchiodi (Ed.), *Handbook of art therapy* (pp. 387–398). New York: Guilford Press.

Riley, S. (2004). The creative mind. *Art Therapy, 21,* 184–190.

Riley, S., & Malchiodi, C. A. (1994). *Integrative approaches to family art therapy*. Chicago: Magnolia Street Publishers.

Riley, S., & Malchiodi, C. A. (2003). Family art therapy. In C. A. Malchiodi (Ed.), *Handbook of art therapy* (pp. 362–374). New York: Guilford Press.

Robbins, A., & Sibley, L. B. (1976). *Creative art therapy*. New York: Brunner/Mazel.

Rogers, E. J. (2007). The basics of grief and loss. In E. J. Rogers (Ed.), *The art of grief: The use of expressive arts in a grief support group* (pp. 21–30). New York: Routledge.

Rogers, N. (1999). The creative connection: A holistic expressive arts process. In S. K. Levine & E. G. Levine (Eds.), *Foundations of expressive arts therapies: Theoretical and clinical perspectives* (pp. 113–131). London: Jessica Kingsley Publishers.

Root, M. P. P. (1989). Family sculpting with bulimic families. In L. M. Hornyak & E. K. Baker (Eds.), *Experiential therapy for eating disorders* (pp. 78–100). New York: Guilford Press.

Rosal, M. (2001). Cognitive-behavioral art therapy. In J. A. Rubin (Ed.), *Approaches to art therapy* (2nd ed., pp. 210–225). New York: Brunner/Mazel.

Rosal, M., & Lehder, D. M. (1982). The effect of tempo upon form and reflective distance. *Proceedings of the Thirteenth Annual Conference of the American Art Therapy Association, 13,* 142–144.

Roth, E. A. (1987). A behavioral approach to art therapy. In J. A. Rubin (Ed.), *Approaches to art therapy* (pp. 213–232). New York: Brunner/Mazel.

Rozum, A. L., & Malchiodi, C. A. (2003). Cognitive-behavioral approaches. In C. A. Malchiodi (Ed.), *Handbook of art therapy* (pp. 72–81). New York: Guilford Press.

Rubin, J. A. (1984). *Child art therapy* (2nd ed.). New York: John Wiley & Sons.

Rubin, J. A. (1999). *Art therapy: An introduction.* New York: Brunner/Mazel.

Safran, D. S. (2003). An art therapy approach to attention-deficit/hyperactivity disorder. In C. A. Malchiodi (Ed.), *Handbook of art therapy* (pp. 181–192). New York: Guilford Press.

Sakaki, T., Ji, Y., Ramirez, S. Z. (2007). Clinical application of color inkblots in therapeutic storytelling. *The Arts in Psychotherapy, 34,* 208–213.

Schore, A. N. (2002). Dysregulation of the right brain: A fundamental mechanism of traumatic attachment and the psychopathogenesis of posttraumatic stress disorder. *Australian and New Zealand Journal of Psychiatry, 36,* 9–30.

Schwartz, A. E. (1995). *Guided imagery for groups: Fifty visualizations that promote relaxation, problem-solving, creativity, and well-being.* Duluth, MN: Whole Person Associates.

Sher, K. J., & Grekin, E. R. (2007). Alcohol and affect regulation. In J. J. Gross (Ed.), *Handbook of emotion regulation* (pp. 560–580). New York: Guilford Press.

Sholt, M., & Gavron, T. (2006). Therapeutic qualities of clay-work in art therapy and psychotherapy: A review. *Art Therapy, 23,* 66–72.

Siegel, L., Gottfried, N. W., & Lowe, R. H. (1988). Emotional distress 18 months after a train derailment and chemical spill. In C. D. Spielberger & L. N. Butcher (Eds.), *Advances in personality assessment* (Vol. 7, pp. 23–48). New York: Lawrence Erlbaum Associates.

Siegel, D. J., & Hartzell, M. (2003). *Parenting from the inside out.* New York: Jeremy P. Tarcher/Putnam.

Signell, K. (1990). *Wisdom of the heart: Working with women's dreams.* New York: Fromm International Press.

Silver, R. A. (1987). A cognitive approach to art therapy. In J. A. Rubin (Ed.), *Approaches to art therapy* (pp. 233–250). New York: Brunner/Mazel.

Silver, R. A. (2002). *Three art assessments.* New York: Brunner-Routledge.

Silveri, M. D., Reali, G., Jenner, C., & Puopolo, M. (2007). Attention and memory in the preclinical stage of dementia. *Journal of Geriatric Psychiatry and Neurology, 20,* 67–75.

Silverman, D. (1991). Art psychotherapy: An approach to borderline adults. In H. B. Landgarten & D. Lubbers (Eds.), *Adult art psychotherapy: Issues and applications* (pp. 83–110). New York: Brunner/Mazel.

Simon, R. M. (1992). *The symbolism of style: Art as therapy*. New York: Routledge.

Simonton, D. K. (2000). Creativity: Cognitive, personal, developmental, and social aspects. *American Psychologist, 55*, 151–158.

Singer, J. L. (2006). *Imagery in psychotherapy*. Washington, DC: American Psychological Association.

Slater, A. (2004). Healing and stone carving. *Art Therapy, 21*, 226–230.

Slingerland Institute for Literacy. (2007). *The Slingerland approach* [On-line]. Retrieved April 30, 2007 from http://www.slingerland.org/organization/approach

Smith, J. C. (2005). *Relaxation, meditation, and mindfulness: A mental health practitioner's guide to new and traditional approaches*. New York: Springer.

Smucker, M. R., Dancu, C., & Foa, E. B. (2002). Imagery rescripting: A new treatment for survivors of childhood sexual abuse suffering from posttraumatic stress. In R. L. Leahy & E. T. Dowd (Eds.), *Clinical advances in cognitive psychotherapy: Theory and application* (pp. 294–310). New York: Springer Publishing.

Sobol, B., & Williams, K. (2001). Family and group art therapy. In J. Rubin (Ed.), *Approaches to art therapy: Theory and technique* (pp. 261–280). New York: Brunner/Mazel.

Staton, A. R., & Lucey, C. F. (2004). The family construction project. *Journal of Family Psychotherapy, 15*, 87–91.

Steele, W. (2003). Using drawings in short-term trauma resolution. In C. A. Malchiodi (Ed.), *Handbook of art therapy* (pp. 139–151). New York: Guilford Press.

Stewart, E. G. (2004). Art therapy and neuroscience blend: Working with patients who have dementia. *Art Therapy, 21*, 148–155.

Stewart, E. G. (2006). *Kaleidoscope … Color and form illuminate darkness: An exploration of art therapy and exercises for patients with dementia*. Chicago: Magnolia Street Publishers.

Stone, B. O. (1968). Art therapy with nonverbal patients: In I. Jakab (Ed.), *Psychiatry and art: Art interpretation and art therapy* (Vol. 2, pp. 191–204). New York: Karger/Basel.

Stone, H., & Stone, S. (1993). *Embracing your inner critic: Turning self-criticism into a creative asset*. San Francisco: Harper Collins.

Swados, E. (2005). *My depression: A picture book*. New York: Hyperion.

Taylor, G. J., Bagby, M., & Parker, J. D. A. (1997). *Disorders of affect regulation: Alexithymia in medical and psychiatric illness*. Cambridge, England: Cambridge University Press.

Taylor, J. B. (2008). *My stroke of insight: A brain scientist's personal journey*. New York: Viking.

Thomas, G. V., & Silk, A. M. J. (1990). *An introduction to the psychology of children's drawings*. Washington Square, NY: New York University Press.

Trombetta, R. (2007). Art therapy, men and the expressivity gap. *Art Therapy, 24*, 29–32.

Trostli, R. (1998). *Rhythms of learning*. Hudson, NY: Anthroposophic Press.

Ulman, E. (1975a). Art therapy: Problems of definition. In E. Ulman & P. Dachinger (Eds.), *Art therapy: In theory and practice* (pp. 3–13). New York: Schocken.

Ulman, E. (1975b). Therapy is not enough: The contribution of art to general hospital psychiatry. In E. Ulman & P. Dachinger (Eds.), *Art therapy: In theory and practice* (pp. 14–32). New York: Schocken.

Ulman, E. (1987). Variations on a Freudian theme: Three art therapy theorists. In J. A. Rubin (Ed.), *Approaches to art therapy* (pp. 277–298). New York: Brunner/Mazel.

Ulman, E., & Levy, B. I. (1973). Art therapists as diagnostician. *American Journal of Art Therapy, 13*, 35–38.

Ulman, E., & Levy, B. I. (1975). An experimental approach to the judgment of psychopathology from paintings. In E. Ulman & P. Dachinger (Eds.), *Art therapy: In theory and practice* (pp. 393–402). New York: Schocken.

Vandendorpe, M. M. (1990). Three tasks of adolescence: Cognitive, moral, social. In V. P. Makosky, C. C. Sileo, L. G. Whittemore, C. P. Landry, & M. L. Skutley (Eds.), *Activities handbook for the teaching of psychology* (Vol. 3, pp. 126–127). Washington DC: American Psychological Association.

Verkuil, B., Brosschot, J. F., & Thayer, J. F. (2007). A sensitive body or a sensitive mind? Associations among somatic sensitization, cognitive sensitization, health worry, and subjective health complaints. *Journal of Psychosomatic Research, 63*, 673–681.

Vick, R. M., & Sexton-Radek, K. (2005). Art and migraine: Researching the relationship between artmaking and pain experience. *Art Therapy, 22*, 193–204.

Wadeson, H. (1980). *Art psychotherapy*. New York: John Wiley & Sons.

Wadeson, H. (2000). *Art therapy practice: Innovative approaches with diverse populations*. New York: John Wiley & Sons.

Wadeson, H. (2002). The anti-assessment devil's advocate. *Art Therapy, 19*, 168–170.

Wald, J. (1984). The graphic representation of regression in an Alzheimer's disease patient. *The Arts in Psychotherapy, 11*, 165–175.

Wald, J. (2003). Clinical art therapy with older adults. In C. A. Malchiodi (Ed.), *Handbook of art therapy* (pp. 294–307). New York: Guilford Press.

Wallace, E. (1987). Healing through the visual arts—A Jungian approach. In J. Rubin (Ed.), *Approaches to art therapy: Theory and technique* (pp. 114–133). New York: Brunner/Mazel.

Wallace, E. (1990). *A queen's quest: Pilgrimage for individuation*. Santa Fe, NM: Moon Bear Press.

Waller, E. (2006). Somatoform disorders as disorders of affect regulation: A developmental perspective. *International Review of Psychiatry, 18*, 13–24.

Warriner, E. (1995). Anger is red. In D. Dokter (Ed.), *Arts therapies and clients with eating disorders: Fragile board* (pp. 21–28). London: Jessica Kingsley Publishers.

Wiener, D. J., & Oxford, L. K. (Eds.). (2003). *Action therapy with families and groups using creative arts improvisation in clinical practice*. Washington, DC: American Psychological Association Press.

Williams, H. C. (2002). *Drawing as a sacred activity: Simple steps to explore your feelings and heal your consciousness.* Novato, CA: New World Library.

Wilson, L. (1987). Symbolism and art therapy: Theory and clinical practice. In J. A. Rubin (Ed.), *Approaches to art therapy* (pp. 44–62). New York: Brunner/Mazel.

Wilson, M. (2003). Art therapy in addictions treatment: Creativity and shame reduction. In C. A. Malchiodi (Ed.), *Handbook of art therapy* (pp. 281–293). New York: Guilford Press.

Winkelman, M. (2003). Contemporary therapy for addictions: Drumming out drugs. *American Journal of Public Health, 93,* 647–651.

Wix, L. (2000). Looking for what's lost: The artistic roots of art therapy: Mary Huntoon. *Art Therapy, 17,* 168–176.

Wright, K. J. T. (1976). Metaphor and symptom: A study of integration and its failure. *International Review of Psychoanalysis, 3,* 97–109.

Wysuph, C. L. (1970). *Jackson Pollock/Psychoanalytic drawings.* New York: Horizon Press.

Yalom, I. D. (1995). *Theory and practice of group psychotherapy* (4th ed.). New York: Basic Books.

Yates, W. R. (1999). Medical problems of the athlete with eating disorder. In P. S. Mehler & A. E. Andersen (Eds.), *Eating disorders: A guide to medical care and complications* (pp. 153–166). Baltimore: Johns Hopkins University Press.

Zaidel, D. W. (2005). *Neuropsychology of art: Neurological, cognitive and evolutionary perspectives.* New York: Psychology Press.

Zeff, T. (2004). *The highly sensitive person's survival guide.* Oakland, CA: New Harbinger Press.

Index

A

Abstract family collage, 52, 131, 143, 249
Abstract representations, 131
Abstract thought, 124, 126, 132–133, 141
Action painting, 41
Adolescence, 11, 29, 103, 124–125, 170
Adolescent art, 103
Adolf Hitler, 179
Affect
    appropriate expression of, 11, 102, 137, 227,
      243
Affect regulation, disturbances of, 101, 113, 137
Affective Component
    blocks to, 111–114
    emergent function, 110–111
    healing function, 104–105
    promoting, 106–108
    overuse of, 114–116
    reflective distance, 107–108
Alcoholics Anonymous, 3, 248
Alexithymia, 42, 102, 114, 120, 256
    normative male alexithymia, 114
Alzheimer's disease, 12, 76, 124, 244
Ambiguous forms, 32, 154–155, 168, 224
American Art Therapy Association, xvii, 5, 17,
    21, 192, 218
Analytic touch, 63
Anorexia Nervosa, 72, 213
Anxiety reduction, 82, 102, 127, 138–139, 141,
    177, 219. 223–225, 228
Anxiety disorders, 115
Archetypal contents, 217
Archetypal images, 149, 166–167
Art instruction, 22, 180
Art process, 25, 30, 49, 94, 104, 108, 202, 220,
    232, 258
Art psychotherapist, 18, 24
Art therapy pioneers, 22, 192
"Artist as therapist", 18
Assertiveness, 97, 127, 236
Assessment, 213–219, 235, 239, 240 251, 262
    boundaries and limits, 196, 198–199
    choice of medium, 197
    color use, 192, 196, 201, 203, 206
    commitment, 193, 196, 198, 199–200, 213, 215
    content, 196, 201, 204
    coping skills, 196, 198, 200–201
    developmental level, 196, 201
    expressive elements, 196, 201
    free choice of art materials, 192
    frustration tolerance, 193, 196, 199, 200, 213,
      215
    learning style, 251
    level of energy, 196, 200, 202
    line quality, 196, 202, 205, 208
    logic displayed, 196, 211, 213
    organic indicators, 196, 201, 203
    organizing functions, 201, 204
    Risk taking, 196, 198, 213, 215
    Preferred medium, 196–197, 215
    Series of tasks vs. one task, 197, 214
    Space use, 202, 205, 206, 208, 215
    Stylistic elements, 214
    Symbolism, 196, 201, 202, 204, 207, 212
Assisted living facilities, 65, 134
Attention-Deficit/Hyperactivity Disorder, 46,
    48–56, 125, 175, 200
Attention to detail, 94, 103
Autism, 43, 68, 70–71, 76, 128, 159
Autistic spectrum, 62, 128, 159

B

Bilateral art, 259
Binge eating disorder, 92–98
Bipolar disorder, 200, 203, 212
Blind contour drawing, 83, 99
Blocked functioning, 56, 221, 226
Blot painting, 32, 154, 168, 174
Bodily rejection, 69
Bodily symptoms, 113
Bodily tension, 40
Body image, 223, 247
Body map of feelings, 114, 121
Borderline personality disorder, 115
Boundary determined media, 33, 45, 85, 155
Boundary setting
    in group therapy, 244
Bridge
    bridging the opposites, 149–150, 166
    family construction project, 258
    P/A level as bridge between K/S and C/Sy, 16

Sensory modulation disorder-under responsive type, 70
Sensory processing disorder, 62, 70, 76
Sequencing, 124, 130, 141, 143, 212
Shadow characteristics, 158, 164
Silence
    adolescent, 232–233
    therapist comfort with, 233
Social skills, 48, 52, 245
Somatic disorders, 114
Somatoform disorder, 111, 113, 120
Sorting, 111, 128
Space use
    decreased, 202–203
    increased, 202–203, 205, 206, 208, 215
Spatial relationships
    illogical, 209
    incomplete, 209
Spiritual art therapy, 207, 210
Spiritual practices, 255
Sponge printing, 168
Stages of creativity
    illumination, 182
    incubation, 181
    preparation, 180
    verification, 182
Stereotypical expectations, 171–172
Stereotypical images, 91–92, 206, 232–233
Stimulus drawing technique, 128
Stone carving, 42, 57
Stress management, 66, 116, 138
String painting, 154
Stylistic elements, 19, 163, 214, 234
Sublimation, 25–26
Subjective health complaints, 113, 138
Substance use disorder, 91
Survival on an island, 135, 144
Symbol
    as bridge, 231
    as defense mechanism, 146, 156
    cultural, 156–157
    emotional charge, 148
    externalization, 148, 152
    formation, 150
    latent content, 146
    manifest content, 146
    multidimensional nature of, 145, 153–155
    of destruction, 158
    over identification with, 160
    personal, 147
    progressive, 148, 155–156
    regressive, 148
    resolution, 145, 147–148, 154

universal, 35, 147, 156, 165, 166
Symbolic component
    blocks to, 158–160
    emergent function, 157–158
    healing function, 147–148
    overuse of, 158–160
    promoting, 156–157
    reflective distance, 155–156
Symbolic content, 24–25, 150
Symbolic experiences, 32, 148, 167
Symbolic journey, 149, 167
Symbolic transformations, 147
Synthesis, 22, 35, 126, 169–170, 252, 260
Synthetic touch, 63
Synthetical thought, 145

T

Tactile exploration, 63–64, 68
Task complexity, 33–35, 224–225
Task instructions
    customizing, 248
    modification, 249
Task structure, 33–35
Tempo, 45, 102, 169, 244
Tension release, 239
Termination from therapy
    avoiding premature, 231
    couples therapy, 259–260
    family therapy, 259–260
    group therapy, 250–251
    group ritual, 250
    individual therapy, 230–231
    review of artwork, 231–232, 259–261
Therapeutic change
    avoiding non-therapeutic change, 229–230
    effects of media properties, 223–224
    effects of task instructions, 224–225
    gradual movement, 224, 229
    planned change, 221, 223
    questions and discussion to promote change, 223
    too many changes, 230
    unplanned change, 227–228
Therapeutic obstacles
    attitude, 235
    belief, 235
    emotion, 235
    lack of skill, 235
    working through, 235